CRIMINAL LESSONS

DISCARD

CRIMINAL LESSONS

Case Studies and Commentary on Crime and Justice

Frederic G. Reamer

COLUMBIA UNIVERSITY PRESS

NEW YORK

COLUMBIA UNIVERSITY PRESS
Publishers Since 1893
New York   Chichester, West Sussex

Library of Congress Cataloging-in-Publication Data
Reamer, Frederic G., 1953–
    Criminal lessons : case studies and commentary on
crime and justice / Frederic G. Reamer.
        p.   cm.
    Includes bibliographical references and index.
    ISBN 0-231-12930-0 (cloth : alk. paper) —
    ISBN 0-231-12931-9 (paper : alk. paper)
    1. Crime—Case studies.   2. Criminal behavior—
Case studies.   3. Crime—Prevention—Case studies.
4. Criminal justice, Administration of —Case studies.
I. Title.

HV6251.R44 2003
364—dc21

                                        2003043466

For Deborah, Emma, and Leah

Contents

CRIMINAL LESSONS

First Lessons

Like many people—the general public, politicians, human service profession-als, and professionals in the criminal justice field—I have spent years trying to understand crime and criminals. My journey started early. I clearly recall my first horror-filled realization that some people commit crimes so serious that they are imprisoned. When I was six years old my father took my older brother and me to the local library in my Baltimore neighborhood. While a librarian assisted my brother, I scanned books on the lower shelves in the stacks. Quite by accident my eyes landed on a book jacket that featured a photograph of an inmate in a prison cell. Intrigued, I reached for the book and sat on the floor staring at photo after photo. I remember feeling startled, curious, and unnerved. What, I wondered, had these people done to deserve being locked up in these cages? Why would these men do such terrible things? What was it like for them to be in prison?

During many subsequent trips to that library, I headed straight for that book. In a sense, I still have not put it down. Little did I know then that my naive fascination at six would turn into a lifelong preoccupation with these questions. Along the way I have spent considerable time working with con-victed criminals. My tour of duty has included a stint as a group worker and social worker in a U.S. Bureau of Prisons institution in Chicago in the mid-1970s (the Metropolitan Correctional Center), the maximum-security state penitentiary in Jefferson City, Missouri, in the early 1980s, and the forensic unit of the state psychiatric hospital in Rhode Island in the mid-1980s. Since 1992 I have served on the Rhode Island Parole Board.

This book sums up what I have learned from these experiences about crime and criminals. It is based primarily on the more than thirteen thousand cases in which I have been involved as a parole board member, supplemented by my earlier experiences working in a federal correctional facility, a state penitentiary, and a forensic unit in a state psychiatric hospital (the forensic unit housed mentally ill prisoners and "patients" who had been found not guilty of a crime by reason of insanity or were not competent, psychiatrically, to stand trial). My purpose is to reflect on my encounters with a remarkably diverse group of criminals and to speculate about what leads to crime and what we, as a society, can do to prevent and respond to it meaningfully.

Of course, I am hardly the first person to pursue this topic. Hundreds of books address the subjects of crime, criminal behavior, and the criminal justice system. Serious scholarly observations and conclusions about the causes and consequences of crime fill these thoughtful tomes. There is no need for me to be redundant or to cover the same ground.

Put simply, the vast majority of authors of books on crime and criminal behavior are writing deductively, from the top down. That is, authors offer conceptual frameworks and typologies—rigorous and thoughtful ones, I should add—that readers may use to understand crime and criminal behavior (see, for example, Barkan 2000; Bernard, Vold, and Snipes 2002; Crutchfield, Kubrin, and Bridges 2000; Gottfredson and Hirschi 1990; Reid 1999; Schmalleger 2001; Sheley 2000; Siegel 2000; Wilson and Petersilia 1995). These frameworks and typologies are of two types. The first group—which I will describe more fully shortly—focuses on different causal (or, to use more formal terminology, *etiological*) theories, to explain why people commit crimes by exploring the relevance of, for example, psychological, biological, economic, political, community, and familial factors. The second group focuses on different types or categories of offenders, based on the patterns of their criminal activities and behaviors. Gibbons (1982), for example, distinguishes among a wide variety of "criminal role careers," such as professional thieves, embezzlers, white-collar criminals, naive check forgers, semiprofessional property offenders, violent sex offenders, amateur shoplifters, addicts, and so on. Clinard and Quinney (1973; also see Clinard, Quinney, and Wildeman 1994) differentiate groups by types of criminal behavior: violent personal crime, occasional property crime, occupational crime, corporate crime, political crime, public-order crime (victimless crimes such as prostitution and drunkenness), conventional crime, organized crime, and professional crime. D. Glaser (1978) also classifies offenders according to types of crime: predatory crime, illegal performance offenses (vagrancy, disorderly conduct), illegal selling offenses (drug selling, prostitution), illegal consumption offenses, disloyalty offenses, and illegal status offenses. Abrahamsen (1960) compares and contrasts "acute criminals" (including situational, associational, and accidental offenders) and "chronic offenders" (including neurotic, psychopathic, and psychotic offenders), while Schafer (1976) classifies offenders based on their "life trends," for example, occasional, professional, abnormal, and habitual criminals.

The Typology of Criminal Circumstances

In contrast, my approach in this book is to present a typology that integrates a number of useful elements found in other typologies but that classifies offenders on the basis of the *circumstances* that led to their crimes. This "typology of criminal circumstances" incorporates what we have learned about three key dimensions of crime and criminal behavior: the causes of crime, the diversity of types of crimes, and various types of criminal careers and patterns during the offenders' lives. Also, this typology is unique in that I based it on inductive inquiry, from the bottom up. I have systematically collated information about the thousands and thousands of offenders whom I have encountered, along with a significant number of their victims, and have used qualitative research methods to create a typology of the *circumstances* that lead to serious criminal behavior (that is, criminal behavior that is serious enough to warrant incarceration).[1] Using what academics call "grounded theory"—which entails deriving theories, concepts, propositions, and new hypotheses from qualitative data collected in the field—I have developed a seven-category typology of the circumstances that appear to lead to serious criminal behavior.[2]

Briefly, these categories include crimes that are the result of

Desperation. Put simply, people who find themselves in desperate circumstances—for example, as a result of sudden debt or family crises—sometimes engage in desperate acts. Examples of crimes of desperation include burglaries committed by parents living in dire poverty who need money to feed their children, fraud committed by people who are under intense pressure to pay their debt to organized crime figures, and embezzlement by white-collar offenders whose financial world has crumbled around them.

Greed, exploitation, and opportunism. For all kinds of reasons—some psychological, some cultural, and some, perhaps, biochemical—some people are eager to outdo the neighbors, even if they cannot afford the competition. They want more money and trappings, and they want them yesterday. For some, crime is the fastest route to big bucks, late-model cars, and large houses. Examples of crimes of greed, exploitation, and opportunism are financial schemes and Internet scams that take advantage of vulnerable people (for example, the elderly), corporate fraud, drug deals that generate large profits, racketeering, murder for hire and arson for hire, and warehouse thefts to obtain goods for black-market sales.

Rage. Everyone becomes angry at times, and most people are able to control their aggressive impulses during these episodes. But some people are unable or unwilling to contain their rage. They respond to conflict by lashing out or worse. Examples of crimes of rage include stabbings and murders that arise from fierce domestic disputes, assaults that arise from "road rage" conflicts, and spontaneous intergang warfare.

Revenge and retribution. Some crimes are mere payback. Party A becomes enraged with party B, and no easy resolution is apparent. The disagreement and resentment escalate and time runs out. Examples of crimes of revenge and retribution are planned (as opposed to spontaneous or impulsive) murders, assaults, and thefts whose goal is to "pay back" the victim for some perceived wrong or injustice.

Frolic. Many crimes occur in the context of people doing their best to have a good time—a *really* good time, often laced with mayhem and mischief. Examples of crimes of frolic are teenaged high-speed drag races that lead to serious injury or death, serious vandalism preceded by heavy drinking or drug use, and death caused by recreational gunplay (e.g., Russian roulette).

Addiction. This is the elephant in the room that we need to acknowledge. An overwhelming portion of crime is related to addiction. Examples include drug possession, prostitution by drug addicts to pay for their habits, pathological gambling, driving under the influence with death or serious injury resulting, and a wide range of property crimes committed to obtain goods to sell on the black market to finance addictions (for example, auto theft, breaking and entering, burglary, receiving stolen goods).

Mental illness. One sad and rather well-kept secret in this business is that many crimes are committed by people with diagnosable, although not always diagnosed, mental illness or brain damage. Typically, these crimes can be linked directly to psychiatric problems. For a variety of complex reasons—some justifiable and some not—a significant number of these offenders end up in the criminal justice system rather than the mental health system. Examples include sex offenders who have been diagnosed with pedophilia or mental retardation, individuals with bipolar disorder who have been arrested for domestic violence, and people with schizophrenia who have been convicted of murder or assault.

Although these seven categories of crime are compelling, these broad distinctions are not sufficient. Within each group we must distinguish many different subtypes of crime if we are to truly understand patterns of criminal behavior. With respect to crimes of addiction, for example, we need to distinguish among addictions related to drugs, alcohol, and gambling. With respect to crimes of rage we need to distinguish among offenses involving, for example, strangers (road rage) and offenses involving family and acquaintances (domestic disputes). With respect to crimes of greed, we need to distinguish among street offenses (such as drug dealing for profit), white-collar financial schemes, and crimes involving serious personal injury (such as murder for hire).

Although I firmly believe that typologies provide a useful way to conceptualize crime and criminals, I recognize that they have their limitations. Typologies sometimes oversimplify remarkably complex phenomena, forcing into tidy categories a diverse array of elements that are not nearly as homogeneous as the categories of the typology suggest. As Gibbons (1982:263, cited in Hagan 1990:111) says, criminals "defy pigeonholing." Criminals are complicated and many do not specialize in particular types of offenses or engage in linear criminal careers. Criminals who commit offenses that fall within the category of crimes of addiction, for example, may also manifest symptoms of mental illness. Criminals who commit crimes of frolic may have been under the influence of cocaine at the time. That is, the seven categories in the typology that I present are not mutually exclusive.

In my experience, however, most offenders have a center of gravity, so to speak; their behavior and the challenge that they present tend to have a central theme that must be addressed if we are to prevent and control crime. For some, the central theme pertains to their struggles with substance abuse, while for others the central theme is mental illness or rage-filled interpersonal conflict, and so on. The typology that I present here will, I believe, help criminal justice professionals to focus on key central themes in offenders' lives in constructive ways. As Hagan observes: "The real value of criminal typologies is their heuristic benefit in providing a useful, illustrative scheme, a practical device which, although subject to abstraction and overgeneralization, enables us to simplify and make sense of complex realities. Any ideal types are prone to oversimplification, but without them the categorical equivocations in discussing reality become overwhelming" (1990:112–13).

This book includes a large collection of case studies based on my experience with offenders. The cases serve two purposes. First, they provide readers with real-life portraits of criminal activity and the circumstances that surround it. These cases may provide criminal justice educators and professionals with valuable material for discussions about and analyses of crime, etiology, prevention, sanctions, and public policy. Second, the cases provide points of departure for my own observations about these topics and, in particular, my typology of criminal circumstances. These prototypical examples come directly from my extensive encounters with offenders to illustrate and support my points about conceptually distinct groups of criminals and crimes. These cases will bring to life what might otherwise be a relatively sterile discussion of abstruse concepts. With the exception of several case examples that are unusually well known and unique (for example, the conviction of a prominent judge for accepting a bribe and a governor for racketeering), I have modified the case examples to disguise the identities of the principals (both offenders and victims). All cases are based on actual circumstances and hence provide readers with realistic accounts of crimes, criminals, and offenders' lives.

Lessons Learned

My discussion will focus mainly on factors that appear to explain criminal behavior, ways to prevent criminal behavior (for example, the role of primary prevention programs and services, economic policy, school reforms, drug interdiction) and appropriate responses to individual offenders (that is, the role of community-based and residential treatment, counseling, incarceration, probation, parole, electronic monitoring). Throughout the book I will offer succinct recommendations related to social services, criminal justice, and public policy.

Interestingly, the conceptual frameworks that I learned as an undergraduate student in criminology courses in the early 1970s are still taught today. Many intellectual debates about the subject in today's literature—where authors speculate about the relative influence of diverse psychological, biological, economic, political, and environmental factors—are virtual clones of the debates that I first encountered in the 1970s. In one sense this is frustrating, in that little evidence exists that our collective understanding of the crime problem has advanced significantly, save for modest gains in empirically based knowledge about the correlates of crime and the effectiveness of various preventative and rehabilitation efforts. In another important respect, however, the sameness of the intellectual and conceptual contours of the debate—including our persistent attempts to sort out the relative influence of diverse psychological, biological, economic, political, and environmental factors—suggests that our initial instincts were on target: crime and criminals are complicated, and the multiple and complex reasons why people commit crimes force us to dissect the issue carefully, mindful that we will not find simple answers. Every crime and criminal produce a unique case study that requires in-depth analysis and subtle, complex interpretation. Fortunately, we can aggregate cases and find patterns and themes, which is what I will offer in subsequent pages.

Here is a précis, with supporting details to follow: Many of the public's impressions and conclusions about crime and criminals are based on high-profile offenders, the cases that reach the public's eye because of the journalistic flashlight that shines on them. This is regrettable because these are the remarkably *atypical* cases and circumstances. News reports about the more prosaic crimes and criminals—which are far more representative of the risks that each of us faces on a day-to-day and night-to-night basis—tend to be buried in the police blotter on page five of the metropolitan section of the paper and squeezed into twenty seconds during the thirty-minute local television newscast.

I am not suggesting that we ignore the dramatic, high-profile cases. These too are significant and, human nature being what it is, impossible to ignore. For me, several cases stand out: the senior official in a state child welfare department who was sexually involved and used drugs with a youngster who was in the department's custody; the prominent judge who accepted a bribe from a lawyer; the incorrigible organized crime figure who seemed right out of central casting; a former governor who pleaded guilty to corruption-related charges.

But these headline cases—cases that deserve to be the lead story—are not the ones from which I have learned most of my lessons. The big lessons come from the sea of inmates—most of them poor—convicted of such crimes as drug dealing and possession, automobile theft, breaking and entering, robbery, credit card fraud, prostitution, domestic violence, and vehicular homicide. These inmates are the product of all that is wrong with our world, and their fractured lives offer messages about what we need to do to repair it.

Here is what I have learned, repeatedly, based on my face-to-face conversations with convicted criminals and my review of their remarkably diverse life circumstances: Most inmates are serving sentences for some drug- or alcohol-related offense or were heavily involved with alcohol or drugs during the period just before their arrest. These cases include armed robberies committed while under the influence or to get quick cash to buy drugs, heroin sold to undercover police officers, cars stolen to finance drug deals, and women stabbed by drunk partners. The connection between drugs and crime is stunning, and the general public needs to understand this. Effective drug- and alcohol-abuse prevention will lower the nation's crime rate. Drug- and alcohol-involved inmates who leave prison without serious treatment are likely to return. This we know.

And we know more. Especially in recent years, I have seen a steady rise in the number of gambling-related offenses—crimes as diverse as bank robbery, insurance fraud, auto theft, and stealing credit cards from rural mailboxes. Most gamblers are not criminals, of course, but we cannot ignore the result of our national casino fever.

Over the years I have been struck especially by the women inmates. The vast majority are serving sentences for drug-related offenses, and many have prostitution charges as well. In important respects they are cookie-cutter cases: victims of childhood sexual abuse by their step-fathers, biological fathers, or mothers' boyfriends . . . which led to poor self-esteem and a series of relationships with abusive men . . . which led to substance abuse to numb the pain . . . which led to some sort of addiction and, often, prostitution and shoplifting to finance the addiction . . . which led to prison. Incarceration in such cases can accomplish only so much; these women have coped as best they can under remarkably abusive, stressful circumstances. Their emotional scars are so deep that only the most sustained counseling and treatment are likely to make a meaningful difference. Stopping sexual abuse is key.

There is no simple solution, no one-stop shopping. Some criminals are fiercely mean and dangerous and should never, ever be released. Some are wickedly greedy and deserve to be punished. Some are mentally ill, desperately poor, and unemployable and need considerable help, in the form of sustained social services, to stay out of trouble. Some—especially those with substance abuse histories—are likely to repeat their crimes if not supervised closely and provided with substantial treatment. And quite a few, I am happy to say, are able to turn it around and put all their crime in their rearview mirror—usually with the help of caring, earnest, and committed human service professionals.

My principal argument is that a thoughtful approach to the problem of crime must take into account the diverse *circumstances* that lead to criminal behavior. Crime-prevention policies, interventions, and legislation are destined to have limited success if they fail to consider the unique etiological factors associated with different forms of crime. By way of analogy, no singular, comprehensive treatment strategy exists for cancer. Like crime, cancer is a simplistic, one-dimensional term that is used to characterize a remarkably diverse array of phenomena. Effective cancer treatment protocols necessarily consider the many forms of cancer (for example, lung, prostate, brain, tongue, bone, pancreatic, ovarian, breast) and the diverse etiological factors (for example, biochemical, genetic, environmental, dietary, occupational, lifestyle) that cause them. To address cancers thoughtfully and effectively, health care professionals identify specific subtypes, explore the unique causal factors associated with them, and tailor meaningful responses that are designed with the traits and attributes of the subtypes in mind. The health care professionals then adjust and tweak the interventions in response to lab results and symptom reports obtained along the way.

Similarly, meaningful responses to crime must be based on our understanding of specific subtypes, the unique causal factors associated with them, and current knowledge about which responses are most likely to succeed, given the unique characteristics and attributes of the subtypes. Residential drug treatment programs may have a positive effect on addiction-related crimes, but little effect on crimes of greed. Addicts who have a major mental illness, such as schizophrenia, need to be treated differently than addicts without a major mental illness. The threat of incarceration may deter some offenders who orchestrate crimes of revenge but may have relatively little effect on offenders whose crimes are a function of their severe mental illness. My claim is that a fuller, richer grasp of the diverse subtypes of crimes and offenders will help policy makers and practitioners fashion more effective prevention and treatment strategies.

A Primer on Etiology

My discussion throughout this book will draw extensively on historic and contemporary thinking about the causes of crime, a body of information known as etiological theory. Thus it will be helpful for me to present a succinct overview of major perspectives and schools of thought, to facilitate my subsequent shorthand references to these views.

Serious scholarly writing on criminal behavior and theories of causation began in the mideighteenth century. Since then hundreds of authors have posed a staggering number of explanatory etiological theories, ranging from narrowly focused speculation about the influence of genetic and biochemical factors on behavior to broad, expansive disquisitions on the pernicious consequences of market economies.

A comprehensive overview of etiological theories would be both distracting and exhausting.[3] Throughout my discussion I will draw on and cite specific theories to highlight and clarify key conceptual points that I wish to make about meaningful responses to crime. For now it will be more useful for me to provide a broad summary of major strains in the evolution of etiological theory.

In general, theories of crime causation are of three types. The first group includes theories that focus on the role of the "free will" that some individuals exercise when they decide to commit crimes. From this perspective, generally known as the classical point of view, criminals make conscious choices to break the law; thus prevention and treatment programs, public policy, and judicial responses should assume that people have the capacity and tendency to make deliberate, rational choices about whether to engage in criminal conduct. Put simply, the classical theorists argue that criminal conduct reflects offenders' free will, which is motivated by their hedonistic pursuit of pleasure. According to the classical view, criminals rob banks, steal cars, commit fraud, and assault people because of the pleasurable sensations associated with these activities. These acts are the product of rational choices that take into consideration the tradeoffs involved in pleasurable consequences and the various risks, or "pain," associated with the criminal activity (such as the risk of physical injury, monetary penalties, legal expenses, and incarceration). Hence, crime is the product of a cost-benefit calculus by the offender.

The earliest serious writings on the classical perspective began with Cesare Beccaria's 1764 publication of *On Crimes and Punishments*. Early adherents of classical theory also included the well-known nineteenth-century British philosopher Jeremy Bentham (1748–1832), who argued that human nature leads people to act in a way that produces the greatest ratio of good to evil (the so-called utilitarian perspective).

The second prominent school of thought approaches etiological issues from a fundamentally different vantage point. From this perspective, generally known as the positivist point of view, people commit crimes as a result of a variety of factors that are entirely or largely beyond their personal control.[4] Typical positivist theories assert that a variety of environmental, geographic, economic, psychological, cultural, and biological factors cause crime. For example, in the nineteenth century, Cesare Lombroso argued in *The Criminal Man* (1876) that criminals have unique physical stigmata, or characteristics, such as their facial features, cheekbones, arches, palm lines, and so on (in other words, he was arguing that he knew a crook when he saw one). Also in the nineteenth century, Karl Marx foreshadowed the economic theory of crime, which claims that capitalism creates inequality, poverty, and forms of social conflict that lead to crime (see Willem Bonger's *Criminality and Economic Conditions* [1910] for a prototypical application of Marxist concepts to the analysis of crime). During this same general period Charles Darwin, in *Origin of the Species* (1859), introduced theories of evolution and natural selection that provided the conceptual foundation for biological positivism. Other noteworthy positivist views include the claims of Robert Dugdale (1877) and Henry Goddard (1912) about the hereditary nature of criminality based on their analyses of generations of criminals in the notorious Jukes and Kallikak families; the twentieth-century hypotheses of Ernst Kretschmer (1926) and

Sheldon and Eleanor Glueck (1956) about the correlation between distinct body types and personality traits; and the conclusions of Charles Goring (1913) about the prominence of feeblemindedness among criminals.

A wide range of twentieth-century sociological theories of crime—which are largely positivistic in nature—have also been highly influential. Among the best-known and most-cited perspectives are the so-called anomie theories, which focus on the breakdown (or lack) of social norms that constrain criminal behavior (Durkheim 1951, 1964). The concept of anomie provided a conceptual anchor for a number of prominent theories, including Robert Merton's "strain theory" (1957), according to which crime is a by-product of society's failure to provide everyone with the means to attain the material goods to which they aspire; Richard Cloward and Lloyd Ohlin's "differential opportunity" theory (1960), which emphasized offenders' selective use of "illegitimate opportunity structures" to get what they want (social status, goods, and so on) because these items either are or seem to be unattainable through more legitimate avenues; and Albert Cohen's "subculture theory" (1955), which focused on the reactions of lower social class members to middle-class values and aspirations.

Other prominent sociological theories include social process theories, labeling theories, and radical theories. Social process theories view criminal behavior as a product of learned behavior, typically learned through cultural norms (Hagan 1990). Prominent social process theories include Robert Park's emphasis on "natural areas" or subcommunities that produce crime (1952) and Ernest Burgess's discussion of geographic "zones of transition" (1925) that breed crime; Clifford Shaw and Henry McKay's "social disorganization theory" (1942), which was based on the authors' extensive use of maps and arrest statistics to find the ecological patterns associated with crime; Edwin Sutherland's "differential association theory" (1947), which argues that individuals who have extensive contact with people who engage in deviant behavior are themselves more likely to engage in criminal conduct because of their opportunity to learn these behaviors; and Walter Miller's "focal concerns theory" (1958), which identified a number of supposed preoccupations in lower-class culture: trouble, toughness, smartness, excitement, fate, and autonomy.

Labeling theory emerged in the 1960s, based on the argument that individuals engage in criminal behavior in large part because the broader society has labeled them as deviant. That is, many crimes are not inherently deviant; rather, the broader society has labeled them as such and, in so doing, exacerbates criminal conduct. Key assumptions under labeling theory are that no act is inherently criminal in nature; those in positions of authority (for example, legislators, policy and administrative officials) define what is and is not criminal; the act of being caught sets the labeling process in motion; certain demographic traits (such as age, social class, gender, race/ethnicity) increase the likelihood of being labeled criminal; and the labeling process strengthens offenders' identification as criminal as well as their "rejection of the rejectors" (Hagan 1990:192; see also Becker 1963, 1964; Lemert 1951; Schrag 1971; Schur 1969, 1971; Tannenbaum 1938).

Perhaps the best-known labeling theory is based on Edwin Lemert's distinction between "primary deviance" and "secondary deviance" (1967). Primary deviance refers to the initial offense itself, such as stealing a car, committing a robbery, or assaulting someone. Secondary deviance entails the formation of a deviant or criminal identity as a result of being caught, prosecuted, convicted, incarcerated, and otherwise processed as a deviant. According to labeling theory, this new identity greatly increases the likelihood that the individual will continue to engage in criminal activity (a form of self-fulfilling prophecy).

In contrast, radical theory—sometimes known as Marxist theory—is rooted in the belief that capitalism and the forces of free-market economies create the conditions for criminal behavior. Richard Quinney (1970, 1974, 1977, 1979) and William Chambliss (1975) argue forcefully that in capitalist nations the criminal law is an instrument of the privileged and elite ruling class, and the elite use it to maintain social order by controlling and oppressing those who are poor and otherwise subordinate (the proletariat). According to Anthony Platt (1974), a noted radical theorist, criminologists have become conservative handmaidens of state repression.

The third major group of theories incorporates elements of the classical and positivist perspectives. From this perspective—which has been dubbed the neoclassical view, the mixed view, or soft determinism—crime is best understood as the product of, to varying degrees and in different proportions, both individual choice and structural or environmental circumstances that are largely or entirely beyond the control of the individuals. A prototypical example of this perspective is David Matza's "drift theory" (1964). Matza argues that while outside forces determine human behavior to some extent, individuals nonetheless have the capacity to exercise some degree of free will. Matza argues that offenders tend to drift between criminal and conventional behaviors and rationalize (or, to use Matza's term, *neutralize*) their conduct by blaming it on their toxic home life or communities, denying that their actions have harmed their victims, condemning people in positions of authority as corrupt, and so on.

Other prominent examples of the mixed view include so-called social control theories. Social control theories typically focus on the influence of social institutions and norms as mechanisms that contain crime. Walter Reckless (1961), for example, advanced the so-called containment theory, arguing that crime is the result of flawed external conditions (for example, poverty, chaotic neighborhoods and families, unemployment) and internal conditions (for example, poor self-concept and impulse control). Travis Hirschi (1969), in his discussion of the "social bond theory," stresses the importance of social connections between individuals and family, friends, schools, employers, neighbors, and religious institutions, as mechanisms that enhance the ability of an individual to engage in law-abiding behavior and avoid criminal behavior.

Responding to Crime

It seems clear to me that people's opinions about how we ought to respond to criminal behavior have a great deal to do with our beliefs about the extent to which offenders are responsible for their behavior. Those who claim that offenders have the ability to exercise control over their behavior, consistent with the "free will" view, are much more inclined to endorse punitive sanctions. Those who embrace a more deterministic view, believing that misconduct is a function of a range of circumstances and phenomena beyond the control of the offender, are much less likely to be punitive and much more likely to embrace rehabilitative efforts.

The concept of punishment, and its proper place in criminal justice, is key. Historically, moral and political philosophers have espoused one of three perspectives on the issue. The first, known as the teleological view (from the Greek *teleios,* "brought to its end or purpose"), maintains that punishment, such as imprisonment, is morally justifiable when its aim is to produce a specific beneficial consequence, such as rehabilitating an offender, deterring the individual offender from committing crimes in the future (known in the trade as specific deterrence), and deterring members of the general public from committing crimes (general deterrence). In moral philosophy teleology—also known as consequentialism—is the school of thought that asserts that an action is morally justifiable to the extent that it produces "good" consequences or, more specifically, more good than "evil." As Jeremy Bentham argued in his classic eighteenth-century commentary on utilitarianism (the most common form of teleology), *An Introduction to the Principles of Morals and Legislation* (1789), "An action may be said to be conformable to the principle of utility, or, for shortness sake, to utility (meaning with respect to the community at large), when the tendency it has to augment the happiness of the community is greater than any it has to diminish it" (1973:362). With regard to punishment specifically, Bentham argued that while punishment is inherently evil, it is justifiable to the extent that it prevents some greater harm:

I. *The end of law is to augment happiness.* The general object which all laws have, or ought to have, in common, is to augment the total happiness of the community; and therefore, in the first place, to exclude, as far as may be, every thing that tends to subtract from that happiness: in other words, to exclude mischief.

II. *But punishment is an evil.* But all punishment is mischief: all punishment in itself is evil. Upon the principle of utility, if it ought at all to be admitted, it ought only to be admitted in as far as it promises to exclude some greater evil. (1789, cited in Ezorsky 1972:56)

Perhaps the earliest argument that punishment is morally justifiable as an effort to "cure" the offender appears in the dialogue between Socrates and Polus in Plato's *Gorgias*:

SOCRATES: Of two who suffer evil either in body or in soul, which is the more wretched, the man who submits to treatment and gets rid of the evil, or he who is not treated but still retains it?

POLUS: Evidently the man who is not treated.

SOCRATES: And was not punishment admitted to be a release from the greatest of evils, namely wickedness?

POLUS: It was.

SOCRATES: Yes, because a just penalty disciplines us and makes us more just and cures us of evil. (cited in Ezorsky 1972:37)

The second major perspective—known as the retributivist view—reflects the widespread belief that the primary purpose of punishment is to convey the community's anger, indignation, and resentment toward the offender—what Feinberg refers to as the "expressive function" of punishment (1965). Whether the punishment "cures" or deters the offender or deters others is not critically important; what matters is that members of the broader society have an opportunity to condemn the offender for the misconduct and to "restore the moral balance disturbed by crime" (Ezorsky 1972:xvii). According to Ezorsky, "For all retributivists punishment has moral worth independently of any further desirable effects. *Ceteris paribus,* the world is better, morally speaking, when the vicious suffer. Thus it is not surprising that retributivism is sometimes characterized as the vindictive theory of punishment" (1972:xviii).[5]

Among the earliest classic commentaries on the retributive functions of punishment are Immanuel Kant's nineteenth-century observations in his *Philosophy of Law*:

> Juridical punishment can never be administered merely as a means for promoting another good, either with regard to the criminal himself or to civil society, but must in all cases be imposed only because the individual on whom it is inflicted has committed a crime. For one ought never to be dealt with merely as a means subservient to the purpose of another, nor be mixed up with the subjects of real right. . . . The penal law is a categorical imperative; and woe to him who creeps through the serpent-windings of utilitarianism to discover some advantage that may discharge him from the justice of punishment, or even from the due measure of it.
>
> (1887, cited in Ezorsky 1972:103–4)

The third—and I think most sensible—perspective reflects a blend of the teleological and retributivist perspectives: teleological retributivism. This point of view acknowledges the legitimate right of the community to express its indignation and resentment toward those offenders who have the ability to exercise some measure of control over their behavior (this would not include, for example, offenders whose crimes are the result of serious mental illness). However, according to teleological retributivism, reasonable constraints must temper these understandable instincts; any punishment imposed on an offender must serve a constructive purpose with respect to some beneficial consequence, such as public safety, deterrence, or rehabilitation. As Ezorsky notes, teleological retributivists are pluralists in that they "mediate between a teleological principle, i.e., utilitarianism, and principles of justice held by retributivists" (1972:xix). In other words, punishment serves multiple aims, which may vary from circumstance to circumstance and case to case. Moral indignation may be particularly important in some circumstances (for example, when a judge accepts a bribe meant to influence his handling of a case being tried before him, or when a man makes a deliberate decision to sexually exploit his stepdaughter), while deterrence and rehabilitation are more compelling in others (for example, when a loving, caring mother who is earnestly trying to conquer her drug addiction shoplifts in order to feed her hungry children, or when a homeless man suffering from untreated schizophrenia is arrested after he accidentally starts a fire in a warehouse where he sought shelter in freezing temperatures).

I would add to this mix a major commitment to the goal of restorative justice, a concept of ancient origin that has resurfaced in the criminal justice field only in recent years (especially since the 1980s). Put briefly, restorative justice is based on a belief that an important goal of the criminal justice system should be to restore victims who have been harmed or injured by offenders. *Victims* can be defined broadly to include individual victims (as in cases of robbery, rape, and murder, for example), organizational victims (as in cases of embezzlement or fraud), and the broader community (as in cases of vandalism or theft of public property).

Original notions of restorative justice have their roots in Jewish, Buddhist, Taoist, Greek, Arab, Roman, and Hindu civilizations, among others (Braithwaite 1998; Van Ness 1986). According to Braithwaite, "Taken seriously, restorative justice involves a very different way of thinking about traditional notions such as deterrence, rehabilitation, incapacitation, and crime prevention. It also means transformed foundations of criminal jurisprudence and of our notions of freedom, democracy, and community" (1998:323).

Restorative justice programs can take various forms, the most common of which include

1. Victim-offender mediation. Canada and the United States pioneered this form of restorative justice in the 1970s (Umbreit 2001). The victims and offender meet with a facilitator to address their conflict and to explore meaningful ways to resolve the conflict and find ways for the offender to compensate victims for their injuries.
2. Conferencing. New Zealand introduced the concept of conferencing in the late 1980s (G. Maxwell and Morris 1992, 1993). This restorative justice approach builds on the concept of victim-offender mediation but broadens it to include relevant family members, clergy, social service professionals, law enforcement officials, and attorneys. The principal goal is for the offender to acknowledge the wrongdoing and for the group to reach consensus about what constructive steps the offender can take to make reparations.
3. Circles. The concept of circles (of relationships) has a long history in Native American (United States) and First Nation (Canada) cultures (Galaway and Hudson 1996). These communities use circles to provide offenders with an opportunity to acknowledge their misconduct and to address problems and conflicts between people. The criminal justice system has used circles since the 1980s. Circles usually include diverse participants concerned about the victim and offender (professionals, community leaders, family, and so on). In turn, each participant holds the "talking piece" and has an opportunity to express his or her views about the crime, the offender, the victim, and opportunities to make reparations.

4. Restitution. Restitution programs typically provide offenders with an opportunity to repay their victims for the economic injuries that they have incurred. Individual victims may receive compensation for their property and economic losses, and organizational victims may receive compensation for theft of property or money (for instance, as a result of fraud or embezzlement).

5. Community service. Community service is a popular option in restorative justice programs, especially when the crime had no individual or organizational victims per se. Community service programs provide the offender with an opportunity to "pay back" the community for the misdeeds. The service may take the form of teaching (for example, when offenders convicted of killing someone while driving drunk lecture high school students about the dangers of drunk driving), labor (for example, when an offender paints or repairs public buildings or cleans public property), or service (for example, when an offender provides assistance at a shelter or soup kitchen).

Restorative justice can achieve various goals (Braithwaite 1998), including the restoration of

Property. Offenders who broke into a home can return stolen jewelry or, if it has already been sold, pay restitution to compensate for the loss.

Injury. Offenders who injured others in a fight can pay the victims' medical bills or lost wages. They can also express their sincere remorse—either in person, by telephone, or in writing—for the pain that they have caused. Offenders who have somehow harmed the community but whose actions did not harm individuals can compensate by performing some form of community service (for example, volunteering to work with disabled people, painting a neighborhood health clinic, removing litter from a public park).

Sense of security. Offenders who become acquainted with their victims may provide reassurance that they did not target these individuals specifically and that the victims need not fear retaliation.

Dignity. Offenders who engage in sincere attempts to restore their victims can enhance their own sense of dignity and reduce their sense of shame. Restorative efforts may be an important step in the offender's rehabilitation.

Sense of empowerment. Both offenders and victims may enhance their sense of empowerment. For victims, restorative justice provides an opportunity to confront crime and criminals and to assert their rights and indignation. For offenders, taking responsibility for their misdeeds can provide a strong sense of empowerment for those who are eager to change their conduct.

Deliberative democracy. Restorative justice is but one expression of the true democratic process, actively engaging citizens in the administration of justice. That is, justice is not rendered only from on high—in the form of judicial sanctions and oversight—but within the commonweal itself.

Harmony based on a feeling that justice has been done. Consistent with ancient traditions, restorative justice can help people make amends for their wrongdoing. An increased sense of justice among citizens has the useful by-product of increased harmony. This is especially true when restorative justice programs take the form of reconciliation meetings between victims and offenders.

Social support. Here too both victims and offenders may find healing. Through restorative justice efforts victims may gain a sense that the broader community in general, and the criminal justice system in particular, are behind them, in their corner, and supportive. Similarly, offenders may gain a sense that those responsible for administering justice have more than punishment and retribution in mind, that they are genuinely concerned about the offender's well-being and future.

Restorative justice programs are gaining in popularity in part because of their nearly universal intuitive appeal and the opportunity that they provide to engage common citizens in the administration of justice. Braithwaite states it well:

> All cultures value in some way repair of damage to our persons and property, security, dignity, empowerment, deliberative democracy, and harmony based on a sense of justice and social support. These are universals because they are all vital to our emotional survival as human beings and vital to the possibility of surviving without constant fear of violence. The world's greatest religions recognize that the desire to pursue these restorative justice values is universal, which is why some of our spiritual leaders offer hope against those political leaders who wish to rule through fear and by crushing deliberative democracy. (1998:332)

My pluralistic approach to crime and the treatment of offenders—which blends features of incapacitation for public safety, punishment and retribution, rehabilitation and treatment, and restorative justice—is based on honest acknowledgment that the responses to crime should be thoughtful, selective, and tailored to individual circumstances and that we need to resist the understandable but naive temptation of one-size-fits-all dispositions and sentencing guidelines. In our wish for clarity and simplicity, too often we end up with simplistic, uniform responses to wildly diverse criminal and life circumstances. The noted legal philosopher H. L. A. Hart echoes this sentiment in this profoundly important and levelheaded passage from *Punishment and Responsibility*, about the relevance of abstruse philosophical principles in the face of real-life crime and criminals:

> No one expects judges or statesmen occupied in the business of sending people to the gallows or prisons, or in making (or unmaking) laws which enable this to be done, to have much time for philosophical discussion of the principles which make it morally tolerable to do these things. A judicial bench is not and should not be a professorial chair. Yet what is said in public debates about punishment by those specially concerned with it as judges or legislators is important. Few are likely to be more circumspect, and if what they say seems, as it often does, unclear, one-sided and easily refutable by pointing to some aspect of things which they have overlooked, it is likely that in our inherited ways of talking or thinking about punishment there is some persistent drive towards an over-simplification of multiple issues which require separate consideration. To counter this drive what is most needed is *not* the simple admission that instead of a single value or aim (Deterrence, Retribution, Reform or any other) a plurality of different values and aims should be given as a conjunctive answer to some *single* question concerning the justification of punishment. What is needed is the realization that different principles (each of which may in a sense be called a "justification") are relevant at different points in any morally acceptable account of punishment. What we should look for are answers to a number of different questions such as: What justifies the general practice of punishment? To whom may punishment be applied? How severely may we punish? In dealing with these and other questions concerning punishment we should bear in mind that in this, as in most other social institutions, the pursuit of one aim may be qualified by or provide an opportunity, not to be missed, for the pursuit of others.
>
> (cited in Ezorsky 1972:154–55)

Understanding the causes of crime and the purposes of punishment and other interventions is helpful to the extent that such insights enable us to prevent crime and fashion meaningful responses to it. Like etiological theories of crime causation, the organized responses to crime by a community also have evolved over time. Historically, responses to crime have been of three types: institutional (such as traditional prisons and less traditional correctional facilities or units with specialized missions, for example, those designed to treat prisoners diagnosed with major mental illness, drug and alcohol addictions, or sex-related disorders); community-based residential programs (such as privately operated drug and alcohol treatment programs and programs designed to provide offenders, many of whom are on parole or probation, with vocational and educational tools); and community-based nonresidential social service programs (such as outpatient mental health counseling, group treatment for sex offenders, job-training programs, and restitution programs). Other innovations in the field include intensive probation, home confinement, electronic monitoring, mediation and other restorative justice programs, day reporting centers, residential treatment for sex offenders, and corrections-oriented boot camp.[6] Throughout the book I will comment on the lessons that I have learned about the most appropriate use of the available options.

The Calibration-Recalibration Model of Crime Prevention and Control

Once criminals have been identified—either through arrest or conviction—the criminal justice system has, in principle, four goals or aims: public safety through containment (through electronic monitoring, secure residential care, or incarceration); treatment and rehabilitation (in the form of residential or outpatient social services and counseling); restorative justice (victim restitution or community service); and punishment or retribution (in the form of incarceration or the payment of fines). My principal argument is that, in light of the best available knowledge and centuries of reflection about and experience with criminals and criminal behavior, the most sensible and rational response to crime should entail several key elements. These constitute what I call the calibration-recalibration model of crime prevention and control.

When the criminal justice system first identifies offenders, it should make assertive efforts to assess the circumstances in offenders' lives that have led them to commit crimes—that is, the degree of an offender's desperation, rage, greed, frolic, revenge, addiction, and mental illness or mental retardation. The focus should not be limited to the crime or crimes that triggered the current offense (known in the trade as the "instant offense"). In addition, justice should consider the offender's criminal career, to determine whether enduring and persistent themes exist. Some offenders' criminal careers and patterns are long standing, consistent, and predictable; they have a modus operandi that is rooted in their chronic drug addiction, mental illness, or greed. The careers of other offenders are much more diverse, uneven, and curvilinear—and much less predictable. For example, earlier chapters in their criminal careers may have been a function of youthful frolic and opportunism, crimes of rage may have dominated the middle chapters, and the most recent chapter may have arisen from a problem with alcohol. In some instances—a very small percentage, I find—a pattern may not be discernible. And, of course, some offenders are just getting started, so no historical pattern or criminal career exists to assess. However, comprehensive assessments of the circumstances that surround criminal activity almost always yield themes and patterns that suggest prominent core issues that the criminal justice system must address. Typically, these core issues include some combination of problems related to desperation, rage, greed, frolic, revenge, addiction, and mental illness or retardation.

Upon completion of this initial assessment, criminal justice must carefully consider its four key goals—public safety through containment, treatment and rehabilitation, restorative justice, and punishment or retribution—and pursue those goals that best suit each offender's unique circumstances. This is the process of calibration. Which goal, or combination of goals, the system pursues will, and should, vary from offender to offender. As I will show throughout the book, some offenders—a relatively small percentage, fortunately—are so dangerous and incorrigible that the only reasonable goals are public safety and containment through long-term incarceration. In many cases the most sensible course of action is the development and implementation of a comprehensive treatment plan and set of social services, for example, substance abuse treatment, mental health counseling, literacy education, and vocational training. Restorative justice—in the form of victim compensation or community service—may be a useful adjunct. In some instances some form of punishment, for retribution's sake, may be appropriate to reflect the legitimate indignation of the community.

Another key feature of this approach to crime prevention and control is that the degree of emphasis on the goals of public safety, treatment and rehabilitation, restorative justice, and punishment or retribution will vary from offender to offender. That is, in some cases the primary emphasis may be on the goal of public safety through incarceration, because of the offender's violent behavior, while the secondary emphasis may be on the goals of punishment and treatment or rehabilitation within the correctional institution. In other cases the proportions may be reversed, for example, when the offender does not pose a major threat to public safety and can be supervised through electronic monitoring; the primary aim may be to engage the offender in meaningful treatment and rehabilitation. In sum, the goals of public safety, treatment and rehabilitation, restorative justice, and punishment or retribution should be "mixed and matched" in varying proportions, depending upon the unique features of the current and historical life circumstances of each offender.

Once the system has set initial goals for an offender—the calibration stage—it is critically important that the professionals working with the offender (for example, probation and parole officers, parole boards, judges, mental health and social service professionals) monitor the individual's progress consistently, diligently, and thoroughly. Beyond the practical reasons for such monitoring (to determine whether the offender is complying with court orders or parole plans, for instance), the principal aim here is to regularly gather information in order to assess whether the plan for the offender—specifically, the degree of emphasis on the goals of public safety, treatment and rehabilitation, restorative justice, and punishment or retribution—need to be adjusted or recalibrated. That is, society cannot assume that a sound plan implemented when an offender is placed on probation, sentenced to prison, or released on parole will never need modification. Life does not work that way. New and unanticipated issues emerge in offenders' lives, often with little or no notice, and these may require some adjustment in the master plan and goals. An offender may function just fine for months in a drug treatment and restitution program but then relapse when he learns that his wife has filed for divorce. The relapse may lead to a new crime, such as a robbery to get money for drugs, which requires some recalibration, for example, that the goal of public safety becomes more compelling for a period of time than the goals of community-based treatment and restorative justice. Treatment should continue, of course, but it may need to occur within the context of a secure environment. That is, new circumstances and events will lead to a change in the constellation of goals for this particular offender. The overarching purpose of recalibration is to increase or decrease emphasis on the goals of public safety (periodically tightening or loosening the leash), treatment and rehabilitation, restorative justice, and punishment or retribution based on information gathered at regular intervals. The mix of responses should always be proportionate, based on principles of justice and the long-standing concept of the least restrictive intervention necessary.

I think several analogies will help to convey the conceptual basis for the calibration-recalibration model.

Sailing entails constant navigation—processing data from a variety of sources, and making many adjustments along the way, to ensure safe passage toward one's ultimate destination. Sailors who fail to pay attention to key pieces of information, such as wind and wave conditions, weather forecasts, water currents, and boat condition—do so at their peril. When they begin their journey, sailors plot their course based on the best information available at departure time (comparable to the calibration stage involved in the management of offenders). Throughout the journey competent sailors pay close attention to and monitor various on-board gauges, radio reports, and maps, supplemented by their own eyeball observations, to chart their course and modify their tacking. They make adjustments in direction, speed, sails, and so forth, based on changes in the data that they receive (comparable to recalibration in work with offenders). Sailors' ability to keep their boat on course and to proceed safely depends on their ability to factor in steady streams of new and changing information and make wise adjustments accordingly. The goal is to keep the wind in the sails; the goal of criminal justice professionals is to keep offenders on course.

Diabetes—a disease in which the body does not produce or properly use insulin, the hormone needed to convert sugar, starches, and other food into energy—requires constant monitoring and feedback once the condition is diagnosed. Patients' conditions and needs vary, of course, but generally the initial treatment plan (calibration) for people with diabetes entails some combination of diligent nutrition and meal planning, exercise, and, especially for people with Type 2 diabetes, weight loss. Initial calibration is not enough, however. People with diabetes know that they must be vigilant about monitoring their blood glucose levels. Diabetics routinely prick their fingers throughout the day, obtain a drop of blood, and check the sugar level with a glucose meter. Based on this data, patients adjust their food intake and activity levels (recalibration). The measurement-adjustment-measurement-adjustment sequence is constant, just as it must be with the supervision of offenders.

Every thoughtful parent knows that child rearing is a never-ending work in progress. Each child has a unique temperament and personality, physical and genetic endowment, and proclivities. Parenting approaches and strategies that are effective with one child may be ineffective and counterproductive with another child in the same family. Parenting techniques that were effective with a child at age six may lose their effectiveness when the child is nine. Effective parenting requires constant and consistent monitoring of the child's physical, cognitive, emotional, and behavioral development.

Information about the child typically comes from various sources, including the parents' observations, as well as feedback from child care providers, teachers, camp and after-school activities counselors, clergy, friends, relatives, neighbors, and so on. Ideally, parents take in all this information, which is typically provided sporadically and in diverse forms, review it critically and constructively, and make parenting decisions accordingly (recalibration). Effective parenting requires varying degrees of emotional support, nurturance, therapeutic intervention, discipline, and punishment, which are adjusted over the days, weeks, months, and years according to the child's needs. The proportions vary over time depending on the information available to parents. At times children need much more emotional support and solace than at other times, when some degree of discipline or punishment may be more necessary. As with sailing, diabetes management, and the supervision of offenders, parenting requires nonstop monitoring and adjustment, or recalibration.

The Stages of Change

Several components of the calibration-recalibration model are relatively easy to conceptualize and implement. The key ingredients of institutional care, for example, are well understood. Although implementation may be flawed, we know how to incarcerate offenders when this form of segregation is necessary for public safety. Similarly, we now know how to design and implement all manner of victim compensation and community service programs in our efforts to promote restorative justice (Braithwaite 1998; Nugent et al. 2001; Umbreit 1997, 2001). Much debate continues about which models, strategies, and approaches are most valid and effective, of course, but the consensus on the basics is considerable.

What is especially challenging in criminal justice, however, is the design and implementation of various rehabilitation, educational, and vocational programs whose goal is to change unlawful and destructive behavior. What is clear to me from my experience over the years is that offenders vary considerably with respect to their willingness and readiness to change. This is not unusual, of course, with involuntary clients (Rooney 1994).

I do not believe that behavior change can be coerced or mandated. Offenders who struggle with problems related to substance abuse, gambling, sexual molestation, domestic violence, impulse control, greed, and so on can be helped only when they reach a point where they genuinely want help. This is hardly a novel concept; mental health and social service professionals have known and embraced this idea for years. Yet this concept, which is so widely accepted in work with voluntary clients—in various mental health, domestic violence, and substance abuse treatment settings, for instance—is much less prominent in the criminal justice system. Because of their coercive approaches to involuntary clients, professionals in criminal justice settings are likely to *impose* treatment and social services as a requirement of probation, incarceration, or parole.

The best available evidence of the importance of clients' readiness for change comes from a widely cited model that is based on the concept of stages of change (Prochaska 1994; Prochaska, Norcross, and DiClemente 1995; Prochaska and Velicer 1997). The model, which is based on extensive empirical research, describes how people modify a problem behavior or engage in a positive or desirable behavior. The approach focuses on the individual's emotions, cognitions (ways of thinking), and behaviors and focuses on intentional change, that is, efforts to change that begin with the individual (as opposed to being imposed externally). Research on the model has focused mostly on behaviors such as smoking, diet, exercise, alcohol and drug abuse, condom use for HIV protection, and stress management. Although research on the stages-of-change approach has not typically focused explicitly on criminal conduct per se, the model is clearly relevant to many behaviors that lead to a significant portion of criminal conduct (such as alcohol and drug abuse).

The stages-of-change approach is organized around five specific stages that occur over time.

Precontemplation

At the stage of precontemplation people are not planning to engage in any meaningful change. This may be because the individual does not have sufficient information about the problem or the options available or because past attempts at change have been frustrating and unsuccessful. Some inmates I have met are not willing or able to acknowledge that they have a problem that warrants change. On occasion, although this is relatively infrequent, inmates tell me that they are not guilty of the crime—that they were "set up" or that someone else is the one who needs to change (for example, the domestic partner whom the inmate abused). Or the inmate may acknowledge having a serious problem but will say that prison is no place to address it. For example, I have heard many sex offenders plead with me to grant them parole, claiming that they have their problem "under control." They add that if my colleagues and I insist on it, they would enroll in a community-based sex offender treatment program. Some of these inmates are willing to admit their guilt, but they are not willing to join a prison-based sex offender treatment program because of their fear of harassment from other inmates. They may want help, but during the time that they are in prison, they are still treading water in the precontemplation stage.

Contemplation

In the contemplation stage individuals are beginning to think about change and hope to change within the near future (the model suggests a time frame of six months within which the individual plans to engage in serious efforts to change). The individual may assess the potential benefits and costs of change and may be quite ambivalent. For example, I have heard many inmates and parolees talk about the difficult decisions that they need to make concerning enrollment in an ambitious treatment program. Some acknowledge the potential benefits but are afraid of the program's intensity and demands or are reluctant to change their lifestyle, while others are afraid to expose themselves during group discussions. For some individuals, the prospect of genuine change is highly threatening. Some inmates are remarkably pragmatic, saying that they do not want to enroll in a program because they would have to give up their prison job and would lose their per diem pay.

Preparation

Preparation is the stage in which individuals actively engage in plans to make changes in the immediate future. In the corrections field this would include planning to join a substance treatment or twelve-step program (such as Alcoholics Anonymous, Narcotics Anonymous, or Gamblers Anonymous), seeking mental health counseling to address problems with depression, enrolling in a literacy course or vocational training program, or joining a domestic violence therapy group.

Action

In the action stage individuals take actual steps to change their behavior. Examples of behaviors by offenders in prison or under supervision in the community that would "count" include abstaining from alcohol consumption (in the case of an alcoholic offender who is in recovery), stopping all physical aggression toward one's spouse (in the case of an offender convicted of domestic violence), learning how to read (in the case of an offender who is illiterate), and having no contact with children while alone (in the case of an offender convicted of child molestation).

Maintenance

In the maintenance stage individuals have achieved some degree of positive behavior change and are engaged in actions to prevent relapse.

According to the stages-of-change approach, movement toward change occurs as a function of several factors. Individuals weigh the relative pros and cons of changing their behavior. The pros include an assessment of the benefits for the individual and others. With offenders, for instance, the benefits of changing behavior might include avoiding or being released from prison, reconciling an estranged relationship with a spouse or partner, regaining custody of one's child from the state child welfare agency, and enhancing one's self-esteem. The down side includes an assessment of costs to the individual and others. With offenders the down side might include being away from family while enrolled in a residential drug treatment program, having to wear an electronic bracelet, performing community service by picking up litter in a public park, and enduring the scorn of neighbors who know from television and newspaper coverage that the individual has been convicted of a heinous crime.

The stages-of-change model is particularly appropriate in criminal justice settings. At any moment one can find offenders at every stage, ranging from stark precontemplation, where no evidence of intent to change exists, to earnest forms of action, where offenders are actively and eagerly involved in programs and behaviors designed to help them change for the better. Offenders may be at one stage with respect to one problem but another stage with respect to another. For example, I once interviewed an inmate who was at the action stage with respect to his heroin problem but at the precontemplation stage with respect to his alcohol addiction.

As a parole board member, I could talk to an inmate forever about the importance of enrolling in this, that, or the other mental health, substance abuse, educational, or vocational program. It is clear to me, however, that if the inmate is at the precontemplation stage and not ready to actively pursue change, my words are like cotton candy at the county fair—once tasted, they dissolve instantly. More than once an inmate has told me that she or he would prefer to serve the entire sentence rather than increase her or his chances for parole by participating in a treatment or educational program. My goal with such an inmate should be to help him or her explore the relative benefits and costs of changing a specific behavior so that he or she can contemplate—really contemplate—behavior change. But if the inmate is not ready to change, no persistence on my part or anyone else's is likely to lead to change. Quite the contrary: a pointless tug-of-war is likely to ensue; the more the criminal justice professional demands change, the more the offender asserts the right to autonomy by resisting.

The artful practitioner who wants to help an inmate move beyond the precontemplation stage skillfully listens with genuine respect and empathy, reflects the offender's ambivalence about change, and gently offers information about options. The professional is patient, not insistent or demanding, empathic and not punitive. Change, or at least the offender's interest in changing, may come in time, but preaching, lecturing, admonishing, or coercing is not likely to accelerate it. From the perspective of the stages-of-change model, client resistance arises from client-practitioner interaction and is entirely avoidable when the practitioner maintains a truly respectful, reflective listening stance, allowing the client to guide the process, focusing on the client's hopes and goals.

I have met many inmates who clearly are at a more advanced stage, such as the action stage, where they are actively involved in rehabilitation, educational, or vocational programs. In these instances the criminal justice professional's main job is to encourage and facilitate these efforts, as a coach and cheerleader, and help the offender move toward maintenance and relapse prevention. I have witnessed many such successful attempts.

• • •

Clearly, during the last several centuries we have seen a remarkable proliferation of theories concerning crime causation and creative attempts to respond to it. Some etiological perspectives are as different as black and white, and some are merely different shades of gray. As with arguments about any intensely provocative subject, such as the morality of abortion and whether God exists, I suspect that we will never achieve true consensus on the issue. Rather, people are destined to disagree about the nature and causes of crime and about the most appropriate way to respond to and prevent crime.

Nonetheless, over time the debates have become richer, more nuanced, and refined. In my view, competing perspectives do not necessarily require a stark choice between that which is right and that which is wrong. As I will make clear throughout this discussion, a wise, mature, realistic, and informed approach to understanding, preventing, and responding to crime necessarily entails careful, thoughtful, judicious, and selective use of different theoretical, ideological, programmatic, and policy perspectives and assumptions. Although some conceptual views have been completely discredited or are terminally simplistic or antiquated, our selective use of many of the perspectives that have emerged over the centuries can be effective. My claim is that our selective use of these theoretical perspectives and assumptions should be guided by the unique and diverse circumstances before us in the form of the different categories of crime that I will now explore: crimes of desperation; rage; greed, exploitation, and opportunism; frolic; revenge and retribution; addiction; and mental illness.

2

Crimes of Desperation

Perhaps the most common refrain I hear from inmates is that they committed their crimes—offenses as diverse as robbery, breaking and entering, automobile theft, bank fraud, and embezzlement—because they were desperate. The dictionary definitions of *desperate* include "reckless or dangerous because of despair or urgency," "having an urgent need, desire," "leaving little or no hope," and "undertaken out of despair or as a last resort" (*Random House Webster's College Dictionary* 1991). These certainly are accurate descriptions of the state of mind described by the "desperate" offenders I have met. Briefly, they claim to have run out of options, and some may have. Others simply gave up and, for a variety of reasons, did not pursue reasonable, legal alternatives in the form of, for example, employment or loans to carry them through a difficult cash-flow crisis.

There are several ways to think about the kinds of desperation that lead to crime. First is the distinction between actual and perceived desperation. I have no doubt that some offenders truly believe that they have hit the proverbial brick wall. These individuals have applied for job after job or have tried to "work things out" in a family relationship, without success. In contrast, some offenders claim that desperate circumstances led to their crimes when, in fact, the circumstances fell short of true desperation. But for lack of skill, ability, knowledge, motivation, or effort, the offender would have pursued alternatives.

Some crimes of desperation involve acute, immediate pressure that leads to risky, dangerous offenses in an effort to fix a problem fast: the heroin addict whose withdrawal symptoms are so intense that he grabs a pedestrian's pocketbook for quick cash, or the lover whose abusive partner was so threatening that she grabbed a kitchen knife and stabbed him.

Other crimes of desperation, however, are the result of circumstances that simmer for some time before they reach a full boil. A classic example is the gambler who borrows money from an organized crime figure to pay off a gambling debt. The organized crime lender offers the gambler a payment schedule, but the borrower's delinquency leads to threats that become increasingly intense and earnest. The gambler's mounting fear leads him to rob someone to pay the gangster, that is, to commit a serious crime to obtain the money to pay off the debt.

Many crimes of desperation have financial overtones. They arise from debt or offenders' efforts to meet their basic needs or provide for others' basic needs, such as food, shelter, and clothing. By definition, crimes of desperation are not committed in pursuit of gratuitous or "luxury" items—a fancier car, a bigger home, a flashy diamond ring.

Other crimes of desperation have no link to money per se. Typically these occur because of interpersonal desperation, where nonfinancial life crises and domestic or other relationship conflicts lead people who are fearful to act in ways that they might not have otherwise. In short, these people see no realistic way out of a bad situation without committing a desperate act.

Financial Desperation and Poverty

Case 2.1 Barney S., the thirty-two-year-old married father of three young children, was serving a four-year sentence for robbery. For twelve years Barney S. was employed as a machinist at a local manufacturer of heating equipment. About a year earlier Barney S. was laid off when the manufacturer closed its plant and relocated the factory to Mexico. For several months Barney S., who had a ninth-grade education, looked for work. During the interim he performed a series of odd jobs to help make ends meet—lawn care, snow shoveling, and dish washing. At one point he was so desperate that he scavenged for soda cans to exchange for cash at a nearby recycling center.

During this unemployment period Barney S.'s wife was diagnosed with ovarian cancer and his sixteen-year-old daughter had a baby for whom she was caring in her parents' home. According to Barney S., he reached a point where, no matter how hard he worked, he was not able to keep up with the rent or put food on the table for his family and infant grandson. "I know it was wrong to hold up that gas station," he said. "I know better, and I'm smart enough to know right from wrong. But no one I know could loan us money—we had already been down that road too many times—and I was feeling more and more like a complete failure. Hell, I didn't even use a real gun. I decided on the spur of the moment to empty the cash drawer of the station where I had just bought my kids some milk in their minimart. I sure regret it now, but at the time I didn't know where else to turn."

Case 2.2 Mary L. was eighteen and the mother of a severely disabled infant. The child was born with a rare respiratory disorder that required constant supervision.

Mary L. had been involved with Tony, the thirty-one-year-old father of her child, for about two years. As Mary L. describes it, "I was just a teenager when I met Tony. We spent an awful lot of time drinking and drugging together. My parents were so bad to me that I thought Tony would save me. Boy, was I wrong, but I was real young, you know?"

According to Mary L., Tony physically abused her, mostly when he was drunk. After her baby was born, Mary L. knew she had to leave Tony. After leaving a shelter where she stayed for a short time, Mary L. was having a difficult time finding an affordable apartment and paying for food. Mary L. was arrested for shoplifting an expensive video camera from a department store; this violated her probation on earlier shoplifting charges, and the judge sentenced her to eighteen months in prison.

The close connection between poverty and crime is indisputable. Although most people living in poverty do not commit serious crimes, a significant percentage of offenders are living in poverty when they commit their crimes. Some people respond to poverty by committing crimes to extract themselves from their desperate circumstances. For some offenders, poverty is a chronic and lifelong condition; for others, such as Barney S. and Mary L., poverty is more acute, often the result of sudden illness or disability, divorce, and unemployment. Here is a summary of what we know:

People who are poor commit a disproportionate amount of crime (Lauritsen and Sampson 1998; Wilson and Herrnstein 1985). Although the correlation is strong, there are many exceptions. Most poor people do not engage in criminal careers. Poverty increases the likelihood of criminal behavior, but it does not guarantee it. As Piehl concludes, "From the body of empirical research, we know that economic disadvantage, criminal offending, and criminal victimization are concentrated in similar populations. At the same time, however, most of those who are poor do not regularly commit illegal acts" (1998:315).

Although police may be more likely to arrest poor people who engage in criminal activity, bias among police does not fully explain the correlation between income (or, more broadly, socioeconomic status) and crime. As Hagan notes, "Criminality for traditional crimes is higher among lower class individuals despite bias in statistics or the administration of justice" (1998:88).

Unemployment and underemployment can affect the likelihood that individuals will commit crimes (Piehl 1998; Sullivan 1989; Sampson and Laub 1993). People who lose their jobs or who have difficulty finding jobs or who are paid low wages (the so-called working poor) may feel financially desperate.

Women face special challenges when they divorce, separate from partners, or are the victims of domestic violence (Alarid et al. 1996; Belknap 1996; Chesney-Lind 1989; Daly 1994, 1998; Denno 1994; Gilfus 1992; E. Miller 1986; Simon and Landis 1991; Steffensmeier and Allan 1996). Some women— such as Mary L.—commit crimes because of the dire economic straits in which they find themselves when they live on their own. We know that female offenders are most likely to be arrested for property crimes, such as theft and fraud, and that most female offenders have low incomes (Gabel and Johnston 1995). Most female offenders whom I have interviewed have told me, in so many words, that their crimes arose from desperation.

ALTHEA: I had to take my baby and get away from that man. He hurt us bad, real bad. I've got bruises up one side and down the other to prove it. I had to feed my baby and find us a place to live, you know? What choice did I have? I know it's wrong to steal, but it's also wrong to starve a baby.

NANETTE: Sam and I lived together for four years, off and on. I left, I came back, I left, and I came back. Each time I thought we could work things out, but I was just fooling myself. Thinking back on it, I can't believe what I put my kids through, all that craziness. Anyway, I knew I shouldn't steal from my boss at the dry cleaners; I feel real bad about that. He was real good to me. But what was I supposed to do? Everyone I turned to for help said, no, no, no.

CALIBRATION-RECALIBRATION

It is no great surprise that some individuals who believe that they have hit a financial brick wall decide to commit crimes to bail themselves out of desperate circumstances. I find that many offenders who commit these crimes do so rather impulsively. A significant percentage of such offenders have only modest formal education—usually less than a high school degree—and spotty employment histories. Many are illiterate or struggle with basic reading and writing skills. They assess their acute financial needs and conclude, quite predictably, that more legitimate avenues—in the form of gainful employment and conventional loans—are beyond their grasp and that crime is their only real option (see chapter 1 for the discussion of Merton's strain theory [1957] and Cloward and Ohlin's differential opportunity theory [1960]).

When there is no evidence of a concurrent illness or disability, such as substance abuse, realistic goals for such offenders should include several components. (This agenda is most appropriate for offenders who are at the contemplation, preparation, or action stage, which I discussed in the chapter 1 overview of the stages-of-change model. At the very least, counselors can share these options with offenders who are at the precontemplation stage and can encourage them to pursue these options.) The first component includes a package of social services designed to enhance the offender's employment prospects. For many offenders, this should entail some combination of remedial education, usually in the form of GED (general educational development) classes, a literacy program, and vocational training. GED and basic literacy programs are available in most correctional institutions and, if necessary, can be incorporated in the offender's probation, discharge, or parole plan.

Vocational training programs are also available in many communities for offenders on probation or parole, and in correctional institutions, although the content and quality of these programs vary considerably. Some states sponsor ambitious and comprehensive vocational training programs, while others do not. Some states periodically revise their programs to keep pace with changing employment trends, while others are less current. For prison inmates, manufacturing license plates—an age-old tradition in many state prisons—hardly qualifies as meaningful vocational training for future employment on the streets. In contrast, in-depth instruction using the most current equipment and pedagogical techniques—related to, for example, automobile repair, plumbing, electrical work, computer technology, and sheet metal work—would certainly constitute authentic vocational training. For offenders whose crimes are primarily the result of acute or chronic financial distress, high-quality educational and vocational services are essential. Without them the broader community is living on borrowed time; for a significant number of individuals who are poor, lacking employable skills, and feeling desperate, it is simply a matter of time before crime resurfaces as an appealing option.

Ideally, offenders on probation or parole who have limited employment histories and skills would be enrolled in meaningful vocational training programs. Incarcerated offenders with limited employment histories and skills would progress through their respective institutional system (moving from more secure to less secure facilities) with the aim of participating in the corrections department's work-release program. These programs consider inmate enrollees to be low security risks (typically inmates who committed nonviolent crimes and are near the end of their sentence) and permit them to spend their days working in private-sector, community-based jobs, returning to the prison each afternoon or evening. Ideally, the work-release job would provide the inmate with real vocational training. Unfortunately, work-release jobs too often provide little, if any, opportunity for genuine skill development. Instead of bona fide vocational training, some inmates on work release spend their days making telemarketing calls or picking up litter—activities that turn the phrase "vocational training" into meaningless rhetoric.

Offenders on probation or parole who need to cultivate solid work habits and learn how to structure their time may benefit from the close supervision that accompanies electronic monitoring (where offenders wear an electronic ankle bracelet that enables correctional officials to keep constant track of their whereabouts). Typical electronic monitoring programs entail frequent contact with probation or parole officers and require offenders to account for every minute of their time. These demands provide a useful opportunity for inmates who have struggled with time management and accountability—some of whom have gotten into trouble because of the lack of structure in their daily lives—to develop critically important time-management skills.

Apart from the mechanics of continuing education, vocational training, employment, and intensive monitoring, it is also important to explore the more subtle psychological aspects of an offender's decision to commit a crime as a way out of a financial bind. Some offenders display considerable insight about their offenses and some do not. Offenders who "get it," that is, offenders who can articulate why they behaved as they did, understand that committing a crime is wrong and show some ability to empathize with their victims; they are eager to enhance their job prospects through schooling and vocational training and are much better "rehabilitation prospects" than those who show little insight, compassion for their victims, or determination to turn their lives around with more education and vocational training. (See chapter 3 for in-depth discussion of offenders whose personality traits make them poor rehabilitation prospects.)

Many offenders can benefit from counseling and "psycho-educational" programs that focus explicitly on their patterns of criminal thinking. Briefly, criminal thinking is characterized by the tendency to view crime as a legitimate, defensible option when faced with difficult circumstances. The psycho-educational programs (which I will discuss more fully in chapter 3) typically guide offenders through a series of structured stages or phases to help them grasp the harmful and self-destructive approaches that they have taken in the past when they have encountered financial and other pressures (Yochelson and Samenow 1976). Such programs go by various names, such as "Cognitive Restructuring," "Corrective Thinking," and "Choosing New Directions."

We must be particularly sensitive to the unique needs of female offenders. In addition to counseling, educational, and vocational services, we must recognize that female offenders often begin their involvement in the criminal justice system at a distinct disadvantage: compared with male offenders, on average they have lower earning power, lower income, fewer resources, and greater family and parenting responsibilities. The vast majority of female offenders are mothers who hope to maintain or regain custody of their children. For women who are on probation or parole, juggling the simultaneous responsibilities of employment or job training, counseling, visits to probation or parole officers, and child care is a monumental task. For incarcerated mothers, maintaining contact with their children is vitally important. According to Gabel and Johnston, "Continuing contact between parent and child is perhaps the most significant predictor of family reunification after parental incarceration" (1995:1023). Unfortunately, in recent years incarcerated mothers have been less able to maintain contact with their children because of

Restrictions on prison telephone privileges (for example, requiring inmates to call home collect, which increases the cost of telephoning)

Construction of the majority of women's prisons in rural and relatively remote areas not easily accessible to inmates' children, most of whom reside in cities

Lack of financial assistance and social service support to facilitate visits between female inmates and their children (for example, funding for transportation services for children in the custody of state or county child welfare agencies)

The unanticipated economic consequences of this family disruption are extreme. In many cases children of incarcerated mothers require expensive (financially and emotionally) foster care and/or adoption, as well as mental health, institutional, and welfare services.

Offenders who commit such crimes as robbery, larceny, theft, and breaking and entering as a result of financial desperation often have individual victims. Some also have organizational victims, for example, when they steal from their employer or a business. These cases often provide an ideal opportunity for creative restorative justice. Judges, parole boards, and probation and parole officers should actively consider the use of victim-offender mediation, conferencing, restitution, and community service. Restorative justice in these instances should be used selectively and only when all participants agree that it makes sense. At a minimum the offender must be willing to acknowledge the misconduct and demonstrate genuine remorse and an earnest interest in the concept of restoration. Such offenders are ideal candidates for meeting with their victims and other interested and concerned parties (along with a skilled facilitator) and enrollment in restitution programs and community service (which might include lecturing to vulnerable and receptive audiences about their experiences with crime and the criminal justice system).

Recognizing that most offenders are poor, we must also think about the broad economic issues involved in the relationship between poverty and crime. It is certainly tempting to believe that crime rates are strongly correlated with economic conditions. That is, as unemployment falls and economic conditions improve, people become less desperate financially and crime rates decline; conversely, as unemployment rises and economic conditions worsen, people become more desperate and crime rates accelerate. Although this apparent correlation has great intuitive and commonsense appeal, evidence suggests that the relationship between economic conditions and crime rates in general is complicated and not linear. According to Piehl,

> While many citizens, policy makers, politicians, and academics assume that economic conditions drive crime rates, evidence of this relationship has proved elusive. As a result, there is a large disconnect between theory and empirical evidence on this point. For theory building, the notion that crime is a function of economic opportunity has great intuitive appeal. Economic theorists, for example, have long assumed that individuals allocate their time between legal work and crime depending on the relative returns of each activity. Advocates of employment-based solutions to the crime problem also rely on such a causal notion. Nonetheless, there has been surprisingly little convincing evidence to support this belief. (1998:302)

Although the relationship between economic conditions and crime rates in general is complex, significant evidence exists of a significant correlation between economic conditions and the kind of crime—property crime—committed by people who feel desperate. Crime data clearly suggest that property crimes increase when economic conditions worsen. After thoroughly examining the empirical evidence, Piehl concludes that "we do know that property crime increases in recessions, whereas homicide either falls in recessions or is not responsive to the business cycle. We know that individuals with worse economic prospects are more likely to be involved in crime and in the criminal justice system, and that neighborhoods with fewer working residents have high crime rates" (1998:303).

One particularly compelling study (Needels 1996) provides strong evidence of the relationship between unemployment and crime. Needels followed the employment, earnings, and criminal justice system involvement of a group of offenders released from Georgia prisons. Those who continued to have legal troubles had lower earnings and lower employment rates than those who did not recidivate. Needels also found that those who had better employment (labor market) opportunities had lower recidivism. According to Piehl, this study "reports the most convincing evidence that there is a link between earnings and criminal activity among releasees" (1998:310).

White-Collar Financial Desperation

Of course, crimes of financial desperation are not limited to poor people. A significant number of financial crimes that occur out of a sense of desperation are committed by white-collar workers, people with relatively high levels of education and professional and social status.

Case 2.3 Howard G. was an attorney with a thriving practice in real estate law. Howard G. invested heavily in three real estate developments during an economic boom. Two of the investments involved the construction of apartment complexes for middle-income people, and one involved a shopping center in an expanding suburban community. About ten months after Howard G. committed substantial funds to these projects, the real estate market underwent an unexpected and sudden downturn. Demand for the apartments and for houses in the suburban community dried up rapidly, creating major cash-flow problems for Howard G. He was unable to make several mortgage payments and received demand notices from the banks that held the financial notes. Howard G. was afraid that in the process he would lose his own home to foreclosure. In a fit of desperation Howard G. wrote himself checks for large sums of money that he held for several affluent clients in trust accounts and escrow accounts. He intended to pay the money back but was unable to do so. Eventually, these clients discovered that Howard G. had illegally appropriated money from their trust and escrow accounts and notified local law enforcement officials. Howard G. was arrested and convicted.

Case 2.4 Irving S. was the president of a large automobile dealership. In addition to selling new cars, the dealership had a large auto repair division. For years Irving S. earned a large income and lived lavishly. He and his wife owned two homes and traveled extensively. The couple belonged to an exclusive country club and bought expensive clothes and jewelry. Over time Irving S. had more and more difficulty paying his bills. He did not acknowledge to his wife that they were in over their heads financially; for a long time Irving S. assumed that his income would increase significantly, especially after he opened a second car dealership. Eventually, however, Irving S. discovered that he and his wife were deeply in debt, amounting to $275,000. In desperation Irving S. approached several childhood friends who had connections with local organized crime figures. The group conspired to stage a large number of automobile accidents and brought their cars to Irving S. for "repair"; the automobile owners processed fraudulent insurance claims and split the substantial profits from the bogus repairs with Irving S. The state police investigated the ring, and a grand jury indicted all the parties. Irving S. eventually was sentenced to three years in prison.

Although some white-collar crime—including corporate crime—is the result of pure greed (see chapter 3), a significant portion stems from the offender's sense of financial desperation. Typically, the white-collar offender is in a deep financial hole, usually as a result of bad investments or out-of-control spending. These individuals usually have access to large sums of money—sometimes through access to trust accounts or escrow funds, sometimes through lines of credit with financial institutions, and sometimes through bribery or fraudulent transactions such as securities fraud, tax fraud, and bank or business embezzlement.

Interest in white-collar crime has surged recently, primarily because of worldwide publicity surrounding the collapse of, or fraudulent activity in, major multinational corporations, such as Enron, WorldCom, Adelphia Communications, and Tyco International. The general public has become much more cognizant of insider stock trading, banking fraud, and complex financial conspiracy.

The concept of white-collar crime was introduced in 1940 by the well-known criminologist Edwin Sutherland, who was critical of social scientists who were preoccupied with the criminal activity of low-income people. White-collar crimes typically involve the abuse of trust, "exploitation of a fiduciary position by an agent responsible for custody, discretion, information, or property rights" (Shover 1998:135).

It is hard to estimate the prevalence of white-collar crime in general and, in particular, by individuals who are feeling financially desperate. Valid data summaries are hard to come by, in part because a considerable portion of white-collar crime remains hidden from view. According to Shover,

A great deal of white-collar crime goes unreported for the simple reason that many of its victims are unaware they have been victimized. Unlike robbery, burglary, and other street crimes, acts of white-collar crime frequently do not stand out in victims' experiences; they characteristically have the look of routine legitimate transactions. Victims who realize or suspect what has happened may have no idea where to report the incident; it is also characteristic of white-collar crimes that the appropriate places or agencies to report to are either unknown or unfamiliar. Many victims do not report. Those who do so are typically motivated by hopes of recovering lost funds and protecting others from a similar experience. Victims who do not report frequently believe that the incident either was not worth the trouble of doing so or that no real harm was done. Others elect to handle the matter privately. This is not appreciably different from what is known about the reporting decisions of street-crime victims. Another reason victims of white-collar crimes do not report is because they often reserve a measure of blame for themselves. Believing they should have been more careful in the first place, victims often feel a sense of embarrassment and shame, and prefer that others not learn what happened to them. (1998:142)

Some white-collar offenders are free agents who act alone and without any affiliation with an employer or organization (Weisburd, Waring, and Chayet 1995). Examples include a financially desperate, self-employed investment counselor who obtained down payments for a bogus investment from a number of elderly clients, and a psychologist who was convicted of submitting fraudulent insurance vouchers for clinical services that he never provided:

MARK G. (FORMER INVESTMENT COUNSELOR): I was recently divorced and was having a real hard time keeping up with alimony payments and child support. I also had large monthly payments for college and car loans. I can't explain how I managed to get myself in this mess. I mean, I know it's wrong to swindle elderly people out of their money. Everybody knows that. All I can tell you is that my whole world was crashing down on me. It's like some other guy, not me, was taking those people's money.

SIMON L. (FORMER PSYCHOLOGIST): I know this isn't much of an excuse, but what I was doing [submitting fraudulent insurance claims] was pretty common. I've met a number of therapists who do this. They may not be as bad as I was—billing for sessions that never happened—but I know people exaggerate diagnoses in order to increase their reimbursement. I guess most clinicians are good people, but I can tell you there are some bad ones out there too. I know; I was one of them.

Many white-collar offenders are employed when they commit their crimes. Some employers are the offender's victim (as in cases of embezzlement), some are co-conspirators (as when business partners and colleagues enter into a conspiracy to defraud investors or customers), and some are merely unwitting bystanders. Here are illustrative comments from a woman who embezzled cash from her employer, and a former partner in a manufacturing company who defrauded an insurance company:

MELANIE B. (FORMER BUSINESS MANAGER AT A TRUCKING FIRM): I'm a spender, you know. That's my problem. I maxed out several credit cards big time. I just can't seem to stay away from the stores—clothing, jewelry, you name it. I'm in way over my head. What happened is that I started getting threatening letters from the credit card companies. I know I screwed up by skimming cash and writing checks out of my boss's business account. I can't believe I was so stupid. I just kept fooling myself.

HERB Y. (FORMER PARTNER IN A MANUFACTURING COMPANY): What happened is that a few of our investments soured. We thought the real estate market around here was going to take off. Little did we know that the bottom would fall out after interests rates soared. My two partners and I were all in this together; in fact, I'm in protective custody now because I testified against them and they have connections to OC [organized crime]. I got sucked into submitting phony thefts of some very expensive equipment at our plant. The only reason I went along with this is that I was on the verge of declaring personal bankruptcy.

CALIBRATION-RECALIBRATION

I find that the majority of white-collar offenders acknowledge their misdeeds. They may quibble some about the nature and magnitude of their crimes—for example, they may claim that they pleaded guilty to avoid trial but did not commit all the offenses charged in their indictment—but they generally admit their wrongdoing.

Such admissions bode well, of course, for rehabilitation. Many of these offenders are at the contemplation or action stage. Although a percentage of white-collar offenders are recidivists, many cease their criminal activity. Coun-seling and mental health services may be helpful with respect to self-destructive decision making, financial planning, lifestyle choices, priorities, family and re-lationship dynamics, depression, self-esteem, and so on. Further, some degree of punishment—in the form of incarceration and fines—is often in order to convey the indignation of the victims and of the broader community. Howev-er, with white-collar offenders who commit their crimes as a result of financial desperation, the psychological dynamics are often different from those found with white-collar offenders who are much more exploitative and more likely to act out of greed (see chapter 3). The latter, I find, are less responsive to sanc-tions and counseling. Shover's observations reflect my own:

> What is the impact of sanctions and other control measures on white-collar offenders? Deterrence-based notions of crime control suggest it should be substantial, in large measure because these offenders are thought to be more rational than street offenders (Weisburd, Waring, and Chayet 1995). Unlike the latter, they do not routinely make decisions to offend in hedonistic contexts of competition and display where drug consump-tion clouds both judgment and ability to calculate beforehand. Coupled with the fact that many live and work in worlds structured to promote, monitor, and reward rational decision making, this suggests that sanctions should have greater deterrent impact on their conduct. Whether or not this assumption is correct, however, is unknown. For one thing, the im-pact of external controls probably varies with severity; notices of violation for regulatory offenses are one thing; imprisonment or large fines are an-other. The possibility that some convicted white-collar offenders see crime as a good bet is suggested by their surprisingly high rate of recidivism (Weisburd, Waring, and Chayet 1995). Evidence of this point is extreme-ly limited, however, and recidivism may be concentrated among unem-ployed and economically marginal offenders. (1998:145)

White-collar offenders who acknowledge their wrongdoing and feel re-morse are also particularly good candidates for restorative justice options. Victim-offender mediation, conferencing, restitution, and community service are very appealing in these cases. In one soon-to-be-famous parole board hear-ing at which I presided, I built in, with the inmate's enthusiastic consent, the requirement that this former banker, whose financial world was collapsing around him at the time of his offenses, arrange a series of lectures to high school students and undergraduate and graduate students in college and university business programs about his unwise choices as a business executive and about ethical decision making in the business world. In this case, which received widespread publicity for months, the inmate, Joseph Mollicone Jr., was convicted on twenty-six counts of embezzlement, conspiracy, and violation of banking laws. Mollicone was the president of a loan and investment company when bank examiners determined that millions of dollars were missing from the institution. This failure triggered the collapse of forty-four other credit unions and savings institutions that were also covered by a private and vulnerable insurance system. The newspaper account of Mollicone's release from prison captured his remorse and interest in restorative justice:

> As the sun rose on a new beginning for Joseph Mollicone, Jr. yesterday, the bank embezzler left prison after 10 years, clutching a television and plastic bag of belongings.
>
> His face thinner and lined with the years of hard time, Mollicone, 59, stopped for a moment to talk to news media gathered outside Medium Security.
>
> "I have a lot to make up to a lot of people," he said, speaking contritely. "Hopefully I will be able to do that."
>
> Mollicone said he spent much of his incarceration thinking, and "you only think of the bad things, naturally. And there were a lot of bad things."
>
> While Mollicone will want to put the past behind him, he won't quietly disappear.
>
> As part of his release agreement with the Parole Board, Mollicone will speak regularly to high school and college students about the years he looted the savings accounts of friends, family and business partners, and $12 million from his own institution, precipitating the worst state banking crisis since the Great Depression.   (Mooney 2002:A-1, A-13)

During my discussions with Mollicone it was clear that he was at the preparation stage and ready to move into the action stage.[1]

Crimes of Fear

Not all crimes of desperation are financial in nature, although many are. Some offenders commit crimes because of their fear of unwanted and dire consequences that have nothing to do with money. As in the following cases, many such offenders have no significant criminal records.

Case 2.5 Terrance M. was a martial arts instructor. Late one evening he was driving home. About a mile from his home, Terrance M. hit something in the road. He continued to drive, looked in his rearview mirror, and did not see anything amiss. When Terrance M. reached his home and got out of his car, he noticed some damage to his front left headlight. He drove back to the site of the collision and found the body of a young man on the side of the road. Terrance M. panicked when he realized that he had probably killed the man. He decided not to notify the police for fear that he would be charged with leaving the scene of a serious automobile accident. Two days after the accident a detective contacted Terrance M.; someone had seen Terrance M.'s car hit the victim and contacted the police with a description of the car. Terrance M. was convicted of manslaughter and sentenced to eight years in prison.

Case 2.6 Melanie D. was a secretary in the local traffic court. Part of her duties included processing payments that the court received for traffic fines. Melanie D.'s cousin contacted her and asked her to fix a large number of outstanding traffic fines for him and his friends. Melanie D.'s cousin knew that Melanie D. could alter the computer code for the infraction to reduce or eliminate the fines. Melanie D.'s cousin told her that it would be in her best interest to help him out. He knew that she was in the United States illegally with forged immigration documents. He threatened to blow the whistle on Melanie D. if she did not cooperate. Melanie D. fixed the traffic violations, but an internal audit conducted by the state accounting office uncovered her crime. Melanie D. was sentenced to three years in prison and then was deported.

These two cases include features commonly found among offenders who commit crimes primarily because they suddenly become afraid. Both offenders had lived law-abiding lives up until the crimes for which they were serving sentences, with the exception of Melanie D.'s entering the United States illegally. Terrance M. had never received more than a parking ticket. After he struck the pedestrian, he panicked and, as he admitted, used very poor judgment. According to Terrance M., the immediate threat of repercussions and "downright fear paralyzed my mind. In that moment I sensed that something was terribly wrong, but all I could think about was my life going down the tubes. I'm ashamed to admit it now, but all I could think of at the time was my own situation, my own future. I know it sounds awful. It *is* awful."

Similarly, Melanie D. had no formal criminal record. True, she had entered the United States illegally. Since immigrating, however, Melanie D. had never been involved in any criminal activity.

I came to the United States for a better life. My world in the Dominican Republic was so small and bleak. I had heard from relatives how much opportunity there was for me in the U.S. I just had to come. I know it was wrong to enter illegally, but I didn't know what else to do. I had such a good life here—I worked hard, I obeyed the law, I started my family. And now look. I can't believe my cousin did this to me. I can't believe I did this to myself. It's my fault that I told him I would fix those tickets. But I was so afraid, so afraid. All I could imagine at the time was that if Carlos turned me in, I would be deported and my whole family's life would be ruined. Now I *will* be deported.

CALIBRATION-RECALIBRATION

In both cases the threat to public safety was minor. Neither offender has a sustained criminal record or a pattern of criminal activity. Although Melanie D.'s violation of immigration laws should not be minimized, beyond that she does not present the profile of someone in the midst of a criminal career. Thus incarceration primarily for public safety purposes is indefensible.

Terrance M.'s case is somewhat different. He killed a man while driving and therefore may appear to be a threat to public safety. However, Terrance M. was not driving under the influence of drugs or alcohol at the time, and the police found no evidence that he was speeding. He is guilty of using extremely poor judgment following a serious accident, not driving to endanger. (The forensic evidence showed that the victim was walking down the remote, rural, unlighted road, which had no sidewalk. He died as a result of an unfortunate accident, not a crime per se.) Terrance M.'s personal history and his lack of a criminal record suggest that he does not pose a serious public safety threat.

Nonetheless, some degree of punishment is in order for both. Terrance M. and Melanie D. committed serious crimes that had significant repercussions. In Terrance M.'s case the victim might have received emergency medical care and survived had Terrance M. contacted the police and rescue personnel immediately. He acted irresponsibly and a man died. Melanie D. violated the public's trust and undermined the justice system by circumventing the traffic court's computer system to alter records on behalf of her cousin and his friends.

Both inmates appeared to be quite amenable to rehabilitation services. Terrance M. was overcome with guilt and made good use of individual counseling sessions with a social worker while in prison. In his counseling he spoke at length about his poor judgment and explored the reasons why he acted as he did. Terrance M. also participated in a "cognitive restructuring" group sponsored by the prison. Clearly, he was in the middle of the action stage.

Similarly, Melanie D. met with a psychologist to talk about her grief. She felt quite remorseful with respect to her crime and letting her family down: "What I did was wrong, but what's even worse is that I've ruined my family's life. There I was, doing everything I could to make a good life for them. Now it's all turned upside down. I'm going to be deported and my family will have to go back with me to the DR [Dominican Republic]." Melanie D. was also a regular participant in a women's support group that met weekly at the prison.

In principle, both offenders would be good candidates for restorative justice. Ideally, Melanie D. would make restitution for the amount of money she cost the state by fixing the traffic tickets. In addition, Melanie D. could perform community service. Victim-offender mediation would not be appropriate in this case because of the absence of direct victims. Restorative justice was not feasible in Melanie D.'s case, however, because soon after her release from prison she was deported to the Dominican Republic, as required by federal law.

Restorative justice was particularly appropriate in Terrance M.'s case. This offender acknowledged his mistakes and was eager to make amends. Although his attorney advised Terrance M. not to contact the victim's family after his arrest or during his trial (this is common legal advice, designed to protect the defendant's interests during criminal and civil proceedings), Terrance M. was now determined to apologize to the victim's family: "I need to do this for myself as a way to deal with my own guilt. But more important, it's the right thing to do. I'll do whatever I can to help that family heal. I know it's going to be hard, but I have to do it." Through his attorney Terrance M. contacted the state's victim's advocate to begin the process of victim-offender mediation and to determine whether the relatives were willing to participate. As part of his parole plan, Terrance M. agreed to provide a series of lectures to high school students about using good judgment and about life in prison.

Desperate Personal Circumstances

Many crimes of desperation involve offenders' attempts to resolve personal problems—problems that are not primarily, although may be indirectly, financial in nature. Typically, these personal problems involve relationships with family, friends, and acquaintances.

Case 2.7   Wendell S. was serving a nine-month sentence for driving with a suspended license. Wendell S. did not have a substantial criminal record before this sentence. His downfall was a series of traffic violations (speeding, driving an uninsured vehicle, failure to pay fines after two automobile accidents, unauthorized use of a motor vehicle) that ultimately led the court to suspend his license to drive. Despite the suspended license, Wendell S. continued to drive. One afternoon, as he was driving to his girlfriend's house to settle an argument, a police officer who was tailing Wendell S.'s car signaled for him to pull over. The officer found that Wendell S. was driving on a suspended license and arrested him. During his relatively short sentence Wendell S. received twelve disciplinary infractions; seven were serious, resulting in several stints in punitive segregation (for fighting, drug use, and sexual misconduct in the visiting room) and five were not (these were more modest infractions, such as taking an extra sandwich from the dining hall, having an extra pair of sneakers, and talking too loudly in the cell block).

Case 2.8   Richard A. was serving an eighteen-month sentence for possession of cocaine with intent to distribute. He had a stellar prison record; he had no major disciplinary infractions and received high praise from institutional staff. About six months into his sentence Richard A. was transferred from a medium-security prison to a minimum-security prison. The minimum-security prison provided inmates with considerably more privileges than the medium-security prison. Richard A. and the other inmates slept in dormitories rather than cells, the prison yard was surrounded only by a low fence rather than barbed wire and razor wire, and inmates in the yard were supervised by only one correctional officer.

One evening Richard A. called his wife and learned that one of their children had been rushed to the hospital and diagnosed with a serious heart condition. Richard A.'s wife was upset and distressed about their child and talked about how hard it was for her to manage the family on her own while Richard A. was in prison. The next afternoon, during a recreation period in the prison yard, Richard A. jumped the fence and escaped. He was arrested two days later while hiding out at a cousin's house and received an additional eighteen-month sentence for the escape.

CALIBRATION-RECALIBRATION

In both cases the offenders used poor judgment to resolve pressing personal problems. One significant difference is that Richard A.'s decision to escape from prison was much more impulsive and spur of the moment than was Wendell S.'s. Wendell S.'s decision to drive on a suspended license was much more deliberate.

In both cases a period of incarceration is warranted for purposes of public safety and punishment. Wendell S. had demonstrated over a period of time that he did not take the court's injunctions or legal requirements seriously. His prison record was poor, and his driving-related behavior posed a threat to the public. Richard A. also posed a threat to the public by virtue of his involvement with drug dealing and his prison escape. Although Richard A. had no history of violence, drug dealing has disastrous consequences in the community (triggering all manner of property crime, for example) and warrants punishment.

Both offenders could benefit from rehabilitation and treatment services. In principle, Wendell S. would be a fine candidate for group treatment and discussion related to his long-standing pattern of criminal thinking. However, he demonstrated no interest in rehabilitative services during his prison stay, despite repeated encouragement from staff and the parole board. According to the stages-of-change model, he was clearly in the precontemplative stage. Further, for Wendell S. restorative justice options were not appropriate; he did not acknowledge his destructive behavioral pattern and was not interested in performing community service as a form of restitution. In fact, the parole hearing for Wendell S. was unusually short and clipped. When asked whether he was at all interested in enrolling in a "cognitive restructuring group," he replied, "No, man. I ain't into none of that. I'll just flatten my bid [serve out the sentence]. I don't want no parole." Wendell S. then got up and walked out of the hearing room.

In contrast, despite his ill-advised escape from prison and his involvement with illegal drugs, Richard A. was an appealing candidate for both treatment and restorative justice. Until his escape Richard A. was a model inmate who was actively involved in a drug education class and a GED program. Also, he had no significant disciplinary infractions on his institutional record. Clearly, Richard A. was in the action stage until his escape; he was taking deliberate steps to address issues in his life. His prison escape, and the poor judgment that led up to it, represented a significant, but not fatal, setback. "I know I messed up," Richard A. told me. "I was doing so good and I threw it all away, just like that. I can't believe I was so stupid. Sometimes I can't see beyond the nose on my face. But I've got to get back to the program and really work it. I know I can do it. I've done it before, and I can do it again."

• • •

Crimes of desperation arise from a wide range of circumstances. The gamut includes efforts to produce a quick fix for day-to-day financial problems (paying the rent, putting food on the table, and so on), stem long-term cash-flow problems (for example, when real estate investments sour), and resolve anxiety-producing personal circumstances (for instance, when an individual escapes from prison in order to address a family crisis).

Offenders who commit crimes of desperation are a diverse lot. Some clearly acknowledge their mistakes and are ready to engage in genuine problem-solving, rehabilitative, and restorative justice efforts. Others are only at the most preliminary stage of change and may not be inclined to move beyond it. In these instances judges, probation and parole officers, parole boards, and other criminal justice professionals should do their best to offer information about the options available and provide sincere and sustained encouragement. What social workers and other social service professionals refer to as "engagement skills" can be critical at this stage. The principal challenge with offenders who are not ready to embark on the difficult process of meaningful change is to remain available, offer support, listen empathetically, guide the offender through the process of reflecting on the benefits and costs of change, maintain respectful and sincere hope for the person, and trust that when the offender is ready, genuine contemplation will begin. Criminal justice professionals must resist the understandable, instinctive temptation to lecture, scold, and push. This does not mean we should coddle offenders. Rather, it means we may need a paradigm shift, a new weltanschauung, in our approach to offenders whose lives teeter. For some, readiness to change may not occur until years after their first encounter with the criminal justice system, not until they have experienced multiple arrests and prison sentences. Many recidivists mature over time or simply tire of the criminal lifestyle. For all but the most incorrigible, readiness to change is a matter of time.

3

Crimes of Greed, Exploitation, and Opportunism

According to the positivist school of thought in criminology, people commit crimes because of a variety of circumstances beyond their control. Economic forces, biological factors, psychiatric torment, abusive conditions, and peer pressure, for instance, are key determinants. It is true, no doubt, that a significant portion of criminal conduct is influenced, to greater or lesser degrees depending on the facts of the case, by factors over which offenders have little, if any, control.

Over the years, however, I have met a number of offenders whose crimes appear to be primarily a function of their out-and-out greed, wish to exploit, and opportunism. The dictionary definition of *greed* is "excessive or rapacious desire, especially for wealth and possessions; avarice; covetousness" (*Random House* 1991). Exploitation is "the use or manipulation of another person for one's own advantage," and opportunism is "the policy or practice, as in politics or business, of adapting actions, decisions, etc., to expediency or effectiveness without regard to principles or consequences." What these offenders have in common is remarkable self-centeredness and lack of disregard for the effect of their crimes on other people.

Dismissing such offenders as individuals who are simply morally corrupt and bankrupt is tempting. But the phenomenon is much more complex. Beneath the veneer of callous disregard for other people and the self-centeredness usually are complicated psychological and psychiatric phenomena. In many instances one or two major psychological and psychiatric forces are at work: antisocial personality disorder and narcissistic personality disorder. Both disorders are part of a large collection of what the American Psychiatric Association (2000:686) dubs "personality disorders." Personality disorders occur when individuals' personality traits—the way they perceive, relate to, and think about themselves and their environment—are inflexible and maladaptive and cause significant functional impairment or subjective distress.

The essential feature of a personality disorder is an enduring pattern of inner experience and behavior that clashes with the individual's culture and is problematic in the following areas: cognition, affectivity, interpersonal functioning, or impulse control. This pattern is consistent, emerges across a broad range of personal and social situations, and leads to personal problems or impairment in social, occupational, or other important areas of functioning. The pattern persists over a long period of time and typically begins in adolescence or early adulthood.

Among the many personality disorders, antisocial personality disorder and narcissistic personality disorder are the most prominent among offenders who commit crimes of greed, exploitation, and opportunism. Understanding these disorders is essential if we are to grasp why these offenders commit their crimes and if we are to fashion reasonable responses to them.

According to standard psychiatric criteria, the essential feature of antisocial personality disorder (formerly known as psychopathy or sociopathy) is a "pervasive pattern of disregard for, and violation of, the rights of others that begins in childhood or early adolescence and continues into adulthood" (American Psychiatric Association 2000:701–3). Deceit and manipulation are common elements. Individuals with antisocial personality disorder typically violate social norms and engage in unlawful behaviors that may or may not lead to arrest, such as destroying property, harassing others, stealing, or pursuing illegal occupations. These individuals often disregard the wishes, rights, or feelings of others. They are frequently deceitful and manipulative in order to enhance their personal profit or pleasure (e.g., to obtain money, sex, or power). They may repeatedly lie, manipulate and con others, and use assumed names and identities. Individuals with this disorder usually have difficulty with impulse control and have a hard time planning for the future. They make decisions on the spur of the moment, without much forethought and without considering the effect of their decisions and actions on themselves or others. These individuals often change jobs and residences suddenly and move in and out of relationships.

Individuals with antisocial personality disorder tend to be irritable and aggressive and often get into physical fights or assault others (including spouse beating or child abuse). They often behave recklessly, disregarding the safety of themselves and others. One prominent example is high-risk driving (recurrent speeding, driving while intoxicated, multiple accidents). Also, these individuals may engage in risky sexual behavior or substance use. They may neglect or fail to care for a child in a way that puts the child in danger.

Individuals with antisocial personality disorder often act quite irresponsibly. They may be unemployed for long periods of time, even though jobs are available to them. They may be absent from work repeatedly, even though there is no personal or family illness. They also have difficulty with finances, as reflected in acts such as defaulting on debts, failing to pay child support, or failing to support other dependents on a regular basis.

Individuals with antisocial personality disorder show little remorse for the consequences of their acts. They may be indifferent to, or provide a superficial rationalization for, having hurt, mistreated, or stolen from someone (e.g., "life's unfair," "losers deserve to lose," or "he had it coming anyway"). They may blame the victims for being foolish, helpless, or deserving their fate; minimize the harmful consequences of their actions; or manifest complete indifference. They generally show no interest in compensating people whom they have harmed or making amends for their behavior. They may believe that everyone is out to "help number one" and that they should not accept being pushed around.

Perhaps the most significant challenge in the criminal justice field is intervening meaningfully and effectively with offenders who manifest symptoms consistent with antisocial personality disorder. Their ways of coping with life's challenges, which often entail illegal and otherwise harmful behavior, is deep-seated and ingrained. Many, although not all, have grown up in families and neighborhoods where crime, petty or otherwise, is commonplace. Many such offenders have reported to me that confrontations with police, arrests, and occasional jail or prison time are preordained, taken in stride, and occupational hazards—in other words, the cost of doing business. Altering this worldview, this weltanschauung, is not easy.

Some experts argue that antisocial personality disorder is a core element in a so-called criminal personality. The concept of a criminal personality is controversial. The contemporary controversy began in earnest with the publication of Samuel Yochelson and Stanton Samenow's *The Criminal Personality* in 1976. Yochelson, a psychiatrist, and Samenow, a psychologist, worked together at the Program for the Investigation of Criminal Behavior based at St. Elizabeth's Hospital in Washington, D.C. Based on their extensive contact with a wide range of offenders, Yochelson and Samenow reject positivist and deterministic explanations of crime; they conclude that it is a mistake to look for root causes of criminal behavior and that criminals choose their behavior. Any meaningful response to criminal conduct needs to be based on assertive efforts to change "criminal thinking." Yochelson and Samenow (1976) maintain that: (1) the criminal personality is imprinted at birth and is relatively unaffected by the family; (2) criminal personalities seek the excitement of the crime; (3) criminals are exploitative and selfish in interpersonal relationships; (4) criminals are amoral, untrustworthy, intolerant of others, manipulative, lack empathy, and are in a pervasive state of anger; (5) criminals lack trust and refuse to be dependent; and (6) criminals create their own rules for living.

Yochelson and Samenow's views have been quite controversial, especially with respect to their rejection of traditional sociological and economic explanations of crime and their strong belief that offenders develop a "criminal personality" that leads them to commit crimes (consistent with the classical view of criminal behavior discussed in chapter 1). For now, however, it is important to focus on Yochelson and Samenow's claims about criminal thinking, which criminal justice professionals have embraced much more widely than the authors' views about the criminal personality. In fact, many contemporary treatment programs are organized around the concept of criminal thinking—these programs are also known as corrective thinking—and include strategies designed to help offenders change their cognitive patterns, which lead to crime. The criminal justice field is now saturated with programs, workshops, seminars, and institutes designed to help offenders undo their criminal thinking and lead more constructive, law-abiding lives. Typically, these programs begin by confronting a number of key characteristics of the offender's criminal thinking:

1. Infringes on the rights of others
2. Fails to accept responsibility for own behavior
3. Has few, if any, goals in life
4. Does not trust others
5. Blames others for his or her problems
6. Sees herself or himself self as a victim
7. Tells lies
8. Self-aggrandizes
9. Engages in self-centered thinking and behavior
10. Has grandiose thoughts
11. Manipulates and controls other people
12. Makes excuses
13. Does not consider the interests of others
14. Is unreliable
15. Breaks promises
16. Criticizes others

17. Is defensive about own misbehavior
18. Minimizes own misbehavior
19. Diverts attention from himself or herself
20. Is overly optimistic

In contrast to antisocial personality disorder, narcissistic personality disorder—also found among many offenders who commit crimes of greed, exploitation, and opportunism—is more narrowly focused (in fact, a number of central elements of narcissistic personality disorder are contained in antisocial personality disorder, particularly the lack of empathy, a sense of entitlement, and the tendency to exploit others for one's own purposes with little or no sense of remorse or conscience). The American Psychiatric Association's comprehensive summary of the character traits of individuals with narcissistic personality disorder (2000:714–15) perfectly describes a number of the offenders I have encountered. The essential feature of narcissistic personality disorder is a consistent pattern of grandiosity, need for admiration, and lack of empathy that begins by early adulthood and is present in a variety of contexts. Individuals with this disorder typically have a grandiose sense of self-importance. They routinely overestimate their abilities, act pretentiously, and inflate and boast about their accomplishments. They may be surprised when the praise that they expect from other people, and feel they deserve, is not forthcoming. These individuals are often critical of other people's contributions and efforts. They are often preoccupied with their own pursuit of success, power, brilliance, and beauty. These individuals may exaggerate their connections with prominent people (name dropping).

Individuals with narcissistic personality disorder also believe that they are superior, special, or unique and expect others to recognize them for their remarkable qualities. They may feel that they can only be understood by, and should only associate with, other people who are special or of high stature. Individuals with this disorder believe that their needs are special in a way that is not easily understood by ordinary people. It is not unusual for them to insist on having only the "top" person (doctor, lawyer, hairdresser, instructor) or affiliating with only the "best" institutions, and they may denigrate the credentials of those who disappoint them.

Individuals with this disorder generally expect others to admire them, yet they have low and fragile self-esteem. They may be preoccupied with how well they are doing and how favorably they are regarded by others. They may expect their arrival to be greeted with enthusiasm and are surprised and disappointed if others are not jealous of them. They may constantly solicit approving comments and exude a sense of entitlement. They expect to be catered to and become angry and resentful when this does not happen. For example, they may assume that they do not have to wait in line and that their priorities are so important that others should defer to them, and they then become irritated when others fail to assist in their "very important work."

Other people often feel exploited by individuals with narcissistic personality disorder. They are demanding and expect others to cater to their whims and wishes. They tend to pursue friendships or romantic relationships that are likely to "pay off" for them and enhance their self-esteem. They often expect special privileges and extra resources that they believe they deserve because they are so special.

Individuals with narcissistic personality disorder have difficulty empathizing with others and difficulty recognizing the desires, subjective experiences, and feelings of other people. They are surprised if others are not totally concerned about their welfare. They often discuss their own problems and issues in inappropriate and lengthy detail, while ignoring the feelings and needs of others. They often feel contempt toward, and impatience with, others who talk about their own problems. These individuals may be oblivious to the harm that their remarks may cause other people (for example, they may tell a former lover about their wonderful new lover or brag about their good fortune in front of someone who is having serious problems). They may view the needs, desires, or feelings of others cynically and disparagingly as signs of weakness or vulnerability. Those who spend time with people with narcissistic personality disorder usually find an emotional coldness and distance and a lack of reciprocal or mutual interest.

Individuals with narcissistic personality disorder often envy others or believe that others are envious of them. They may begrudge other people's good fortune, believing that they are more deserving of those achievements, admiration, or privileges. They often come across as arrogant and haughty. They often seem snobbish, disdainful, or patronizing.

Crimes of greed, exploitation, and opportunism take many forms. Most, I find, fall into groups related to various types of financial crimes, organized crime, gang exploitation, and sexual exploitation.

Financial Crimes

Crimes involving financial exploitation, greed, and opportunism are different from crimes involving financial desperation (chapter 2). Again, this conceptual distinction can be important in successfully individualizing sentencing, rehabilitation, discharge planning, and prevention. Crimes involving financial exploitation, greed, and opportunism are rooted in a sense of entitlement rather than despair. Offenders who are exploitative, greedy, and opportunistic tend to be much more calculating, cunning, and manipulative than those who act out of a sense of despair, who tend to be much more impulsive and spontaneous. The former typically view their crimes as an option of "first resort," whereas the latter view their crimes as an option of last resort. The difference in motive is key. The greedy, self-centered exploiters are out to get what they want—and they often want a lot—whereas the desperate offenders are out to get what they believe they need to survive. The latter is no more justifiable than the former, but, as I will explore shortly, the difference in motive has enormous implications for potential rehabilitation.

Crimes of greed, exploitation, and opportunism take various forms: white-collar crimes, fraudulent activities, crimes of theft, drug-related crimes, crimes involving personal injury, and racketeering.

White-Collar Crimes

Many crimes of greed, exploitation, and opportunism involve business-related and corporate greed. Hagan makes a useful distinction between occupational and organizational or corporate crime: *"occupational crime* refers to personal violations that take place for self-benefit during the course of a legitimate occupation, while *corporate (organizational) criminal behavior* refers to crimes by business or officials that are committed on behalf of the employing organization" (1990:339–40). White-collar crime takes various forms, including consumer fraud, securities theft, credit card and check fraud, insurance fraud, commercial bribery, embezzlement, bankruptcy fraud, and computer crimes.

Several scholars have constructed useful typologies of white-collar crime. Bloch and Geis (1970; also see Hagan 1990 and Sutherland 1940) distinguish among five major types of offenses by

- Individuals as individuals (for example, lawyers, doctors, and so forth)
- Employees against their employers (for example, embezzlers)
- Corporate officials on behalf of their company (for example, antitrust violations)
- Agents of the corporation against the general public (for example, in false advertising)
- Merchants against customers (for example, in consumer fraud)

Edelhertz (1970) devised another prominent typology of white-collar crime (also see Hagan 1990):

Crimes by people operating on an individual ad hoc basis (for example, income tax violations, credit card fraud, bankruptcy fraud, and so on)

Crimes committed in the course of their occupations by those operating inside business, government, and other establishments, in violation of their duty of loyalty and fidelity to employers or clients (for example, embezzlement, employee larceny, payroll padding, and so on)

Crimes incidental to, and in furtherance of, business operations but not central to the purpose of the business (for example, antitrust violations, commercial bribery, food and drug violations)

Crime as a white-collar business, or as the central activity (such as medical and health frauds, advance fee swindles, and phony contests)

At the national level we recently have witnessed a number of Fortune 500 companies whose top officers have been indicted on charges of insider trading, stock price manipulation, and embezzlement. I have encountered a wide variety of white-collar offenders whose crimes involved comparable deception and manipulation at a local level.

Case 3.1   Morton C. was an attorney who represented many clients who had been involved in automobile accidents. Most of Morton C.'s clients claimed that they were injured as a result of the accident. He typically referred his clients to local physicians, who examined and treated the clients and submitted bills to Morton C. Morton C. would sue the other driver involved in the automobile accident and include the physicians' bills, along with an accounting of lost wages, as part of the legal complaint.

Morton C. colluded with two physicians who agreed to artificially inflate the number of office visits and the number of medical services provided to Morton C.'s clients. Over a period of years these exaggerated bills led to many large settlements with insurance companies and therefore to inflated legal and medical fees for Morton C. and the physicians. All three were convicted of fraud.

Case 3.2   Alma B. was vice president of a large institutional laundry that served area hotels. The business had 125 employees and served hotels throughout the region.

Alma B. grew up in a blue-collar family and thoroughly enjoyed the affluent lifestyle she now had as an adult. She had expensive tastes in clothing, cars, and jewelry. Alma B. was frustrated with her most recent salary raise at work and resented that she needed to cut back on some of her personal expenditures. Over a period of fourteen months Alma B. embezzled $67,000 from her employer by creating false invoices for goods and services and depositing money into a false corporate entity that she had created in an effort to camouflage the diversion of funds. She was sentenced to eighteen months in prison and ordered to pay restitution.

CALIBRATION-RECALIBRATION

Both cases involve white-collar transactions that originated in the offenders' greed. Both Morton C. and Alma B. set out to line their own pockets. In Morton C.'s case he deliberately defrauded insurance companies for no reason other than to enhance his own revenue. Similarly, Alma B. embezzled money from her employer in order to maintain her affluent lifestyle. Neither of these offenders was desperate financially; both simply wanted to add golden feathers to their already plush nest.

Both cases warranted a period of incarceration, not so much for public safety but for punitive purposes. Further, in addition to deterring Morton C. and Alma B. from offending again (specific deterrence), prosecutors hoped that other citizens in comparable positions (physicians and business administrators) would be deterred from committing comparable crimes (general deterrence).

Beyond this similarity, these two cases were quite different in several important respects. Morton C.'s demeanor when I met him can only be described as self-centered, arrogant, defensive, haughty, lacking in insight and remorse, and grandiose. His speech was glib and seemed filled with hubris. Morton C. claimed that he had been not only unfairly prosecuted but persecuted as well: "You have no idea how many people are out there ripping off the system. The AG [attorney general, the prosecutor] made it sound like I was Attila the Hun. I was a little guy who was hung out to dry so the AG could put another notch in his belt and help himself with his next election. I know how these things work; I was railroaded. What I did was nothing compared to the people making big scores in insurance scams."

In short, Morton C. manifested many of the traits associated with antisocial personality disorder and narcissistic personality disorder. He was not at all receptive to suggestions that he participate in counseling while incarcerated, and his willing participation in any gesture of restorative justice was out of the question. Clearly, he was at the precontemplation stage of change, and I found no evidence that Morton C. was ready to take even baby steps beyond it. Given his relatively short sentence, my colleagues and I could do little to help him move in the direction of meaningful change.

Unfortunately, this is not unusual with offenders who have deep-seated personality disorders, especially antisocial and narcissistic tendencies. This is not to say that such individuals will never be receptive to change, but the prospects are not good, at least not in the short run. On occasion I have seen maturation or life crises help such offenders reach a point where they become more eager to change the course of their lives. As always, criminal justice professionals should continue to be as supportive and available as possible with the hope that offenders will respond at some point.

In fact, Alma B. is one such example. During her first parole hearing Alma B. was slightly defensive and demonstrated little insight, telling us, "All right, I know what I did wasn't such a bright idea, but it's only money. I think I've paid my dues here and I have to pay the money back. I'll do that, although it may take me the rest of my life. But no one needs to be protected from me; prisons should be for the real criminals, the ones who really hurt people."

At that point in her sentence Alma B. had not participated in any counseling programs to help her address her poor judgment, which had led to the embezzlement. That fact, combined with her lack of insight, led the parole board to conclude that she was not ready to be released. The board encouraged Alma B. to enroll in a counseling program at the women's prison and informed her that she would receive another hearing in six months. At that hearing Alma B. sounded like a different woman:

To tell you the truth, after the last hearing, when you denied my parole, I was real angry and upset. For awhile I was angry with the board. But about a week later I was talking with the chaplain, and she helped me realize that I was mostly angry at myself for getting into this predicament. I had never thought of it that way. She too encouraged me to get into the counseling group and I'll tell you, it's really opened my eyes. I'm not just saying this. I never realized before why I wanted so many fancy, expensive things. But Marie [the counselor] has helped me to understand that buying these things was the only way I could feel satisfied—my marriage was a mess, I hated my job and used that to justify stealing the money, and it turns out I was depressed. I'm on medication now and with Marie's help I think I'm turning things around. I realize money and fancy things aren't going to really make me happy inside, although more money is always better than less money! But I know now that what really matters is being involved in healthy relationships with people who love me for who I am. It's been a long time since I've had that. You know, even though I hate this place, I think it's been a blessing in disguise.

Alma B. thus had moved from the precontemplation stage evident in her first parole hearing to the contemplation and action stages. She was getting her act together, so to speak, and was headed in the right direction. Part of her parole plan included an ambitious restitution schedule, which was Alma B.'s earnest attempt at restorative justice.

Fraudulent Activities

Fraudulent activities motivated by greed are many and varied. Many involve scams designed to manipulate innocent victims ("marks"), especially elderly people and others who may be particularly susceptible to clever, exploitative schemes.

Case 3.3 Serge F. worked in the warehouse of a large appliance store. He was injured on the job—when a loaded pallet fell on his leg—and he filed a worker's compensation claim. After his claim was processed, Serge F. was eligible for "temporary total disability benefits." That is, the worker's compensation court ruled that he was totally disabled temporarily and should receive benefits until he was able to return to work following rehabilitation. Serge F.'s doctor estimated that he would not be able to work for at least nine months.

About two months after the accident Serge F. began working for a cousin at his supermarket and was paid under the table. However, Serge F. signed papers monthly confirming that he was still disabled and unable to work. Thus Serge F. was receiving disability benefits fraudulently. After appearing in court on the fraud charges, the judge placed Serge F. on probation. However, Serge F. violated the terms of his probation by continuing to work (and being paid off the books) while he received disability benefits. The judge ordered him to serve a six-month sentence.

Case 3.4 Hank L. was a dentist who owned a popular clinic in a low-income neighborhood. Most of his patients were eligible for Medicaid benefits. Hank L. was one of the few dentists in the state who was willing to serve Medicaid patients; most dentists refused to serve Medicaid patients because of the low rate of reimbursement for most procedures.

Over time Hank L. became very frustrated with the Medicaid paperwork and with the reimbursement rate. During a two-year period Hank L. billed the state-administered Medicaid program for $213,000 worth of dental services for patients who did not exist and for services that he never provided. Hank L. was convicted of Medicaid fraud and lost his license to practice dentistry.

CALIBRATION-RECALIBRATION

Neither Serge F. nor Hank L. was desperate for money. Both had steady sources of income. Although Serge F.'s disability benefits were modest, his income was sufficient to meet his monthly expenses. Hank L. was truly affluent. Although he complained about the Medicaid reimbursement rates for his professional services, Hank L. had earned a six-figure income for many years. The bottom line was that both Serge F. and Hank L. wanted more income than they were able to generate legally.

Unlike many offenders whose fraudulent crimes are motivated by greed, Serge F. and Hank L. were genuinely remorseful and demonstrated their insight the first time that I met them. Both had moved into the contemplation stage of change and seemed eager to prepare for real change in their lives and priorities. Hank L. also had good restorative justice instincts:

> It's hard for me to grasp what I've thrown away. Looking back on it, I was the epitome of greed. I had it all but didn't realize it. I didn't need more money; I just got seduced by the dollar signs. I saw my other dentist friends doing so well, and I felt the need to be in their same orbit. In the beginning of my career I wasn't bothered by making less money; I really did get a charge out of providing an important health service to poor people. But over the years I got kind of jaded. The system [Medicaid] just beats you into the ground—the paperwork, the approvals, the low reimbursement, the delayed reimbursement. It just wears you out to the point where you figure if you cheat some, you're simply getting back what they owe you. Well, I know the system is not perfect—hell, it's far from perfect—but that's not a legitimate excuse. There are better ways to try to reform the system. I hope that some day I can get my license reinstated. Maybe one of the things I can do is negotiate a plan with the board [the state licensing board for dentistry] where I could practice under a provisional license, make restitution monetarily, and provide dental services to poor people again.

So did Serge:

> This has been a real wakeup call for me, you know what I mean? I knew so many people who were beating the system the way I was [receiving unemployment or disability benefits fraudulently] that I figured myself for a fool if I didn't do the same thing. Some of my buddies convinced me that this was an easy scam. Now I think about it real differently. You

know, it's interesting—none of those "good" friends visit me here. I just believed what I wanted to believe at the time. Now, when my kids come here to visit me, I think, "Man, look at what you've taught them." There I was, lecturing them about "do this," "don't do that," and now look at me. They come here, see me locked up and wearing this khaki uniform with a prison number on my chest, and they lecture me about doing the right thing. I've got to show them what I've learned, and I've got to be someone they can look up to again.

Theft

An enormous percentage of thefts are crimes of greed and opportunism, as opposed to crimes of desperation. Most involve property crime of one sort or another, although more recently we have begun to encounter incidents of "identity theft" (that is, theft, via computer or otherwise, of an individual's Social Security numbers or credit card numbers). Many offenders whom I have encountered had little, if any, compunction—at least at the time they committed their crimes—about taking other people's personal property. Many instances of breaking and entering, burglary, auto theft, and robbery amount to little more than offenders' wanting more—greed, pure and simple. Here is a mere smattering of the cross section:

Case 3.5 Lawrence A., nineteen, had dropped out of school in the tenth grade. He had a learning disability and found school "boring and frustrating." He spent most of his time "hanging out with my buddies" and working at an occasional odd job (helping out a neighbor who had a junk removal business, shoveling snow, working at a local car wash). Lawrence A. and two friends were arrested for breaking into six lockers at a local self-storage facility and helping themselves to the tenants' possessions.

Case 3.6 Wanda M. was the manager of the computer concession at the bookstore of a major university. She was assistant manager in the department for four years and manager for three. Wanda M. sold fourteen personal computers and twenty-seven laptop computers off the books and at a deep discount to friends and acquaintances and pocketed the money.

Case 3.7 Brandon S. owned a chain of jewelry stores that catered to an affluent clientele. One of his golfing partners contacted Brandon S. and said that he had a proposal. The golfing partner explained to Brandon S. that he had a close relationship with a man who had access to a "steady stream of high-end jewelry that, you know, becomes available. Don't ask me too many questions about *how* the jewelry becomes available. Let's just say that my friend has some *very* good connections." During the parole hearing Brandon S. explained that he "pretty much knew that the jewelry was hot [stolen property], but I figured that if I didn't know too much about the circumstances my hands wouldn't be too dirty."

Brandon S.'s friend was arrested after a state police sting operation. The friend pleaded guilty and received a lighter prison sentence in exchange for his testimony against Brandon S., who was also indicted and convicted of receiving stolen goods and criminal conspiracy.

Case 3.8   Victor D. supervised the loading dock and shipping department at a major department store. Victor D.'s brother-in-law approached Victor and proposed "the deal of a lifetime." The brother-in-law told Victor D. that he had some "great contacts who can easily fence just about anything your store sells—the electronic stuff and jewelry, that's where the big money is." Victor D. diverted nearly $98,000 worth of stolen goods to his brother-in-law before he was caught by an undercover police officer hired by the store to work in the shipping department and investigate unexplained inventory loss that the store's internal audit officer had discovered.

Case 3.9   Dierdre K. was a home health aide employed by a visiting nurse agency. She provided homebound elderly with assistance in the "activities of daily living" (such as bathing, toileting, food preparation). Dierdre K. worked in the home of an eighty-four-year-old woman for about three months. The woman suffered from de-bilitating arthritis and dementia. Dierdre K. stole three of the woman's personal checks, forged the woman's signature, and cashed them at a currency exchange.

Case 3.10   Sid L. was a twenty-five-year-old man who worked in the stockroom of a discount store. His pay was close to minimum wage and, according to Sid L., "just wasn't enough for a man my age who likes the good life. How am I supposed to keep up with the club scene on that pay? I mean, you got to be kidding!" Sid L. and a friend of his were arrested and charged with stealing four high-end automobiles from an affluent community about twenty minutes away (two BMWs, one Lexus, and one Mercedes Benz) and selling them to a "guy in the neighborhood who knows what to do with these cars."

Case 3.11   Jose S. was arrested for utility theft. He was employed at a local super-market in the produce department. Jose S. learned from a former neighbor that he could bypass the cable company's equipment and get "free" cable television and In-ternet services. He stole cable service for nearly eighteen months and was sentenced to six months of home confinement on electronic monitoring.

CALIBRATION-RECALIBRATION

This diverse group of cases provides a representative cross-section of offenders and thefts that are motivated by greed. Within this group I found some offenders who came to understand their wrongdoing, expressed remorse, and were earnest about making constructive changes (consistent with the contemplation, preparation, and action stages of change), some who were just beginning to accept responsibility and move toward treatment and rehabilitation (the contemplation stage), and some for whom insight and the possibility of change were not yet on the radar screen (the precontemplation stage). Selected comments from these offenders reflect their location on the spectrum:

LAWRENCE A. (PRECONTEMPLATION STAGE): Yeah, I know it wasn't such a good idea [breaking into the self-storage lockers], but I ain't really about that stuff no more. You got nothin' to worry about, you know? I'm all set; I don't need no programs.

WANDA M. (PREPARATION STAGE WITH RESPECT TO RESTITUTION AND ACTION STAGE WITH RESPECT TO THERAPY): Thinking back on that period in my life [when she was selling computers stolen from the bookstore], I now realize that I sort of forgot everything I had learned about what's right and wrong. I mean, a person in my position and with my background certainly should know better. I'm amazed at how easy it is for your mind to play games with you. At the time I didn't really think anyone was being hurt. But being in the group [the therapy group in the women's prison] has helped me realize that lots of people *were* being hurt; the university lost money, for example, and that means higher tuition for the students and maybe lower wages for the employees. I guess I never really thought it through like that before. I really want to figure out a way to make this up to the university when I get out.

BRANDON S. (CONTEMPLATION STAGE): Being on home confinement like this [with an electronic ankle bracelet] has given me lots of time to think. Almost every day I have to explain to my kids why I can't go with them to their baseball game, to the school picnic, or take them to their friend's house. People think that being on home confinement is a great deal, and maybe it is compared to prison, but it's a pretty miserable experience.

I haven't really talked to anyone about how I got into this mess, but I was just telling my wife that I really should get the name of a counselor who can help me figure out how to handle this with my kids and avoid problems in the future.

VICTOR D. (PRECONTEMPLATION STAGE): Nope, not interested [in participating in any counseling program]. What I did was a one-time thing, I promise you. I know it wasn't smart, but I have everything under control. There's really nothing anyone in here can do for me.

DIERDRE K. (CONTEMPLATION STAGE): You don't have to be a rocket scientist to know that someone like me shouldn't steal checks from an old lady. For heaven's sake, I'd probably hit the roof if someone did that to my own mother. Just yesterday I told one of the COs [correctional officer] that I ought to talk to one of the chaplains or some counselor about why I did that. Sometimes I lie in my bunk at night and can hardly believe that I would be so stupid. Holy cow.

SID (PREPARATION STAGE BRIEFLY, RETURNED TO CONTEMPLATION STAGE): I was talking to my mom during one of my visits. She convinced me that I really got to get my act together, you know what I'm saying? I know there's no future in stealing cars and coming in and out of this place. I got to go back to school and get my GED and learn a trade. Actually, about three months ago I signed up for the GED class and talked to the teacher about my situation. But then I got a good job as a porter over in medium security [a good prison job] and kind of put the GED on the back burner. I guess I got to move it to the front burner again; hell, I'm going to be getting outta here in eight months, even if you all don't give me parole.

JOSE S. (CONTEMPLATION STAGE): I've been thinking about what I can do to make things right. I feel kinda guilty about getting all the cable for nothing. I know they're a big company and what I took probably doesn't hurt them that much, but I can see why they're so upset. The guilt is what bothers me the most. I'm going to start going to my church more and I'm going to talk to my priest about this. What I did was wrong.

Drug-Related Crimes

Many drug-related crimes—especially drug dealing and selling—are committed by substance abusers themselves, as a way to "finance" their own addiction (I will explore this phenomenon more fully in chapter 7). However, a significant percentage of drug-related crimes are committed by nonaddicts. The prototypical offender in this category has an antisocial personality disorder. The key elements in the following scenario are common:

Case 3.12 Marvin H., twenty-five, dropped out of school when he was in the eleventh grade. He had been suspended from high school two times for fighting and was expelled once for stealing a teacher's pocketbook. Marvin H. spent five months in the state training school for boys after being arrested for automobile theft. Since leaving high school Marvin H. has never held a steady job.

For nearly two years Marvin H. sold cocaine to customers around his neighborhood. He was arrested after police received a tip from a neighbor. Marvin H. was paroled after serving nine months of a one-year sentence. Two years later Marvin H. was arrested again on drug-dealing charges.

CALIBRATION-RECALIBRATION

At his appearance before the parole board I asked Marvin H. why he decided to get involved in selling drugs again after serving prison time for the same crime. His reply was succinct: "I loved the money, man. I just loved the money, and the money's big, you know what I'm saying? That's all there is to it." Marvin H. expressed little regret and no remorse. His modest regret focused almost exclusively on his being caught and the hard time that his family was having without him. Beyond that, I heard no comments about the effect of drug selling on the community, on drug addicts, and so on. None. When I asked Marvin H. whether he understood that many people who buy illegal drugs are addicts and that they often commit crimes (such as breaking and entering, shoplifting, and robbery) to get cash to buy drugs, he responded with, "Yeah, I guess so." Marvin H. may reach a point where he tires of the revolving door (in and out of prison) and is receptive to constructive, legal alternatives to crime, but when I interviewed him he seemed far from it (precontemplation stage of change).

Crimes Involving Personal Injury

A relatively small percentage of crimes motivated by greed and opportunism explicitly aim to harm others. These exceptions, however, tend to involve extremely serious offenses, for example, where criminals agree to burn down a home or business for a fee (arson for hire) or kill someone for a fee (murder for hire).

Case 3.13 Buddy C., forty-seven, had a long criminal record, including such offenses as breaking and entering, assault, violation of a restraining order, credit card fraud, and driving under the influence. He rarely held a steady job. Buddy C. received a call from a friend who explained that he (the friend) had heard from a business-man who was in deep financial trouble. The businessman owned a doughnut and coffee shop, and the bank was about to foreclose on his mortgage. The business-man was trying to locate someone who, for a fee, would be willing to burn down his business so that the businessman could collect the insurance. Buddy C. agreed to commit the arson. When he burned down the building at 2 A.M., Buddy C. did not realize that someone was living in an upstairs apartment. The tenant died in the fire.

Case 3.14 Leo F., now thirty-seven, had gotten out of the army soon after his twenty-second birthday and was struggling to find some direction in his life. He had been dishonorably discharged for selling MDMA—known on the street as ecstasy, a psychoactive drug that has both stimulant (amphetamine-like) and hallucinogenic properties—to other soldiers. Leo F. had been arrested on several occasions as a ju-venile; his parents had hoped that the army would straighten him out.

One afternoon Leo F. was hanging out with a good friend and using cocaine. The friend told Leo F. that he had a serious proposal for him. The friend said that he had just caught his wife in bed with another man, a coworker with whom he had a his-tory of considerable conflict. The friend and his wife had been having some marital difficulty, but he thought they were working things out. Now Leo F.'s friend was so enraged with his coworker that he wanted Leo F. to kill him. The friend knew that Leo had received enough training in the army to know how to commit murder. Leo F. agreed to kill the man for a fee. Leo F. was arrested and charged with murder. After fifteen years in prison Leo F. became eligible for parole.

CALIBRATION-RECALIBRATION

At his first parole hearing Leo F. had little to say. He muttered a few com-ments about how he knew he had made a serious mistake. Beyond that, how-ever, Leo F. demonstrated little evidence of insight. The board encouraged Leo F. to contact a prison counselor to arrange to join a counseling group, preferably the group for inmates convicted of murder (that is, the board hoped to help Leo F. move from the precontemplation to the contemplation and, ideally, the preparation and action stages of change.)

When the parole board saw Leo F. again two years later, he seemed to be a different person. He was much more verbal, articulate, and insightful. He spoke at length about how he was "growing up in prison" and had begun to realize how destructive his youthful indiscretions had been. Leo F. presented the board with copies of certificates that he had earned in several demanding prison-based programs that focus on criminal thinking, alternatives to violence, parenting (Leo F. had a son), and substance abuse. Leo F. also submitted a letter from a prison social worker who summarized the progress Leo F. had made in their counseling sessions.

The parole board was very impressed with Leo F.'s progress. However, given the gravity of his offense and the length of his sentence (thirty years), the board was not yet ready to release him. Incarceration for public safety and punishment continued to be appropriate. The board encouraged Leo F. to continue his program participation and to seek transfer to a lower security facility (that is, transfer from medium security to minimum security).

During the hearing Leo F. talked about his recent involvement in the "murderers' group," inmates who met regularly to discuss the serious crimes that they had committed, their life circumstances, futures, and so on. Leo F. explained that through this group he had learned about the concept of victim-offender mediation and said that he had spoken to his counselor about the possibility of meeting with the surviving family members of his victim. On his own Leo F. had begun to take initial steps toward restorative justice.

The parole board met with Leo F. again fifteen months later. The board continued to be impressed with Leo F.'s program participation and insight. By then Leo F. had participated in two face-to-face meetings with his victim's surviving family members (along with a facilitator). He spoke sincerely and thoughtfully about the profound effect that these meetings had on him. The parole board agreed to release Leo F. in one year for an extended period of supervision on home confinement (electronic monitoring).

This particular case provides a valuable illustration of the ways in which the multiple goals of criminal justice can be served and of the ways in which offenders can progress through various stages of change. Leo F. committed an extremely serious crime. During the first third of his sentence he displayed little interest in rehabilitation and little insight. Clearly, he was at the precontemplation stage, and continued incarceration for public safety and punishment were warranted. Leo F.'s lack of insight at the time made him a poor candidate for restorative justice options. At the next parole hearing two years later, Leo F. had made significant progress. He was able to verbalize what he had learned about himself and the reasons he committed his crime. He had already jumped to the action stage in several important respects, as evidenced by his active participation in several prison-based programs. He had become involved in the murderers' group and had begun participation in victim-offender mediation, a form of restorative justice (Leo F. is an example of an offender who was in the action stage with respect to some changes and the preparation stage with respect to another).

At Leo F.'s third parole hearing, fifteen months after his second hearing, the board was sufficiently impressed with his progress that it was willing to consider gradual release to the community. In order to protect the public, in light of the gravity of Leo F.'s crime, an extended period of home confinement with electronic monitoring made sense. This would be combined with continued rehabilitation, in the form of counseling, and participation in victim-offender mediation. The parole plan also included lecturing to high school students about crime and imprisonment—another form of restorative justice.

Racketeering and Bribes

Some of the more noteworthy greed, exploitation, and opportunism cases that I have encountered entailed some form of racketeering or bribery. Technically speaking, a racketeer is someone engaged in an organized, illegal activity, such as extortion. Typical cases involve public officials who accept bribes in exchange for favorable consideration when public contracts are awarded or to otherwise influence their decisions.

Case 3.15   Antonio Almeida was a prominent judge on the Rhode Island Superior Court. In 1992 he was convicted of soliciting and accepting $45,000 in bribes from lawyers in exchange for favorable rulings and court appointments. He received a six-year sentence (MacKay 1998).

Case 3.16   In 1998 former Rhode Island governor Edward DiPrete pleaded guilty to eighteen counts of bribery, racketeering, and extortion committed during his three terms of office. He had been awarding state contracts in exchange for political contributions (Kirk 1999).

Case 3.17   Raymond Azar, the former director of public works in Cranston, Rhode Island, pleaded guilty to racketeering. Azar was involved in a kickback scheme that earned him more than $350,000 in bribes for awarding public works contracts to contractors. He received a five-year sentence (MacKay 1998).

Case 3.18   Michael Piccoli, former director of the Rhode Island Waste Management Corporation, pleaded guilty to obtaining money under false pretenses in connection with a prominent public corruption case. He served a one-year prison sentence before being paroled (MacKay 1998).

CALIBRATION-RECALIBRATION

As with offenders in general, those convicted of racketeering and related crimes run the gamut, ranging from those who acknowledge their guilt clearly and forcefully to those who continue to deny their offenses or obfuscate the case-related details. Some are eager to make meaningful changes in their lives, and some are unwilling to acknowledge that any change is warranted.

Viewed narrowly, incarceration for such public officials can rarely be based on the "public safety" argument. Without minimizing the effect of their crimes, incarceration is not necessary in these cases in order to keep the typical former public official off the streets. However, in this day and age the public is growing increasingly weary of public corruption and, understandably, clamors for some modest incarceration, at the very least, for retributive and punitive purposes. Also, public corruption cases often provide ideal opportunities for restorative justice in the form of community service.

Organized Crime

Organized crime in the United States has a long, colorful, and storied history, from as far back as the colonial period. By the 1800s various ethnic gangs dominated organized crime. The modern era of organized crime began in the early twentieth century with gangsters of Italian and Sicilian descent; Prohibition provided much of the fuel for mob influence and profit. Since then organized crime has branched out into diverse enterprises, including drug trafficking, firearms smuggling, money laundering, gambling, labor racketeering, loan-sharking, prostitution, pornography, kidnapping, fraud, robbery, stolen property and shipments, and murder (Jacobs and Panarella 1998). Members of various ethnic groups—including Jamaicans, African Americans, Russians, Chinese, Chicanos, and Mexicans—have joined the action.

In addition to the more traditional crime syndicates, a number of nontraditional syndicates and politically organized groups are considered part of organized crime (Abadinsky 1989; Albanese 1989; Bequai 1979). Examples include large-scale narcotics smugglers, organized burglary and robbery rings, and, to some extent, groups such as the Pagans and Hell's Angels (Hagan 1990). In some states and communities organized crime is prominent, whereas others see little evidence of its presence.

With the exception of the relatively small number of organized crime offenders who renounce their affiliation, the majority view crime as a way of life. As with most career criminals, these offenders are archetypes for the psychiatric diagnosis of antisocial personality disorder.

Case 3.19   Frank B. began his delinquent career when he was 10. With his brother and a cousin, Frank B. would shoplift from neighborhood stores and steal hubcaps from cars. By the time he was 15, he had graduated to auto theft and larceny. He served two terms in the state reformatory. When he was 19 Frank B. was recruited by a local organized crime family and became involved in gambling operations (numbers) and pornography. When he was 21 Frank B. began serving a two-year sentence for robbery, and when he was 24, he received a four-year sentence for aggravated assault on his sister's ex-boyfriend. Three years after his release Frank B. was arrested yet again, this time for murdering a man who failed to promptly pay back his loan from organized crime figures for whom Frank B worked. Frank B. was sentenced to fifty years in prison for this offense.

Case 3.20   Since his early twenties, Sanford M. had been actively involved in an organized crime–sponsored pornography enterprise. He helped to finance several adult entertainment establishments and skimmed profits from each of them for his organized crime bosses. Before he was thirty-five Sanford M. served two short prison sentences for contributing to the delinquency of a minor and cocaine possession. Just before his fortieth birthday Sanford M. was indicted on charges of laundering money on behalf of drug traffickers involved with his organized crime family. He was convicted and sentenced to five years in prison during the same week that his wife gave birth to their first child.

CALIBRATION-RECALIBRATION

At his first parole hearing Frank B. was virtually silent. He was reluctant to engage in any substantive conversation about his criminal past and his current sentence. It was a short hearing. At his second parole hearing two years later, Frank B. was in a higher (more restrictive) security facility; he had been moved from medium security to maximum security because of a series of disciplinary infractions involving trafficking in narcotics and contraband within the prison. Once again he was denied parole.

Since then Frank B. has had two more parole hearings. At each one he has been represented by an attorney who argues that Frank B. is a changed man who is no longer interested in living a crime-laden life. However, Frank B. has yet to speak in detail or convincingly about his changed ways and his future. In light of his heinous criminal record and apparent lack of insight, incarceration is the only appropriate option, both for public safety and punitive purposes. Frank B. has not engaged in any substantive rehabilitative programs and has provided no indication that he plans to do so (precontemplation stage). Restorative justice in this case is a moot point.

But while Sanford M. was in prison, he thought long and hard about his criminal career. He told me that having a son changed his outlook on life. Sanford M. talked about how he is overwhelmed with sorrow whenever he sees his young son in the prison visiting room. According to Sanford M., "seeing that little guy come in here is my wakeup call. He has changed my life, and I can't imagine watching him grow up from behind bars. I want him to be proud of me and to know that I can be a good father."

After considerable thought Sanford M. decided to renounce his affiliation with the organized crime family, an act that ordinarily meets with severe repercussions. Once Sanford M. made his decision, he began to keep his distance from other inmates connected to organized crime. They became suspicious and harassed Sanford M. for his apparent "defection." For his own safety Sanford M. entered the protective custody unit, which is segregated from the general prison population. Eventually, the state transferred Sanford M. to an out-of-state prison in order to protect him.

Unlike Frank B., Sanford M. began to move toward significant change in his worldview and priorities. He began to express sincere remorse for his criminal past and seemed to be quite earnest about forging a new path in life. Sanford M. made good use of counseling services available within the prison. Sanford M. was eventually paroled, placed on electronic monitoring because of the breadth and depth of his criminal record, and then moved out of state to begin a new life. Unlike Frank B., Sanford M. moved straight from the precontemplation stage to the action stage, with impressive results.

Gang Exploitation

Many communities throughout the United States struggle with gangs and the destruction that they create. Research on gangs began with Frederick Thrasher's classic 1927 study, *The Gang: A Study of 1,133 Gangs in Chicago.* Although it is difficult to define exactly what constitutes a gang, scholars generally agree that gangs have certain key elements. According to Malcolm Klein, a preeminent researcher on the subject, the best available evidence suggests that

1. Street gangs are composed principally of youths, but with age ranges from nine or ten years to the thirties. Average age is generally between late teens and early twenties.
2. Street gangs are composed principally of racial and ethnic minorities, with whites constituting less than 10 percent (most of the whites are members of supremacist groups).

3. Street gangs are primarily male, but with gender ratios reported from 10-to-1 to 1-to-1. Autonomous female groups exist but are rare.

4. Street gangs are generally located in inner-urban areas, but more recently they have been found in the minority enclaves of many towns that are not generally thought of as "urban."

5. The illegal behaviors of street gangs are generally highly versatile; that is, they participate in a wide variety of crimes rather than specializing in one or a few types (specialty gangs excepted, by definition). Thus most gangs are not violent gangs or drug gangs or conflict gangs. Indeed, given the preponderance of certain nonserious forms of behavior, they might more properly be called alcohol gangs, petty theft gangs, loitering gangs, or graffiti gangs.

6. Street gangs often define themselves as oriented to crime, given their own recognition that they are in fact more crime-involved than are most youthful groups. It is suggested that there is an ill-defined "tipping point" in criminal orientation that effectively separates street gangs from many other groups.

7. In contrast to the public image, street gangs more often than not are relatively loose structures of only moderate cohesiveness, with distributed or unclear leadership, considerable membership turnover and instability, and codes of honor and loyalty strongly felt but often broken when convenient. (1998:113–14)

Malcolm Klein (1998) also describes three prominent street gang structures. Traditional street gangs last for many years with succeeding generations of members. These gangs tend to be large, averaging about two hundred members, with subgroups based on age or neighborhood. Traditional street gangs are quite territorial and commit a wide range of crimes. Compressed gangs have shorter lives, usually ten years or less, and are much smaller than traditional street gangs (the average size is about fifty). These gangs tend to be somewhat less territorial and somewhat "younger" than traditional street gangs. Finally, specialty gangs are the smallest gangs (the average size is about twenty-five) and have the shortest lives. These gangs usually focus on a narrow range of crimes, for example, drug selling, burglary, graffiti, and automobile theft. Their territoriality has less to do with neighborhood of residence and more to do with locations where they can successfully ply their criminal trade.

Adolescents and young adults join and remain in gangs for a wide range of reasons. Extensive research conducted over decades consistently points to a common set of factors: social status and identity; a sense of belonging; excitement; challenge; protection from real or imagined threats; and an alternative to a bleak or troubled home life (Cohen 1955; M. Klein 1971, 1998; Spergel 1964, 1995; Thrasher 1927).

Consistent with patterns found in the empirically based research literature, virtually all the offenders I have met who have gang affiliations have been young. Some were adolescents when they were arrested for remarkably serious crimes and were tried as adults (waived from the juvenile court to adult criminal court because of the heinous nature of the offenses with which they were charged). Many of the eighteen-to-twenty-year-old offenders I have encountered have had gang affiliations to some degree (that is, some belonged to more traditional street gangs and some to what Malcolm Klein [1998] refers to as compressed gangs and specialty gangs).

Case 3.21   Jorge S. was eighteen when he was arrested for cocaine possession and distribution. He had been selling cocaine for nearly two years and was arrested after he sold the drug to an undercover police officer.

Jorge S. was an active member of the Latin Kings, a traditional street gang. Jorge S. joined the gang shortly after dropping out of school in the tenth grade. At the time his father had just been sentenced to a twenty-year prison sentence for attempted murder, and his mother was in a residential drug rehabilitation program. Jorge S. was living with an older sister.

Jorge S. had a hard time adjusting to prison life. He was much younger than most inmates and he was isolated and harassed. The prison administration made sure that Jorge S. was housed in a unit that was separated from other members of the Latin Kings. During his first year in prison Jorge S. was placed in punitive segregation on three occasions for fighting, having "dirty urine" (evidence that he had consumed illegal drugs while in prison), using gang hand signals, and being in possession of gang paraphernalia (literature and drawings).

Case 3.22   Sopheap S. moved to the United States from Cambodia when he was only a year old. The family fled Cambodia because of their fear of the tyrannical Pol Pot and the Khmer Rouge (Communist Cambodians). The family settled in a city that had a small but growing Cambodian population.

When he was seventeen, Sopheap S. was recruited to be a member of a local Cambodian gang, the Original Loco Bloods. Sopheap S. and his fellow gang members were involved in a number of robberies and home invasions. When he was twenty-two, he was arrested, charged with burglary and found guilty, and sentenced to three years in prison.

CALIBRATION-RECALIBRATION

At his first appearance before the parole board, Jorge S. was quite sullen and uncommunicative. His responses to parole board members' questions consisted mostly of grunts and monosyllables. Jorge S. did not seem at all interested in substantive discussion of any aspects of his troubled past, his current predicament, or his uncertain future.

QUESTION: Mister S., can you tell us a little bit about your family situation? Who are you in touch with now? Does anyone visit you here?
ANSWER: There's not much to say.
QUESTION: How long have you been involved with the Latin Kings?
ANSWER: Not too long.
QUESTION: Have you decided whether you want to break away from the gang or stay with it?
ANSWER: No.

Clearly, we were not going to gain much ground in the hearing. We politely encouraged Jorge S. to avail himself of available programs—especially the GED and vocational education programs—and do his best to cut back on the disciplinary problems. We told Jorge S. that we hoped to see him in a lower (less secure) building at his next hearing.

It is not surprising that an offender such as Jorge S. would be reluctant to disclose much to parole board members or, for that matter, any authority figure in the criminal justice system. For a variety of developmental, emotional, and cultural reasons, Jorge S. still felt strong ties to the gang. Gang members were his family, especially considering the chaos and instability in his own family of origin. The gang was probably the only place in the world where Jorge S. felt accepted and supported and had a sense of belonging. A group of highly educated criminal justice professionals were not likely to replace that.

My experience with offenders such as Jorge S. is that they are most likely to remain in the precontemplative stage for quite some time; although the occasional exception arises, few are willing to renounce their gang affiliations. Statistically, these young offenders are likely to cycle in and out of prison.

For these offenders the most critical variable appears to be one that criminal justice professionals and the criminal justice system cannot influence or control: time. The data on criminal careers of gang members suggest that maturation and aging tend to be the most powerful correlates of eventual disaffiliation. Many of these offenders tire of the gang lifestyle as they age. In short, they grow out of it. The exceptions include those who will rise to in-

fluential, lucrative, and stimulating gang leadership positions that they are not eager to abandon. But many of the rank-and-file gang members will move on. Some, especially those inclined toward "criminal thinking" patterns, will venture into other forms of crime—those committed by individuals rather than groups—and some will seek the straight and narrow. Attempts to reduce gang involvement and proliferation depend to a great extent on the effectiveness of diverse factors, including community and economic development in vulnerable communities that provide relatively few legitimate alternatives for residents, suppression by law enforcement (particularly the use of special police gang units, which monitor and work with gangs), and gang truces (attempts to get gangs to enter into peace treaties).

Although they are not the norm, I have encountered some gang-affiliated members who, even at a relatively young age, decided to renounce his (it is usually a male) affiliation and walk away from the gang. This is not an easy task, particularly for members of gangs that have formal protocols designed to prevent renunciation (harassment, death threats, and so on).

When I met Sopheap S., he was remarkably polite and articulate. Almost from the beginning of the interview he spoke about his shame—mainly with respect to his parents' distress about his life of crime and imprisonment—and his wish to forge a new life for himself. Sopheap S. talked calmly and clearly about how his "eyes have opened" within the past year:

> When I was first involved with OLB [the Original Loco Bloods] I was just a kid. I mean, I didn't feel like a kid, but I was a kid. In fact, I remember how grown up I felt when one of the older gang members, Nhol, first approached me about joining. I thought, man, this is what it's all about—I've made it. I now realize that I was swept up by the glamour and the glitter of the gang life. For the first time in my life I felt like I belonged. Before that I was always getting harassed in school and in the neighborhood, people telling me I'm Chinese or that I should have stayed in my country—silly stuff like that. Once I joined the OLB I could hold my head high.
>
> I think differently about all this now. Coming here [to prison] has made me realize what else I can do with my life. I've always been told I'm smart, but I guess I never believed it. Martha [the GED teacher] has really helped me begin to believe that I *am* smart. She's even convinced me that I should go on to college. Imagine that? I've got a kid now, and that's really changed my thinking. I can't just be thinking of myself anymore. I've got to walk the walk.

I asked Sopheap S. whether it would be difficult to walk away from the gang. He claimed that it would not be too hard; he and the mother of his child planned to move out of state and start a new life.

In contrast to many gang members, Sopheap S. seemed eager to make major changes in his life. He had already embarked on the GED program and spoke in detail of his plan to disaffiliate with the gang (evidence that he was in the preparation and action stages of change). Sopheap S. spoke animatedly about his determination to work with high-risk Cambodian children and adolescents to prevent them from making the mistakes that he made; he spoke about this as a way to pay back the community, a form of restorative justice. His success could not be guaranteed, but the signs were hopeful. This is an instance where criminal justice and social service professionals can make an enormous difference by being available, supportive, and willing to offer education, social, and vocational services to provide the offender with the basic knowledge and skills that he needs to succeed.

Sexual Exploitation

It is important to begin this discussion with a key distinction between two types of sex offenders. In this chapter I will focus on offenders whose sex-related crimes appear to be a function of self-centered opportunism that does *not* entail the classic symptoms of what the American Psychiatric Association (2000) refers to as sexual disorders (the technical term for these disorders is *paraphilias,* such as exhibitionism, fetishism, pedophilia, and voyeurism). I will discuss the latter more fully in the chapter on crimes that arise out of mental disorders.

Here I will focus on a pattern that I have encountered among a number of sex offenders whose personalities and behaviors are much more consistent with the characteristics of antisocial personality disorder and narcissistic personality disorder. That is, these offenders take advantage of unique circumstances to sexually abuse victims; they are manipulative and disregard the rights and feelings of others in order to pursue their own pleasure, and they feel little remorse at the time. However, their pattern of behavior does not rise to the level of a sexual disorder in the strict sense of the term. Some of these offenders are able to achieve considerable insight into their behavior—usually as a result of intense sex-offender treatment—although some never do.

Case 3.23 Albert J., forty-one, married a woman he had met at work. Susan J., thirty-seven, and Albert J. were both employees in a hospital cafeteria. At the time of their marriage, Susan J. had been divorced for three years and was raising two children alone, Barry, thirteen, and Amy, fifteen.

Albert J. was arrested after Amy told her mother that he had fondled her and penetrated her vagina with his fingers. Albert J. had taken Amy and Barry on a camping trip one weekend while Susan J. was visiting relatives out of town. According to Amy, Albert J. "drank an awful lot and when he thought I was asleep he laid down next to me and assaulted me." After learning of the assault from Amy, Susan J. confronted Albert J. He said he didn't know what really happened on the camping trip but said that if anything "inappropriate occurred," it would never happen again. He admitted that he had drunk a six-pack of beer and "a lot of bourbon" that evening.

Case 3.24 Lance M. had been living with Tanya R. and her young daughter for a little over a year. Lance M. worked for a landscaping contractor, and Tanya R. was an exotic dancer at a local club for men. Lance M. and Tanya R. had a volatile relationship. They argued frequently and occasionally hit each other. One evening the couple had an intense fight after Lance M. accused Tanya R. of having an affair. Lance M. screamed at Tanya R. that he would "show her who's boss"; he then forced Tanya R. onto their bed and raped her.

CALIBRATION-RECALIBRATION

Neither Albert J. nor Lance M. had a history of sexual assault or manifested symptoms of a sexual disorder. Neither had ever been accused of or arrested for such a crime before. In both cases the men exploited their victims to suit their own purposes. Although it certainly makes sense to regard both men as sex offenders, our approach to them—with respect to public safety, punishment, rehabilitation, and restorative justice—had to take into account the difference between their profiles and those of sex offenders who display clear symptoms of a chronic sexual disorder. Quinsey recognizes this distinction and the importance of treating some sex offenders in much the same way that we would approach other types of offenders:

> Sex offenders are . . . much like other offenders, and the issues of risk pertaining to them are identical. Although there is a technology of assessment and treatment that is specific to sex offenders and a substantial proportion of them are undoubtedly paraphiliacs or sexual deviants, the technology of assessment and treatment that exists specifically for sex offenders is fallible and will not bear the weight of unrealistic expectations. There is no mark of Cain or magic bullet of treatment to eliminate uncertainty. (1998:403)

Specialists in treating sex offenders generally agree that it is important to distinguish between offenders who are high risk and those who are not (Groth and Birnbaum 1979; McCaghy 1976; O'Brien 1986). Research data suggest that high-risk sex offenders have several characteristics related to the extent of their psychopathology, the number of previous sex offenses, whether the victim was a family member, substance abuse history, and marital status (Quinsey 1998). Such factors are key in my assessment of offenders such as Albert J. and Lance M. For example, I was particularly concerned that Albert J. had a history of alcohol abuse. On the other hand, the absence of a known history of previous sex offenses was encouraging.

I was also heartened by Albert J.'s eager participation in the prison-based sex offender treatment program. He had been enrolled in the program for about two years and received glowing reports from the program's director (someone who does not often file glowing reports). According to the program director, Albert J. had forthrightly acknowledged his offense and his inappropriate conduct. The director spoke about Albert J.'s growing understanding of the nature of boundaries in a family (especially a step- or "blended" family) and of the destructive effect of his alcohol abuse. I was also impressed with Albert J.'s apparent insight. In our discussion he talked about how he had let his wife and stepchildren down and violated their trust. Albert J. commented on the influence that alcohol might have had when he assaulted his stepdaughter, but he also said that he did not want to use that as an excuse:

> I know I done wrong. There's no excuse for it. I might be able to come up with a thousand reasons why I did what I did, but all that matters is that I done wrong. I'm working hard to patch things up with my wife and with Amy. I really love them, maybe more than ever. I hope they will give me a chance to show them I can be a good husband and stepfather. I've been working real hard with Steve [the sex offender treatment program director], and I'll work just as hard in counseling when I get out [of prison]. Even if you all [the parole board] don't see fit to let me go, I'm not stopping the program. It's been good for me. AA [Alcoholics Anonymous] has also been good. I'm gonna keep up with that too when I get out.

With someone like Albert J., close supervision is essential, at least initially. Although he may not pose the statistical risk posed by offenders with sexual disorders—such as pedophilia—some risk exists. Accountability is important. So, for public safety purposes, a period on electronic monitoring would be appropriate for some time after Albert J.'s release. Continued participation in an outpatient sex offender treatment group is also important. Fortunately,

CRIMES OF GREED, EXPLOITATION, AND OPPORTUNISM

offenders such as Albert J., who was already at the action stage of change and was preparing for additional steps upon his release from prison, tend to be amenable to such requirements and suggestions, although not all are. Further, Albert J.'s interest in "working things out with my wife and stepdaughter" and "helping the family heal," as he told me, suggests that he has some instincts toward constructive restorative justice. Nonetheless, given his offense, he cannot be allowed to be alone with Amy.

In contrast, Lance M.'s profile was less auspicious. During my first discussion with him, Lance M. was defensive and dismissive, common characteristics of offenders with antisocial personality disorder. He did not acknowledge that he had mistreated his girlfriend and partner; rather, he focused on how Tanya R. had supposedly betrayed him by allegedly having an affair. Lance M. said he had no interest in participating in the prison's sex offender treatment program: "I ain't sittin' around with a bunch of diddlers [prison slang for child molesters] in some group. I'm not like them and never will be. I did what I did and that's all there is to it. I just wanna do my time and be done with all this." As with many offenders who manifest classic symptoms of antisocial personality disorder, Lance M. was in the precontemplation stage of change and showed no signs of moving beyond it.

• • •

Offenders who commit crimes of greed, exploitation, and opportunism are remarkably diverse. At the extremes some are one-time offenders who see the errors of their ways, and some are steeped in their criminal thinking and chronic pattern of antisocial and destructive behavior. Between the extremes are offenders who are able to change over time, often with the help of supportive, skillful professionals who provide encouragement, a meaningful relationship, and opportunities for earnest self-exploration.

4

Crimes of Rage

A large percentage of offenders have committed some kind of violent act. However, only some offenses are planned with, as they say in the legal trade, malice aforethought and plotted out as acts of revenge or retribution (see chapter 5). Most violent acts are far more spontaneous, arising from impulsive instincts ignited by intense conflict.

The crimes of rage that I have encountered fall generally into four major groups: incidents involving family members and partners, social acquaintances, workplace colleagues, and strangers.

Family and Relationship Violence

An overwhelming percentage of violence involves family members. Without question, our awareness of the dynamics involved in family violence has increased exponentially in recent years, especially since the 1960s. What was once a topic only for whispered conversations is now a bona fide academic and professional specialty.

Viewed broadly, family violence takes many forms, including physical attacks, psychological or emotional aggression and abuse, sexual assaults or threatened sexual assaults, and neglectful behavior. Viewed more narrowly, as in this discussion, family violence entails acts of physical violence (Gelles 1998); these are the behaviors that are most likely to lead to arrest and conviction in criminal court.

Acts of physical violence in families and intimate relationships take a variety of forms, including violent spousal abuse, child abuse, elder abuse, and marital or date rape. Here are several representative cases:

Case 4.1   Ronald B. married Jenelle B. soon after they learned that she was pregnant with their child. For the first several years of their marriage the couple got along well. More recently, however, the couple has fought constantly. According to Ronald B., "Our marriage started to fall apart soon after our son was expelled from school. We started to disagree about how to discipline Bobby, and it seems like we've been fighting ever since."

Ronald B. was serving a four-year sentence for aggravated assault. During one of the couple's heated arguments, Ronald B. suddenly flew into a rage, grabbed his wife by the throat, and beat her head against the wall. The police and medical reports show that Jenelle B. had some swelling on the brain as a result. She reports that she has had chronic headaches ever since.

At a victims meeting with the parole board, Jenelle B. reported that her husband had become "very controlling. He needs to know where I am every minute, how much money I've spent and on what, and all that. He even wants to tell me what clothes to wear."

Case 4.2   Hilda T., twenty-four, was a single mother of three children, aged 5, 2, and 6 months. Hilda T. struggled to make ends meet on her monthly public assistance benefits. Her two older chidren were removed from her custody temporarily after allegations of child neglect. Hilda T. was working toward regaining custody when she was arrested on a charge of abuse involving her infant. A neighbor heard the baby shrieking and called 911. The emergency medical technicians rushed the baby to the emergency room, where the medical staff found evidence of physical abuse and shaken baby syndrome.

Case 4.3   Matt I., fifty-one, lived with his father, Dan I. The two had lived together for six years, ever since Dan I. was diagnosed with dementia. Father and son always had a stormy relationship, complicated by Dan I.'s long-term alcoholism and more recent dementia.

Matt I.'s life was somewhat unstable. He had been married twice, had a difficult time holding a job, and was often in debt. He once served a sixty-day jail sentence for simple assault.

One afternoon Matt I. and his father got into an intense argument. Dan I. accused Matt I. of stealing some of his money. The two argued and argued until Matt I. lost control and pushed his father hard. Dan I. fell to the floor unconscious. Matt I. called an ambulance and told the crew that his father had fallen while walking to the bathroom. However, based on Dan I.'s injuries, the emergency room staff suspected that he had been physically abused and called the protective services division of the state department of elderly affairs. Several weeks later Matt I. was indicted on a charge of elder abuse. He was found guilty at trial and sentenced to five years in prison.

Case 4.4 Sarah M. and Zachary S. met when both enrolled in a business class at a local community college. The two started dating. They spent much of their social time going to dance clubs and restaurants.

Late one night, after they left a dance club, Zachary S. and Sarah M. went to her apartment. After they watched some television, Zachary S. asked Sarah M. if she would like to have sex. Sarah M. said no but he persisted. They began to argue and she told him that she wanted him to leave. Zachary S. started yelling at her, accusing her of being a "tease" and yelling that he was "sick and tired" of her "girl games." He then pulled Sarah M. onto the apartment sofa and forced her to have oral sex. Zachary S. then left the apartment and she called the police. Zachary S. was arrested, convicted, and sentenced to two years in prison.

The prevalence of family and relationship violence is difficult to assess. Estimates come from several sources, including reports from clinicians, data from law enforcement agencies (primarily police, prosecutors, and courts), and self-report data from surveys. Each source has its strengths and limitations. For example, although clinicians (social workers, psychologists, psychiatrists, and counselors) are a valuable source of anecdotal information about family and relationship violence, they see only a fraction of the perpetrators of abuse and their victims. Data from law enforcement agencies provide an important glimpse of trends over time, particularly related to arrests, prosecutions, and convictions, but many acts of violence never reach the attention of law enforcement officials. In addition, arrest, prosecution, and conviction rates can be affected by factors other than the actual incidence of violence, for example, increased public pressure on police to arrest abusers, changes in philosophy among prosecutors and judges, and new legislation. Also, self-report data, while providing many insights concerning the public's exposure to violence and its attitudes and perceptions, are of questionable validity because many investigators use nonrepresentative samples and because the subject is sensitive and taboo.

Nonetheless, when one aggregates data from all available sources, consistent patterns begin to emerge. For example, the U.S. Department of Justice's National Crime Victimization Survey, which obtains data from a cross section of about 60,000 households twice each year, found that between 1987 and 1991 "intimates committed an annual average of 621,015 rapes, robberies, or assaults" (Gelles 1998:185; also see U.S. Department of Justice 1994). In 1992, 51 percent of the victims of intimate violence (most incidents involved physical assaults) were attacked by boyfriends or girlfriends, 34 percent were attacked by spouses, and 15 percent were attacked by ex-spouses. Female victims outnumbered male victims by a ratio of 10 to 1. Information from victim surveys suggests that about one million women are victims of violent assaults each year (Gelles 1998). According to the Justice Department (1994), nearly 700 husbands and boyfriends are killed by their wives and girlfriends each year, and more than 1,400 wives and girlfriends are murdered by their husbands or boyfriends.

Information from the National Family Violence Surveys, conducted by Straus and Gelles (1986; also see Davis 1995 and Gelles and Straus 1988), also is compelling. Respondents in 16 percent of the homes surveyed reported that some kind of violence between spouses had occurred during the year before the survey. Nearly 30 percent of the couples reported marital violence at some time in their marriages. Most incidents of violence were part of a pattern over time rather than an isolated event; the average female respondent reported three instances of abuse each year, with the highest frequency among those aged twenty to twenty-four.

Relatively little is known about marital rape. Finkelhor and Yilo (1985) surveyed a sample of 323 women and found that 10 percent reported that their husband had forced them to have sex. Russell (1984) found that 14 percent of a sample of 644 married women reported one or more incidents of marital rape. Information from the Second National Family Violence Survey (Gelles 1998) found that 1.2 percent of the 2,934 married women interviewed reported that their husbands had tried or succeeded in forcing them to have sexual intercourse in the previous year.

Much information is available about child abuse and elder abuse. The National Center on Child Abuse and Neglect (1996) reports that in 1993 more than a half million children (565,000) were seriously injured, 614,100 were physically abused, and 300,200 were sexually abused. The National Child Abuse and Neglect Data System, sponsored by the Children's Bureau of the U.S. Department of Health and Human Services, reports that in 2000, 879,000 children were found to be victims of maltreatment; 19 percent had been physically abused, and 10 percent were sexually abused (National Clearinghouse 2002). Results from the National Family Violence Surveys show that more than 20 parents in 1,000 (2.3 percent) admit to engaging in one act of abusive violence (kicking, biting, punching, hitting, or trying to hit a child with an object, beating up a child, burning or scalding, and threatening the use of or actually using a gun or a knife) during the year before the survey (Gelles and Straus 1987, 1988; Straus and Gelles 1986). Estimates from various studies of child homicide at the hands of parents or caretakers range from 5.4 to 11.6 deaths per 100,000 children younger than four (Gelles 1998; U.S. Advisory Board on Child Abuse and Neglect 1995; also see Brissett-Chapman 1995 and Wells 1995).

Data on elder abuse are also quite sobering, although fewer reliable sources are available. Researchers generally believe that about 5 percent of individuals aged sixty-five and older have been victims of physical abuse, psychological abuse, financial exploitation, and/or neglect within a year's time (Wolf 1995). Pillemer and Finkelhor (1988) found that about 32 elderly per 1,000 report experiencing physical violence, verbal aggression, or neglect in the past year. The rate of physical violence was about 20 elderly in every 1,000 (Tatara 1995). The Justice Department reports that in 1999 the rate of violent crime victimization of people aged sixty-five or older was 4 per 1,000 (Rennison 2000). The first National Elder Abuse Incidence Study estimates that 551,011 elderly people were victims of abuse, neglect, and/or self-neglect in domestic settings in 1996. The study found that physical abuse occurred in about 26 percent of the cases (National Center on Elder Abuse 1998).

Several studies also document the frequency of dating and courtship violence. A range of surveys has found that 10 to 67 percent of dating relationships involve some form of violence. Researchers estimate that "severe violence" among dating couples ranges from about 1 percent each year to 27 percent (Gelles 1998).

Over the years consensus has begun to build about the most effective ways to treat perpetrators of domestic, family, and relationship violence. In general, programs typically aim to help perpetrators identify their patterns of abusive behavior, accept responsibility for their behaviors, understand the nature of the cycle of violence, critically examine their attitudes related to issues of power and control in relationships, learn nonviolent and nonabusive ways to manage anger and handle conflict in relationships, and implement meaningful changes. Intervention approaches primarily include individual counseling, couples counseling (only when appropriate), group therapy, and batterers' groups. Although some perpetrators participate in programs voluntarily, many participate as a condition of probation or parole (Roberts 2002).

CALIBRATION-RECALIBRATION

Not surprisingly, a principal challenge in work with violent offenders is helping them reach a point where they are willing to acknowledge their abusive behavior and commit themselves to change. I have seen the entire range, from offenders who adamantly refuse to accept responsibility (the precontemplation stage of change) to those who are profoundly insightful and contrite (the contemplation stage) and are taking steps to address their domestic violence issues (the preparation and action stages). For example, in my interviews with Ronald B., who battered his wife, he did not acknowledge that he has a problem with violence. In two separate conversations he projected all blame for their physical encounter onto his wife:

> You have no idea what it's like to live with that woman. This is a complete set up. She says I'm always out to get her, telling her how to live her life and what not. She's a liar. Sure, I've yelled at her now and then, mostly when she's drunk and behaving like an idiot. The night this happened she drank a fifth of vodka and went after me. I did what any man would do in that situation. Give me a break. You guys always believe the woman.

In contrast, Hilda T., who was convicted of abusing her infant (shaken baby syndrome), was beginning to acknowledge her problems when I first met her. The institutional reports that I reviewed showed that during the preceding year Hilda T. had not participated in any treatment programs and seemed unwilling to talk about her crime. At the beginning of my interview with her I had the impression that little had changed since then. Hilda T. was relatively quiet and unresponsive to my questions about what happened on the day that her infant was injured. However, about ten minutes into the interview Hilda T. began to cry. Slowly, she began to talk about how horrified she feels about what she did to her child. She said that she had not yet "opened up" to anyone about what had happened. I asked her whether she felt able to begin doing that now, and she said she did. The parole board rejected her application but encouraged her to begin talking with a prison counselor and consider joining a treatment program.

When we saw Hilda T. nine months later, it was abundantly clear that she had heeded our advice and had taken considerable initiative. She had begun meeting weekly with a prison social worker and had enrolled in a group treatment program. She had moved quickly from the contemplation stage of change to the preparation and action stages. About one year later the board paroled Hilda T. to home confinement and electronic monitoring. The parole plan included continued counseling and collaboration with the state child welfare agency to enhance Hilda T.'s relationships with her other children. While her children remained in foster care to ensure their safety, the foster parents arranged weekly supervised visits between Hilda T. and her children, in the hope of eventual family reunification.

Matt I., who was convicted of abusing his elderly father, was more on the fence. At times he seemed to acknowledge that he had mistreated his father and needed to address his anger-management issues: "I guess I was a bit out of control. My dad's sick in the head [dementia], you know, and that can be real hard to live with. Sometimes it's just rough dealing with someone like that day in and day out. Maybe someone can teach me how to do that better." But comments of this sort alternated with those that were less encouraging: "My father is always on my case. He's always been rough on me, and it's only gotten worse as he's gotten older and sicker. We never did get along real well. It's about time I stood up to his crap. No son should have to put up with years and years of abuse from a parent. Maybe I never should have agreed to live with him. This probably never would have happened if he were on his own." Thus, although I saw glimmers that Matt I. was preparing to address his anger-management and relationship issues, I also saw evidence that to some extent he remained in the precontemplation stage of change, unaware of the extent to which he was ready to own responsibility for his behavior.

Zachary S., on the other hand, who had raped his girlfriend, Sarah M., seemed far less ambivalent. While he was out on bail, Zachary S. contacted a program for batterers and began attending counseling sessions. Although Zachary S. admitted that he took this step because his attorney told him to (believing that this might help Zachary S. when he appeared in court to answer the charges against him), he acknowledged that the program has changed his thinking, that he had committed himself to changing his behaviors (action stage of change), and that he was thinking about restorative justice (contemplation stage of change):

> You know, before I started attending the men's group, I was clueless—less than clueless, maybe. I grew up in a family where men ran the show—my dad, my uncles, my grandfather, they all called the shots in their marriages. It never occurred to me that there was another way to live. My mother, my aunts, and my grandmother were all real passive women; until now it never dawned on me that this could be a problem. Looking back on it, I treated Sarah the way I saw the adult men in my world treat their partners. I was in control. What I've learned, painfully, is that it's plain wrong to treat women that way. I know this may sound like what I'm supposed to say, but I think a lightbulb has turned on in my head. When I get parole—sorry, *if* I get parole—I want to spend some time helping young guys avoid the mistakes I've made. I've also got a lot of explaining to do with Sarah—if she'll let me, that is."

Social Violence

In many respects violence between social acquaintances (nonfamily) resembles violence between spouses and partners: most offenders are young. Gelles

(1998), for example, found that people aged eighteen to thirty are most likely to be responsible for violence between intimates *and* nonintimates (social violence) (no evidence exists that youth is a risk factor in elder abuse).

The use of alcohol and other drugs fuels many, although not all, violent incidents between acquaintances.

Case 4.5 Alex H. worked on a construction crew with Paul L. The two had known each other for about a year. Alex H. and Paul L. often would go to a local pool hall after work and drink beer. They got along well most of the time, although they would occasionally engage in heated arguments about women or issues at work.

One Saturday afternoon Alex H. and Paul L. rode their motorcycles with their girlfriends to a local lake. The two couples went swimming and had a picnic. Toward late afternoon Paul L. took Alex H. aside and told him that he thought he was being "a little too friendly" with Paul's girlfriend. Alex H. became very upset and accused Paul L. of being "insecure and paranoid." Their argument escalated into a shoving much and eventually a fistfight. Alex H. fractured Paul L.'s jaw. Alex H. also pushed Paul L.'s motorcycle over with such force that he caused extensive damage.

CALIBRATION-RECALIBRATION

Young men are clearly the group with the highest risk of social violence. They are particularly likely to have difficulty with impulse control that is linked to violence. Some refer to this phenomenon informally as the "testosterone factor," because it is much more likely to occur among males (although there are notable exceptions). More formally, the American Psychiatric Association refers to the diagnosis of intermittent explosive disorder (2000:663–64). This disorder characterizes a wide range of perpetrators of domestic, family, acquaintance, and social violence. The essential feature of intermittent explosive disorder is the occurrence of discrete episodes of failure to resist aggressive impulses that result in serious assaultive behavior or destruction of property. Common examples of serious assaultive acts include hitting, punching, or otherwise hurting another person or verbally threatening to physically assault someone. Property destruction typically involves deliberately breaking something of value (such as furniture, artwork, or an appliance). The degree of aggressiveness expressed during an episode is grossly out of proportion to any provocation or precipitating incident or event (such as an argument or disagreement). Individuals diagnosed with intermittent explosive disorder often describe the aggressive episodes as "spells" or "attacks" in which the explosive behavior is preceded by a sense of tension or arousal and is followed immediately by a sense of relief. After the explosion the individual may feel upset, remorseful, regretful, or embarrassed about the aggressive behavior.

One critical difference between offenders with this sort of explosive disorder and those with antisocial personality disorder is that the former often feel distraught, remorseful, and embarrassed by the episode. As in Alex H.'s case, offenders with intermittent explosive disorder sometimes are eager to address their issues and make amends. When I met with Alex H., he immediately acknowledged that he sometimes has a hard time with his temper and has a "short fuse." He displayed considerable insight and understanding and was actively participating in an anger-management program (action stage of change). Alex H. also showed me the draft of a letter he had written to Paul L., expressing his regrets and apologizing for his actions. Alex H. explained that he wrote the letter as part of his counseling program and is thinking seriously about actually sending it to Paul L. Alex H. said that he has "fantasies about sitting down with Paul, saying I'm sorry, and trying to work things out. We used to be real good buddies" (contemplation stage of change with respect to restorative justice).

Workplace Violence

Media reports seem to be filled with accounts of workplace violence. Some events involve carefully calculated acts of revenge and retribution (see chapter 5). Others, the subject of this discussion, are more impulsive and spontaneous.

Case 4.6 Belinda Y. and Melody N. had worked together at a printing plant for about eighteen months. Both were responsible for processing printing orders.

Belinda Y. and Melody N. both reported that they had difficulty getting along. According to Belinda Y., "You know how you sometimes meet a person and know you're not a good match? That's the way it was with me and Melody." The two "got on each other's nerves a lot," Belinda Y. said. "We'd get pissed off about even little things—whether one of us took too long a break, whose fault it was that a [printing] job got screwed up, whether the heat was on too high. You name it, we argued about it."

One morning, according to Belinda Y., Melody N. told her that she needed to wear less perfume, that the scent was overwhelming. That comment led to an angry exchange, and Belinda Y. ended up stabbing Melody N. with a letter opener that was lying on top of a printing machine. Belinda Y. was charged with assault with a deadly weapon and sentenced to two years in prison.

CALIBRATION-RECALIBRATION

That this case involves women is somewhat unusual statistically, but the incidence of violence perpetrated by women is much higher than many people think. Currently, about 30 percent of women inmates in state prisons are serving sentences for violent offenses (murder, manslaughter, sexual assault, robbery, assault); the comparable figure for male inmates is about 50 percent (Beck and Harrison 2001).

As with any act of violence, dispositions in cases involving workplace colleagues must balance the goals of public safety, punishment, rehabilitation, and restorative justice. In Belinda Y.'s case public safety was a major issue. She had a history of assaultive behavior both in and out of the home. When Belinda Y. was a teenager, she was expelled from school for fighting. When she was twenty-one, she was charged, along with three other young women, with assault and battery for a fight that broke out at a shopping center. Although the label "intermittent explosive disorder" is ordinarily attached to males, the profile fits Belinda Y.

Unfortunately, Belinda Y. was not receptive to counseling or rehabilitation. In my one and only interview with her she was combative and contentious (precontemplation stage of change). When I broached the possibility that she might find it useful to speak with a counselor about her pattern of assaults and join an anger-management group, Belinda Y. asserted that she had a different agenda: "I ain't talkin' to nobody about that stuff. I'm doin' my time and that's all y'all need to know about me. Ain't nobody telling me how to live my life."

My impression, after talking with Belinda Y., was that she was struggling with far more than intermittent explosive disorder. I suspected that she also had more serious psychiatric problems and perhaps some organic brain dysfunction. I recommended that she be assessed by a prison psychiatrist. Perhaps psychotropic medication could help her control her impulses and behavior. Belinda Y. had also been physically and sexually abused as a child and, as a result, may have suffered from posttraumatic stress disorder (see chapter 8). Thus traumatic memories may have triggered some of her outrageous behavior.

In important respects Belinda Y.'s case is symptomatic of widespread issues of violence in the workplace. Although most workplace incidents do not involve coworkers (many involve customers or patients, for example), many do. According to the results of the Victim Risk Supplement to the National Crime Victimization Survey (National Institute 1996), the risk of workplace violence increases when large numbers of workers have face-to-face contact. A comprehensive survey of approximately 250,000 private workplaces by the

U.S. Bureau of Labor Statistics found that 22,400 nonfatal workplace assaults occurred in 1992. The perpetrators were almost as likely to be female (44 percent) as male (56 percent). Most assaults occurred in the service (64 percent) and retail (21 percent) trades. Coworkers or former coworkers (as opposed to a patient or customer) were victims in about 6 percent of the cases. Nearly half of the assaults (47 percent) involved hitting, kicking, or beating; other cases involved pinching, squeezing, stabbing, scratching, biting, or shooting.

Stranger Rage

Many crimes of violence involve people who know each other—family members, acquaintances, intimate partners, and coworkers. However, a significant number of violent incidents occur between strangers who have rage-filled encounters. These cases are prototypical:

Case 4.7 Manuel Z. and his wife were eating at a local restaurant. At the end of their meal Manuel Z. left their table and walked over to the cashier to pay the bill. As he stood in the short line near the cashier, Manuel Z. witnessed an intense argument between the cashier and another restaurant patron. The customer, Warren D., was complaining about the food and refused to pay the bill. Warren D. and the cashier began to argue; Warren D. then picked up a nearby chair and began threatening the cashier. Manuel Z. attempted to intervene and became involved in the argument. Warren D. then slammed the chair into Manuel Z. and fractured his eye socket and jaw, causing permanent damage. Warren D. was convicted of assault and sentenced to three years in prison.

Case 4.8 Frank J. was driving down a two-lane state highway on his way home from work. He looked into his rearview mirror and noticed that the driver of a sports car was tailgating him. Frank J. increased his speed modestly, but the other driver continued to tailgate. Frank J. forcefully motioned with his hand for the other driver to back off. The driver of the other car flashed his lights several times and honked his horn. The other driver also made an obscene gesture to Frank J. Frank J. returned the obscene gesture and deliberately slowed his car to a crawl; the other driver bumped the rear of Frank J.'s car with the front of his car. Frank J. pulled off to the side of the road to inspect the damage. The other driver also stopped and began cursing at Frank J. Frank J. quickly opened up the trunk of his car and pulled out a gun. Frank J. told the other driver to leave. When the other driver continued cursing and refused to leave, Frank J. shot him in the leg with the gun. Frank J. was charged with assault with a deadly weapon, found guilty, and sentenced to four years in prison.

Unfortunately, violent encounters between strangers occur all too frequently. Relatively few data about this specific phenomenon are available. In fact, among the various types of sudden, spontaneous incidents of violence between strangers, only road rage has attracted substantial scholarly attention. Surveying this unique knowledge base may provide some much-needed information about the attributes of people who burst into rages in public settings and the societal conditions that set them off.

Rathbone and Huckabee define road rage as "an incident in which an angry or impatient motorist or passenger intentionally injures or kills another motorist, passenger, or pedestrian, or attempts or threatens to injure or kill another motorist, passenger, or pedestrian" (1999:1). Several studies have identified unique characteristics of individuals who engage in road rage. According to Ellison et al. (1995) and Callahan (1997), the anonymity of the participants is a major factor leading to violence in hostile encounters between strangers. Familiarity between individuals engaged in some form of conflict sometimes constrains violence; the absence of familiarity removes this constraint and can increase the likelihood of violence.

Fong, Frost, and Stansfeld (2001) used self-report data to explore differences among road-rage perpetrators, victims, and a control group of patients at medical clinics. The authors found that perpetrators were more likely than members of the control group to be male, had higher aggression scores on standardized measures, were more likely to use illegal drugs, had higher psychiatric morbidity, and had less driving experience. Deffenbacher et al. (2000) found that high-anger drivers were more likely to engage in aggressive and risky behaviors in general than low-anger drivers. Brewer (2000) surveyed pertinent literature and concludes that perpetrators of road rage tend to lack personal restraints in other areas of their lives, are relatively young, and are more likely than nonperpetrators to have criminal records. Dukes et al. (2001) also note that the majority of aggressive drivers are young, aged eighteen to twenty-six.

While it is always a bit risky to extrapolate from what we know about a narrow phenomenon and apply these findings to a broader phenomenon, I think we can learn much from recent studies of the characters and characteristics of people who engage in, or are likely to engage, in road rage. After all, hostile encounters on the road typically involve people who do not know each other. True, being in one's automobile may provide an inflated, if unwarranted, sense of security and confidence that one might not have while simply walking down the street alongside strangers; that is, people in their cars—where they can exert considerable control over their immediate environment in the form of temperature, music, snacks, direction, speed, and so on—may behave somewhat differently (and more brazenly) than pedestrians, but the personality traits associated with perpetrators of road rage sound remarkably similar to the attributes that I have encountered among offenders convicted of crimes of rage involving strangers: they are predominantly male, young, likely to use drugs, have criminal records, have poor impulse control, and lack personal restraints in other areas of their lives. In short, many offenders who assault strangers have the features found among those with antisocial personality disorder, narcissistic personality disorder, and intermittent explosive disorder.

I would add one other important diagnosis to the list of those often found among offenders with significant histories of conflict with both acquaintances and strangers: attention deficit/hyperactivity disorder. Although much of the literature on this clinical phenomenon and most treatment protocols have focused on children, in recent years professionals have begun to recognize the prevalence of the disorder among adults and the effect that it has on their lives and the lives of their families and acquaintances. As Ellison and Goldstein (2002) assert,

> For many individuals with Attention-Deficit Hyperactivity Disorder (AD/HD), problems in peer relations that start in childhood persist into adolescence and adulthood (Murphy 1998; Weiss and Hechtman 1993). Adolescents with AD/HD tend to have fewer close relationships and have increased rates of peer rejection than teens without AD/HD (Bagwell, Molina, Pelham, and Hoza 2001). Impaired social relations persist even when AD/HD symptoms diminish in adolescence, possibly due to a long history of tenuous peer relationships. Furthermore, as a result of "impulsivity, interrupting, forgetfulness, inattentiveness, hyperactivity, difficulty reading social cues, temper or mood swings, adults with AD/HD frequently report difficulties maintaining friendships" (Murphy 1998). Adults with AD/HD have been described as *self-absorbed, impulsive, intrusive, inattentive, irresponsible, rude, and insensitive in social situations* (Murphy 1998). Poor self-esteem and low self-confidence are common, and are often associated with isolation and feelings of loneliness. Thus, impaired social relationships appear to be a life-long problem for individuals with AD/HD. Many adults feel like they missed important lessons in life—how to express themselves, how to feel at ease, and how to control their emotions in social interactions.   (2002:20; emphasis added)

The formal clinical criteria associated with attention deficit disorder clearly mirror this profile, and one can easily see the childhood origins of so many of these symptoms that later manifest themselves in adulthood.[1]

According to the American Psychiatric Association, the essential feature of attention deficit/hyperactivity disorder is a persistent pattern of inattention and/or hyperactivity-impulsivity that is more frequently displayed and more severe than is typically observed in individuals at a comparable level of development (2000:85–86). Hyperactive-impulsive or inattentive symptoms that cause impairment typically are evident before age seven, although many individuals are diagnosed after the symptoms have been present for a number of years.

Individuals with attention deficit/hyperactivity disorder usually have problems in academic, occupational, or social situations. They may fail to pay close attention to details or may make careless mistakes in schoolwork or job-related tasks. Their work is often messy and performed carelessly and without a great deal of thought. These individuals often have difficulty sustaining attention to tasks or recreational activities and often find it hard to complete tasks. They often appear distracted, as if their mind is elsewhere or as if they are not listening or did not hear what someone just said to them. They may move on to a new task before completing the current task. Often they do not follow through on requests or instructions and fail to complete schoolwork, chores, or other duties that they have been assigned.

Individuals with attention deficit/hyperactivity disorder often are disorganized at work; they may lose important materials or handle them carelessly. Individuals with this disorder are easily distracted by irrelevant stimuli and frequently interrupt ongoing tasks to attend to trivial noises or events that others usually and easily ignore (e.g., a car honking, a background conversation). They often forget about details important to their daily routine (for example, they may miss appointments or forget to bring lunch or pick up a child from day care). In social situations these individuals may have difficulty sustaining conversations, listening to others, keeping their mind on conversations, and following details or rules of games or activities.

These individuals may seem terribly impatient and have difficulty delaying their responses and blurting out answers before questions have been asked completely, waiting their turn, and not interrupting or intruding on others in social, academic, or occupational settings. Other people may complain that they cannot get a word in edgewise when they speak with someone who has attention deficit/hyperactivity disorder. Individuals with this disorder typically make comments out of turn, interrupt others consistently, intrude on others, grab objects from others, touch things they are not supposed to touch, and clown around. Their impulsivity may cause accidents and lead them to engage in dangerous activities without consideration of possible consequences.

The general public and many human service professionals typically associate this disorder with schoolage children. The stereotypical hyperactive child is one who cannot sit still, has difficulty focusing and following through with classroom tasks and homework, and is inattentive. A well-kept secret, it seems, is that many adults manifest the adult version of the same symptoms (substituting workplace behaviors for classroom behaviors); sometimes the hyperactive feature is present and sometimes not, but the difficulty with focus and impulse control is common. I have lost count of the number of times that I have interviewed offenders who are in the middle of adulthood and who continue to get into legal trouble involving assaults, rage, and poor impulse control and who respond affirmatively when I ask whether they were diagnosed as a child with some form of attention deficit disorder. Many report that they have never received treatment or that their treatment ceased some time during childhood. My strong suspicion is that vast numbers of adult offenders would be helped enormously if they were assessed and, when appropriate, treated for attention deficit/hyperactivity disorder. Treatment protocols for the disorder are well known and often quite effective when followed comprehensively and consistently (Barkley and Murphy 1998; Everett and Everett 1999; Hallowell and Ratey 1995; Kelly and Ramundo 1995; Robin 2000).

CALIBRATION-RECALIBRATION

Warren D., who assaulted Manuel Z. in the restaurant, had been diagnosed with attention deficit/hyperactivity disorder as a child. His profile was familiar. Warren D. told me how teachers complained to his parents that he rarely paid attention to them, would often ignore instructions or follow them only partially, and was easily distracted and impulsive. Warren D. also told me that he often felt different from other children, did not have many friends, and felt "blue" much of the time. Throughout adolescence he got into trouble consistently with teachers, neighbors, and the police. Warren D. had been suspended from school on several occasions for fighting and vandalism, and he had been arrested four times for shoplifting and disorderly conduct.

In prison Warren D. was also in trouble; during the first year of his incarceration he had received eight disciplinary reports and sanctions for a steady stream of mostly minor infractions, many of which involved problems consistent with poor impulse control, attention deficit, and depression (for example, sleeping through the morning or afternoon count, failing to respond to a direct order from a correctional officer, reporting to work late, and switching bunks with his cellmate without permission).

I asked Warren D. whether he had ever been referred to a counselor or psychiatrist for a formal assessment. "Nah," he replied. "I think my parents once sent me to a shrink, but I only went once. Also, one of the schools I got kicked out of sent me to talk to somebody. But nothing big ever really happened."

My guess is that Warren D. was never assessed or treated properly by social service and mental health professionals. With proper intervention—for example, a comprehensive strategy involving counseling for Warren D. and his parents, behavior management education for Warren D.'s parents and teachers, and psychotropic medication to help Warren D. with his impulse control and depression—there is a good chance that he would have fared better in childhood, adolescence, and young adulthood. With my encouragement Warren D. agreed to speak with a prison psychiatrist about his impulse control and "attentional" issues. The psychiatrist fully agreed with my hunch and offered to prescribe a combination of psychostimulant medication, which often helps children *and* adults who struggle with impulse control and attentional issues, and antidepressant medication. When I next saw Warren D., six months later, he spoke enthusiastically about how much difference the medication made: "Man, I feel like a different person. I mean, things aren't perfect, but I feel like I'm in more control of myself. Those pills help to take the edge off. I've even started the GED program and I can sit through the classes okay. I could never do that before." Another compelling datum was that since taking the medication, Warren D.'s disciplinary record in prison had improved dramatically. I was not surprised.

Frank J. presented a different challenge. Almost from the moment he was arrested after he confronted and shot another car driver, he expressed remorse for his actions. He had never been in serious trouble in his life and was horrified that he had reacted so violently to the man who was tailgating him. Frank J. explained to me that when he is working, he spends enormous amounts of time driving because of his job as a regional sales representative for a food supplier. He said that over the years he has become increasingly frustrated on the road and intolerant of other drivers. Frank J. told me that while he has never thought of himself as an aggressive person, "something happens to me when I get behind the wheel. I've never been one to speed or cut off other drivers, but I *really* get ticked when other people do that. I feel like I can't let them get away with it. Sometimes I even call the police on my cell phone to report crazy, out-of-control drivers. Come to think of it, that's what I should have done with the guy I shot. I should have just called the cops and reported him instead of taking matters into my own hands."

Frank J. was an outstanding candidate for both rehabilitation and restorative justice. He demonstrated impressive insight, was eager to make the most of his time in prison (he enrolled in many educational and counseling programs), had no disciplinary infractions, and had become a leader in the prison-based program that speaks to high-risk juveniles about life in prison and crime. Frank J. also spoke about how he would like to work with the regional automobile association to help organize a road-rage prevention program when he is released from prison. He showed me the draft of a letter he had composed to the automobile association's president, outlining his ideas. Clearly, Frank J. was in the action stage of change with respect to steps that he could take in prison and in the preparation stage with respect to his plans for restorative justice (paying back the community) upon his release. (Frank J. did not plan to participate in victim-offender mediation. This was a case where such mediation was not feasible. Frank J.'s victim, the man who had tailgated Frank J. on the highway, had a substantial criminal record and significant psychiatric issues. Victim-offender mediation in this instance was not likely to be fruitful.)

• • •

The wide variety of crimes that originate in offenders' sense of rage provides a daunting challenge for criminal justice professionals. Perhaps the greatest challenge involves acts of rage that arise from offenders' relationships with family members—spouses, partners, children, and elderly parents. Hostile encounters between coworkers and strangers also account for a significant portion of crimes of rage.

One prominent theme among these offenders is some degree of difficulty with impulse control. Although impulse control issues do not account for every crime of rage, the correlation is high. Alcohol and drug use often exacerbate impulse control problems, even among those who are not technically alcoholic or addicts.

Comprehensive responses to offenders who commit crimes of rage must be especially sensitive to public safety. These offenders, as a group, seem less willing than many other groups of offenders to engage in constructive rehabilitation programs. Victim-offender mediation is a viable option in some instances, but it is not feasible in many instances because of continuing hostility between the parties.

5

Crimes of Revenge and Retribution

Many offenders who victimize other people do so deliberately, intentionally, and with advance planning. Unlike crimes of rage—which are much more impulsive and spontaneous—crimes of revenge and retribution are calculating and deliberate.

Typically, crimes of revenge and retribution involve a premeditated attempt to harm someone who, in the offender's judgment, deserves to be injured. The harm may be physical, psychological, or financial. Physical attacks are self-explanatory. The perpetrator feels resentful and angry and plans a vengeful attack. Most of these incidents involve domestic partners, friends and acquaintances, and coworkers.

Psychological attacks tend to be more subtle. We have all heard the term *psychological warfare*. As I will show, some offenders manage to turn psychological warfare into an art form, usually through harassing one or more victims. The means of harassment can be remarkably simple—a barrage of threatening telephone calls or messages, for example—or stunningly complicated.

Financial revenge and retribution takes several forms as well. These offenses may involve manipulative financial schemes or some kind of financial harassment. They are not spontaneous acts of rage and they are not motivated by greed. Rather, these acts of revenge and retribution are designed to be provocative and, often, spiteful.

Revenge and retribution are complex psychological phenomena. In a narrow sense, revenge is "to exact punishment or expiation for a wrong on behalf of, especially in a vindictive spirit." Retribution is "requital according to merits or desert, especially for evil" (*Random House* 1991). As one would expect, many offenders who commit illegal acts of revenge and retribution manifest symptoms of antisocial personality disorder, an impulse control disorder, and, in some instances, narcissistic personality disorder (see chapters 3 and 4). In addition, these offenders sometimes manifest genuine symptoms of yet another disorder: paranoid personality disorder.[1]

Offenders with paranoid personality disorder are often suspicious and mistrusting of others; their suspicion and mistrust may lead, ultimately, to acts of revenge and retribution. According to the American Psychiatric Association, paranoid personality disorder is a pattern of pervasive distrust and suspiciousness of others such that their motives are interpreted as malevolent (2000:690–91). This pattern begins by early adulthood and is evident in family, social, and work settings.

Individuals with this disorder assume that other people want to exploit, harm, or deceive them, even if no supporting evidence exists. They may believe that others are plotting against them and may attack them without reason. They often feel that they have been deeply and irreversibly injured by another person even when they have no real evidence for this. They often question the loyalty and trustworthiness of their friends and acquaintances and scrutinize their actions and motives. They are genuinely surprised when a friend or associate shows loyalty. If they get into trouble, they expect that friends and associates will either attack or ignore them.

Individuals with paranoid personality disorder avoid confiding in or becoming close to others because they fear that the information they share will be used against them. For example, an individual with this disorder may misinterpret an honest mistake by a store clerk as a deliberate attempt to shortchange or may view a casual humorous remark by a coworker as a vicious attack. They often misinterpret compliments offered by others. They may view an offer of help as a criticism that they are not performing competently.

Individuals with this disorder often bear grudges and are unwilling to forgive the insults, injuries, or slights that they think they have received. Minor slights often lead to major hostility and conflict, and the angry feelings persist for a long time. These individuals often feel that their character or reputation has been attacked or that friends and acquaintances have slighted them in some other way. They are quick to counterattack and react with anger to perceived insults. Individuals with this disorder may be consumed with jealousy, often believing, without evidence, that their spouse or sexual partner is unfaithful. They may accumulate trivial and circumstantial "evidence" to support their jealous beliefs. They usually want to exert complete control of intimate relationships to avoid being betrayed and may constantly question and challenge the whereabouts, actions, intentions, and fidelity of their spouse or partner.

As with crimes of rage, crimes of revenge and retribution can be directed against family members and partners, acquaintances, coworkers, and strangers (although I find that crimes of revenge and retribution, as I define the terms here, are rarely directed against true strangers). I have also encountered a number of offenders whose crimes of revenge and retribution are directed against individuals in positions of authority who have, or are at least perceived to have, some measure of control over the offender's life, such as public officials, correctional officers, police, judges, and probation and parole officers.

A number of scholars have explored the psychological nature of revenge, including revengers' motives, purposes, and aims (McCullough et al. 2001; Seton 2001; Stuckless and Goranson 1994; Vidmar 2001). Not surprisingly, various inquiries have documented that people sometimes have a deep-seated need to "get even," respond to perceived harm or violation, and restore some sense of balance that has been upset in an important relationship with a person or organization. These factors loom large in studies of revenge and retribution in workplace settings (Bies and Tripp 1996; Bies, Tripp, and Kramer 1997; Douglas and Martinko 2001; Kim and Smith 1993), intimate relationships (Marks 1988), and as a motivation in the commission of crimes such as arson (Bradford 1982; Pettiway 1987) and employee theft (Terris and Jones 1982).

Family and Relationship Revenge and Retribution

Most crimes of revenge and retribution involve people who have some sort of intimate relationship with each other: spouses, partners, children, parents, siblings, and other relatives. This should not surprise us. After all, these are the people with whom most of us spend the most time and share life's most intense, emotion-filled moments. Whatever social veneer and diplomacy we manage to present in our public lives, we tend to let down our emotional guard in our private lives, in our most intimate relationships, and say it like it is (or appears to be). The sometimes raw, unvarnished communication that occurs in families and intimate relationships can be a source of comfort and reassurance. But the same candor and forthrightness can also trigger intense conflict and antagonism of the sort that foments deep-seated anger and resentment and, ultimately, a persistent wish for revenge and retribution. Otherwise rational people—and often people who tend not to think so clearly— become consumed by their anger and resentment toward important people in their lives and feel compelled to do something about it.

In extreme cases I have seen offenders' preoccupation with revenge and retribution rise to the level of a genuine obsession. Obsessions, in the psychiatric sense, are "persistent ideas, thoughts, impulses, or images that are experienced as intrusive and inappropriate and that cause marked anxiety or distress" (American Psychiatric Association 2000:457). Not all individuals who are obsessed with thoughts of revenge and retribution act on them, of course; some people merely play out the fantasy. Others, however, do act on their obsessions and commit crimes in the process.

Case 5.1 Bruce L. was separated from his wife, Dianne L. The couple had been married for nine years. According to Dianne L., Bruce L. was abusive and controlling during most of the marriage. Dianne L. went to the local court and obtained a "no contact order," which prohibited Bruce L. from contacting her by telephone or in person.

Bruce L. heard from a friend of his that Dianne L. was dating an acquaintance of theirs. Bruce L. became angry when he heard this news. He could not bear the thought that his acquaintance was dating his wife. Bruce L. drove by Dianne L.'s house several times a day for several weeks to see whether the acquaintance's car was parked there. Bruce L. then embarked on a series of vengeful acts designed to infuriate his wife. He left threatening messages on her voicemail daily; withdrew all the money from their joint bank account over a month's time; telephoned the gas, electric, and telephone companies and had the utilities shut off; and called Dianne L.'s employer to report that she had lied about her role in a "missing funds" problem that the company was investigating. Dianne L. contacted police, who arrested Bruce L. for violating the no-contact order.

Case 5.2 Lyle A., a computer engineer, was in the process of divorcing Amanda A., an occupational therapist. They continued to live together in their house but slept in separate bedrooms. Their divorce was a long, contentious process. The two argued incessantly about details, ranging from the division of property to custody of their dog. The couple argued when they encountered each other in their home, met together with attorneys, and were together in public settings; the bickering seemed to never stop.

Lyle A. was becoming increasingly incensed and enraged at the divorce settlement terms that his wife was insisting on. He spent hours and hours ruminating about the "unfair deal" that he was being handed in the divorce. He lay awake at night calmly constructing a plot to harm Amanda A. in a way she would never forget. At about 2 A.M. one day Lyle A. climbed out of bed and quietly retrieved a machete that he stored in the family's garage. He tiptoed into Amanda A.'s room while she slept and proceeded to slash her face, neck, and shoulders. Amanda A. survived the assault but was severely traumatized and disfigured as a result. Lyle A. was convicted of assault with a deadly weapon and sentenced to thirty years in prison.

Case 5.3 Warren H., who was married, was having an affair with Hilda P. Warren H. had told Hilda P. for some time that he would leave his wife, but he had not yet done so.

Hilda P. told Warren H. that she was two months' pregnant and that he was the father. Hilda P. told him that it was now time for him to leave his wife and "be responsible to me and this child." He told Hilda P. that he could not yet leave his wife and that he wanted Hilda P. to abort the pregnancy. Hilda P. became upset and threatened to tell Warren H.'s wife about the affair and pregnancy. Hilda P. also told Warren H. that she would not abort the pregnancy. Warren H. argued back and forth for weeks. He became increasingly resentful and angry toward Hilda P.: "It got to the point that I just couldn't stand her no more. I couldn't believe what she was doing to me. I wanted to kill her."

Warren H. invited Hilda P. to accompany him to a state park where they used to hike together to "talk things out." He led her over to a rocky ledge overlooking a ravine—one of their favorite spots. As they got close to the edge, Warren H. pushed Hilda P. Hilda P. survived the fall but was critically injured and in a coma. She also suffered a miscarriage. Upon his conviction Warren H. was sentenced to thirty-five years in prison for assault with intent to murder.

Case 5.4 Belinda W., eighteen, was dating Hal V., forty-two. The couple met when they both worked part time at a county fair. Hal V. was the father of two children and was separated from his wife.

For some time Belinda W. did not tell her parents about Hal V. However, her parents found out about the relationship when they overheard a telephone conversation between the two. Belinda W.'s father became extremely upset and forbade his daughter to see Hal V. Her father said that she should not be involved with a married man twenty-four years her senior.

For weeks Belinda W. and her father were locked in a bitter dispute about the relationship. She was extremely resentful. One night she broke into her father's machine shop, destroyed some of his valuable equipment, and stole cash from his safe.

CALIBRATION-RECALIBRATION

These four cases provide a cross section of crimes of revenge and retribution involving family members and other intimate acquaintances. In some instances the revenge and retribution involved physical assaults on a person (as in Lyle A.'s and Warren H.'s cases) or property (as in Belinda W.'s case), whereas in other instances the revenge and retribution took the form of psychological or financial assaults. Bruce L., for example, engaged in all manner of psychological warfare in his attempt to torment his wife, from whom he was separated. Bruce L. also harassed his wife financially, by gradually and systematically withdrawing money from the only bank account to which she had access.

As with offenders who commit crimes of rage, offenders who commit crimes of revenge and retribution vary with respect to their insight and prospect for rehabilitation. One important difference is that offenders who commit crimes that are truly vengeful and retributive are more likely to manifest symptoms of antisocial personality disorder—characterized especially by their lack of guilt or remorse—and of paranoid personality disorder than to manifest some kind of impulse control disorder (such as attention deficit/hyperactivity disorder or intermittent explosive disorder). Bruce L., for example, embarked on a carefully planned and calculated campaign to harass his estranged wife and make her life miserable. He was bitter, angry, and resentful: "That woman is a curse. I'm doing hard time here because she drove me to distraction. I never would have done any of those things if she hadn't messed up my mind the way she did. Did she tell you about all the times she cheated on me? Did she tell you about her drinking problem? Did she tell you about all the problems she had with her other two husbands? Huh, did she tell you all that?"

Belinda W., who set out to steal from her father and sabotage his business, was also belligerent and remorseless. Her defiance and defensiveness may have been a function, in large part, of her age: "My fucking father thinks he can run my life. I'm nineteen now, and I was eighteen when all this happened. That's an adult, right? So what if he thinks I'm stupid for hanging out with a forty-two-year-old guy? What does he know about relationships? He and my mom haven't gotten along since the day I was born. I'm done with my dad now. I don't have to go home no more. Hal [Belinda W.'s boyfriend] and I are all set."

For offenders such as Bruce L. and Belinda W., who display little or no evidence of insight or remorse, rehabilitation prospects are grim, at least initially (precontemplation stage of change). Following release, close supervision—by either electronic monitoring or frequent contact with the parole officer— is essential. Victim-offender mediation at this stage would be out of the question. Young offenders, such as Belinda W., may develop more insight over time as they mature.

Offenders who harass and harm spouses or partners during a sustained period of time pose another unique challenge: the dynamics of stalking behavior. Some offenders who commit crimes of revenge and retribution against spouses or partners resort to stalking as a form of intimidation; for others the stalking is a manifestation of their emotional obsession with the victim.

In general terms, to stalk is to "pursue prey, quarry, etc., stealthily" and to "proceed in a steady, deliberate, or sinister manner" (*Random House* 1991). Stalking is considered a crime in many countries and is typically defined statutorily as the willful, malicious, and repeated following or harassing of another person that threatens his or her safety:

> The term refers to repeated and often escalating unwanted intrusions and communications, including loitering nearby, following or surveying a person's home, making multiple telephone calls or other forms of unwanted direct and indirect communications, spreading gossip, destroying personal property, harassing acquaintances or family members, sending threatening or sexually suggestive "gifts" or letters, and aggressive and violent acts. The behaviour terrorizes, intimidates, and controls the victim.
>
> (Abrams and Robinson 2002:468).

The first antistalking legislation in the world was enacted in the United States in 1990 (Sheridan and Davies 2001). Research shows that 90 percent of stalkers are men and about 80 percent of victims are women. Most stalking victims are women who are being harassed by men who want to either reestablish or initiate a relationship. Most stalkers are ex-husbands or partners who do not want to accept that the relationship has ended or "*who seek revenge for a perceived rejection or other infraction*" (Abrams and Robinson 2002:469; emphasis added). Sheridan and Davies, British researchers, provide verbatim comments from stalking victims:

> The most serious events took place over a two-year period. I was followed continually, verbally and physically attacked. My property was damaged and I lived under constant threat of the phone continually ringing through the day and through the night. Some of the worst encounters were: being followed by a car which hit the back of my legs every time I got back up. Being threatened with a knife. Bombarded by constant verbal abuse in public places and when passers by intervened they too would be subjected to this. Also having to leave my home knowing after phone calls that the assailant was coming down to cause havoc. This would be anytime between 12 midnight and 4 A.M. (Female, 27 years)

> An ex partner—unbeknown to myself—put paint thinners over my car, slashed my tyres, sent doll figures with no heads on, chicken claws in the post, and apparently put my house and my activities under constant observation. (Female, 35 years)

A man who was known to me declared his interest on several occasions. I was *not* interested. Some time later I discovered that he waited outside my place of work, loitered outside my home, followed me home after social evenings out with my friends. He also obtained photos of me from colleagues under the pretence that he was arranging a practical joke. I was unaware of any of this until about 12 months after. I did actually approach him about this one night in the pub (I was with friends) but he seemed oblivious to my concerns and actually *believed* we were having a relationship! He even expressed worry about how this would affect my husband and how he was sorry my husband would be hurt.

(Female, 45 years) (2001:134)

Research on the characteristics of stalkers conducted independently on three continents identified remarkably similar patterns (Sheridan and Davies 2001). All the studies documented repeated communications, intrusions, property damage, threats to the person, and actual assaults. The majority of stalkers are male, older than most other types of offenders, and likely to have criminal and psychiatric histories. Also, some cultural and religious norms reinforce the instincts of men who believe that they have a right to control women. Various scholars have distinguished among different types of stalkers, for example, based on the nature of the victim (a celebrity, former lover, political or public figure), the stalker's mental status (personality disorder as opposed to a psychotic condition), the stalker's cultural or ethnic group, and the nature of the stalker's relationship with the victim (no relationship or former neighbor, spouse, lover, colleague) (Sheridan and Davies 2001).

Although stalkers as a group pose a daunting challenge for criminal justice professionals, some offenders who commit crimes of revenge and retribution are more amenable to treatment and rehabilitation. Youthful offenders, such as Belinda W., may be increasingly responsive as they mature. There is no guarantee, of course, but youthful indiscretions and poor judgment sometimes yield to the more mature insights that many people develop as they age. I have heard many an inmate who is, say, forty-five or fifty years old talk quite insightfully about the heinous, insensitive, cruel, and destructive behaviors in which he or she engaged as a youth.

The trajectory of offenders such as Lyle A., who assaulted his wife with a machete, and Warren H., who pushed his lover over a ledge into a ravine, is difficult to forecast. Some, such as Warren H., reach a point where they are able to articulate and reflect on what happened and work with counselors and others to address the issues. Other offenders, such as Lyle A., seem to be stuck, for a variety of reasons, in their overwhelming agony and misery. During our first interview, which took place nearly thirteen years after the assault, Lyle A. seemed emotionally paralyzed:

QUESTION: Mister A., how well do you recall what happened the night you assaulted your wife?

ANSWER: Not real well. I sort of block it out.

QUESTION: Do you think much about what happened?

ANSWER: I try not to.

QUESTION: You told one of the prison psychologists that you spent several days thinking about and planning the assault. Do you remember anything about what was running through your head at the time?

ANSWER: No, not really.

QUESTION: Would you like us to recommend that a counselor contact you so you can talk about what happened?

ANSWER: I don't think so. I'm doing okay.

In contrast, Warren H. was eager to talk about what led up to his decision to push his lover over the ledge. He had spent considerable time talking with a prison counselor about what he had done and the surrounding circumstances (action stage of change) and was eager to get his life back on track as soon as possible. In fact, Warren H. was putting together plans to start a self-help support group for inmates who were serving long sentences for crimes of violence (preparation stage).

QUESTION: Can you tell me a little about your relationship with Hilda P. [the victim]? How long had the two of you been involved?

ANSWER: I met her at a neighbor's house and we just hit it off. At the time my wife and I weren't getting along real good, and I figured we were headed for a divorce or at least a separation. I was kinda lonely and upset at the time, so meeting Hilda was real good for me.

QUESTION: How long had you been involved before the incident [at the park] occurred?

ANSWER: I think it was about ten months, give or take.

QUESTION: And what's your understanding of why you pushed her off that ledge at the park? What was going on then for you?

ANSWER: Well, like I told you, Hilda told me she was pregnant with my child. That was a big shock. I mean, I never thought the two of us would be together forever, you know. I wanted her to have an abortion, but she said no. She also threatened to tell my wife about the whole thing. It's not like I panicked or nothin.' I remember being scared, but it's not like

I suddenly freaked out. I remember talkin' to my buddy Sal about the mess. I remember sayin' to Sal that I had to figure out how to get outta this. I remember driving home and thinking and thinking and thinking. What's weird is that I'm not really the kind of person to hurt somebody like that. I never been the type to get in lots of fights or hit people, you know? Somehow—and this is what I've been talkin' to Sandy [the prison counselor] about—I managed to convince myself that Hilda had painted me into a corner and I was forced to take drastic measures to get out of it. I remember being so angry with her and so resentful. I felt like I had to get her back for messin' up my life.

Now, don't get me wrong. I realize now how twisted my thinking was. I mean, that's just a crazy way to think. I can't believe I actually thought like that. But I've grown up a lot in here. I was pretty young and stupid then. I would never do somethin' like that now to get back at someone. I'm smart enough now to know that there's better ways to handle anger and fear.

Acquaintance Revenge and Retribution

Conflict between friends and acquaintances sometimes leads to intense anger and resentment. In some instances, particularly when the conflict is protracted and brews over time, one party will feel the need for revenge and retribution. The assault—whether physical, psychological, or financial—does not manifest itself as spontaneous, "out of the blue" rage (see chapter 4) but rather as the result of a more deliberate, carefully mapped out plot.

Case 5.5 Chhouk P., nineteen, was a member of a gang, the Oriental Rascals, along with his childhood acquaintance, Nuon B. Chhouk P. had just joined the gang, which was responsible for a series of home invasions, burglaries, and robberies.

Nuon B. was arrested after committing his second burglary with gang members. He confessed to the police and, with his parents' encouragement, agreed to testify against other gang members in their upcoming criminal trial on burglary charges. Nuon B. was released on bail. Word quickly spread among Oriental Rascals that Nuon B. was cooperating with the police and prosecutors. Chhouk P. and three other gang members met to discuss Nuon B.'s defection. They agreed that he had to be killed. Chhouk P. called Nuon B. and arranged to meet him at a mutual friend's apartment to party. When Nuon B. arrived, Chhouk P. pulled out a gun and attempted to shoot Nuon B. Nuon B. suffered a bullet wound to the hip but managed to avoid more serious injury. Chhouk P. fled when neighbors heard the gunshot and came to the apartment. He was later arrested and charged with attempted murder.

Case 5.6 Gregory A. owned a chain of laundromats that was struggling financially. He was deeply in debt and was having difficulty paying his home mortgage and business loans. Gregory A. also owed back payments for child support.

Because of his history of financial problems, Gregory A. knew that he would not qualify for another conventional loan. One of his friends, who knew of Gregory A.'s plight, told him that he could put Gregory A. in touch with a "guy who can help you out." Gregory A. borrowed $15,000 from the man, Bobby L., who had organized crime connections. Bobby L. became Gregory A.'s friend, or so Gregory A. thought.

Gregory A., who had recently remarried and had an infant son, was not able to keep up with the payments on the $15,000 loan. Bobby L. contacted Gregory A. regularly to try to work out payment, but he was not able to meet the payment schedule. Bobby L. began to leave a series of increasingly threatening messages on Gregory A.'s voicemail; Bobby L. told Gregory A. that "you better watch your back" and "keep your eye on your wife and that new little baby of yours." Gregory A. feared for his and his family's safety and decided to contact the police. The police arranged a sting and placed a concealed wire on Gregory A. Gregory A. then contacted Bobby L. and arranged to meet with him at a local restaurant to "discuss what I can do about this situation." At that meeting Bobby L. reiterated a number of explicit threats. The police, who were eavesdropping on the conversation from a nearby van, swarmed into the restaurant and arrested Bobby L. Bobby L. ultimately was convicted of extortion.

Friends and more casual acquaintances sometimes become locked into conflict. In most instances the parties manage to resolve their differences and move on. Sometimes, however, the conflict proves to be intractable and spins out of control. One party decides that carefully designed retribution or revenge is the only way to resolve the dispute.

A widely publicized incident that received national attention provides a classic illustration of this phenomenon (Maier 1992). Wanda Holloway was the mother of a teenager, Shanna, who did not win a coveted place on the cheerleading squad at a school in Texas. Next door to the Holloways lived Wanda's best friend, Verna Heath, and her daughter, Amber. Amber was the same age as Shanna, and the two became friends. The friendship between Verna and Wanda ended when Amber made the squad but Shanna did not. Wanda forbade her daughter to have anything to do with Amber.

Holloway then plotted to kill Amber and her mother, whom she blamed for Shanna's lack of success. Holloway hired her ex-brother-in-law, Terry

Harper, to kill Verna and Amber Heath. Harper was mortified by Wanda Holloway's vengeful plan to kill the thirteen-year-old girl and her mother. He could not imagine killing people about something as trifling as cheerleading.

After the meeting Harper decided to play along with the plan and turn Holloway in to the police. He met Holloway again, only this time he took a tape recorder to record their conversation. Harper sent the recorded message, along with background information, to the police. Holloway was arrested and convicted of solicitation of capital murder.

CALIBRATION-RECALIBRATION

As with people who commit crimes of revenge and retribution against family members and partners, perpetrators of crimes against acquaintances also vary with respect to their prospects for rehabilitation. Bobby L., for example, who had organized crime connections and threatened Gregory A. when he could not repay his loan promptly, displayed limited insight and no interest in counseling or any other rehabilitation program (precontemplation stage). He had all the markings of a career criminal steeped in criminal thinking; Bobby L. had been arrested as a juvenile for auto theft and burglary, and as an adult he had served two prison terms for obtaining money under false pretenses and embezzlement. According to prison records, Bobby L. had close ties to two other organized crime figures who were serving unrelated prison sentences. My interview with him was not encouraging:

QUESTION: Mister L., you were convicted of extortion. Can you tell us about the circumstances that led up to the crime?
ANSWER: There's not much to say.
QUESTION: Did you enter a guilty plea or did you go to trial?
ANSWER: I took a deal [prosecutors offered to recommend to the court that Bobby L. receive a reduced sentence in exchange for a guilty plea].
QUESTION: Are you saying that you're guilty of the offense or not?
ANSWER: I'm saying that I took a deal. That's all I'm saying.
QUESTION: I notice in your [criminal] record, Mister L., that you were arrested as a juvenile and you've served time on two other occasions. Do you have any thoughts about why you've been so heavily involved in crime? How do you explain this?
ANSWER: [shrugs shoulders]
QUESTION: Mister L., are you saying that you don't want to get into all that?
ANSWER: Right.

QUESTION: Let me bring up a different topic. Have you ever had a steady
job on the streets?

ANSWER: What do you mean?

QUESTION: I mean, have you ever worked for a regular employer—like in a
business or at a restaurant or something—and gotten a regular paycheck?

ANSWER: No, not really.

QUESTION: Are you at all interested in obtaining a regular job, or would you
prefer to go back to the life you were leading before?

ANSWER: I do just fine. I know how to take care of myself.

In a case such as this, incarceration for public safety and punishment must
be the priority. Granted, at some point—as is the case with nearly every
prison inmate—Bobby L. will be back on the streets. He is in a high-risk category for re-offending because he displays no insight, has a significant criminal record, limited education, no interest in vocational training or rehabilitation, and no history of steady, legitimate employment. In short, Bobby L.
epitomizes the career criminal with prototypical antisocial personality traits.

Cases such as Bobby L.'s raise important issues about the goals, purposes,
and effects of incarceration. There is rich and complex debate among criminal justice scholars and practitioners about the appropriate use of incarceration, particularly with respect to juggling the goals of retribution, public safety, and rehabilitation (see chapter 1).

One bottom-line consideration concerns the extent to which offenders
such as Bobby L. should be incarcerated, for how long, and with what likely
result. In my experience few of these offenders experience something like an
epiphany during their incarceration. At best these career criminals mellow
over time; their criminal engines run out of gas. Some come to understand
the error of their ways and make a 180-degree turn in their values and priorities, but many do not. When they are released from prison, which nearly all
of them will be, even if they are not paroled, they should be monitored and
supervised closely and for as long as their sentences permit (the typical offender has "suspended," or probation, time to serve after being released from
prison).

The good news is that most offenders—that is, everyone arrested by the
police and convicted of some crime—are not career criminals in the strict sense
of the term; many offenders go straight after their first serious brush with the
law. The bad news, however, is that many offenders are career criminals—people who commit crimes as a way of life, to greater and lesser degrees. The reasons why some people pursue the criminal path could fill tomes; they range

from the permanent effect of traumatic head injuries to economic deprivation, biochemical imbalances, mental health issues, learning disabilities, and so on. The extent to which these offenders are or are not fully responsible for their actions does not change the danger that they pose to others.

Several studies have produced some fascinating details about criminal careers. Among the best known is a now-classic study conducted by Marvin Wolfgang, Robert M. Figlio, and Thorsten Sellin (1972). This group followed the criminal careers of about ten thousand boys born in Philadelphia in 1945. Wolfgang and his colleagues found that about one-third of the sample was arrested, but about half terminated their criminal careers after their first arrest (at least judging from arrest records). However, once a boy had been arrested three times, the chance that he would be arrested again was greater than 70 percent. A small percentage of the sample accounted for a very large percentage of the arrests; 6 percent of the group committed five or more crimes before they were eighteen, accounting for more than half of all the recorded offenses of the entire group of ten thousand and about two-thirds of all the violent crimes committed by the group. Thus while only a portion of the population pursues a criminal career, this small percentage wreaks considerable havoc.

Given that a relatively small percentage of offenders who pursue criminal careers are responsible for most of the crime, selective incarceration makes considerable sense. Even though true rehabilitation may be unlikely for many of these offenders (they never proceed past the precontemplation stage of change), keeping them off the street prevents crime. Consider the following data: Shinnar and Shinnar (1975) used an elaborate mathematical model to estimate the extent to which incarceration would reduce crime in New York State. They estimated that the street robbery rate would be reduced by 80 percent if every person convicted of this particular crime spent five years in prison. Peterson and Braiker (1980) interviewed California offenders at length to assess the amount of crime that they committed when out of prison. Even assuming that the offenders tended to underreport their offense rates, Peterson and Braiker concluded that if no one were incarcerated in state prison, the number of armed robberies in California would be about 22 percent higher. Greenwood (1982) examined the number of offenses committed by offenders in California, Michigan, and Texas and concluded that imprisoning one robber who was among the top 10 percent in offense rates (that is, the offenders who committed the largest number of offenses per year) would prevent more robberies than incarcerating eighteen offenders who were at or below the median offense rate (that is, the offense rate that divides the group into the "upper" and "lower" halves).

In a fascinating study of seventeen hundred federal offenders, Forst et al. (1982, cited in Wilson 1983:151) found that more than half were not known to have committed even one crime during the six years after they were released from prison, but the other half committed at least nineteen offenses per person per year. Finally, Petersilia and Greenwood (1978) examined the arrest records of 625 people convicted in Denver of serious crimes during a two-year period. Petersilia and Greenwood concluded that if every individual convicted of a felony were sentenced to prison for five years, the number of felonies committed would drop by 45 percent, although the prison population would increase astronomically (by 450 percent). If the mandatory five-year sentence were limited to repeat offenders, the crime rate would drop by 18 percent and the prison population would increase by 190 percent.

The tempting conclusion, of course, is that the selective incapacitation of high-rate offenders would reduce criminal activity significantly. Although this has great intuitive appeal, we must temper our eagerness to embrace this finding with the realization that, typically, offenders have aged some by the time they accumulate the criminal records that we would use to identify high-risk individuals. But we know that offenders' chances of re-offending decline as their age increases—the effect of maturation or "aging out" of crime. Thus selective incapacitation, especially for older offenders, may be less useful than common sense would suggest. As Nagin notes in his incisive discussion of the deterrence effect of imprisonment,

> A criminal record takes time to accumulate. With time comes age, and age is generally accompanied by a slowing of criminal activity. Perhaps the best-documented empirical regularity in criminology is the age-crime curve. On average, rates of offending rise through adolescence, reach a peak at about age eighteen to twenty, and begin a steady decline thereafter. The central lesson to be learned from this regularity is that for most people rates of offending decline throughout their adult years. Thus, while a long criminal record may be a good signal of very active prior offending, it may also be a signal, due to age, of an individual having entered a period of offending rate decline. Prospectively, such individuals may be poor candidates for incarceration from an incapacitation perspective. (1998:364)

In contrast to Bobby L. and his long-term pattern of criminal conduct, Chhouk P. was a relative novice. At nineteen he was just embarking on what could turn out to be a criminal career. Although Chhouk P. had been arrested twice as a juvenile for relatively modest offenses (disorderly conduct and shoplifting), he did not have a significant criminal record. For Chhouk P., being arrested and imprisoned at nineteen was a major wake-up call. He had shamed and betrayed his Cambodian parents, who were fleeing political oppression in their homeland when they emigrated to the United States; they were keenly distraught at Chhouk P.'s arrest and conviction. After many long talks with his parents Chhouk P. decided to renounce his gang affiliation, and he enrolled in several education and vocational training programs (action stage of change). Chhouk P. paid a big price for his renunciation of the gang and disaffiliation—he decided to "check in" to protective custody to avoid being severely harassed by other imprisoned gang members—but he seemed determine to turn his life around.

> I have always felt like I live between two worlds in this country [the United States]. At home with my parents I'm surrounded by everything Cambodian—the language, the traditions, the religion, everything. Don't get me wrong; I know it's good stuff, you know? But on the street I live in the other world—the American world of fast cars, women, alcohol, action, hustles, you name it. All of that was real exciting to me; I mean, I was a kid when all this was happening. I guess you could say I rebelled against my parents and their world. I understand that now. And look where it got me. But I've decided it's time to grow up, and if that means my old friends are going to give me a hard time, so be it. I can handle that. It won't be easy, but I can handle it.

Chhouk P. turned out to be a fine candidate for parole about two-thirds of the way through his two-year sentence. He was released on electronic monitoring parole and was expected to participate in a demanding job-training program and personal counseling at a community center that specialized in the delivery of services to Southeast Asian clients. Two years after his release a social service agency hired Chhouk P. to work with high-risk adolescents. He also went to a local community college part time and was planning to obtain his associate's degree in human services.

Coworker Revenge and Retribution

As I pointed out in the discussion of crimes of rage, a significant number of conflicts that lead to crimes arise in the workplace. Research shows that many of these incidents occur spontaneously, in the heat of the moment, when workers clash (chapter 4). Words are exchanged, egos are bruised, feelings are scraped, tempers flare, and people lose control.

Other workplace incidents, however, are much more deliberate, premeditated, and calculated, beginning with a plan that culminates in a physical, psychological, or financial "attack." All of us can immediately conjure up television images and newspaper accounts of career employees in the Postal Service, the computer industry, or some manufacturing plant who harbored deep-seated, intense resentment toward one or more colleagues and unexpectedly opened fire with a gun or other automatic weapon smuggled into the work site. The pattern is all too familiar. Sometimes the signs of mental illness are clear (see chapter 8) and sometimes not. Sometimes the assault is the solution.

Of course, not all crimes of revenge and retribution are so extreme. Although some are acutely violent and filled with mayhem, others take the form of psychological or financial warfare.

Case 5.7   Candace J. worked at a local convenience store. For two years Candace J. worked as a clerk and then applied to be an assistant manager. Candace J. deeply resented her low wages as a clerk and was bored by the job's mundane duties but held out hope that she could earn more money, and responsibility, as an assistant manager.

Candace J. did not get promoted. The district supervisor told her that the company did not think she "was quite ready for new responsibilities" but encouraged her to continue working for the company and reapply for an assistant manager's position in six months.

Candace J. decided that she would look for another job. In the meantime she felt so angry and resentful toward the company that she began leaving anonymous, threatening notes for the district supervisor. Candace J. also began to skim cash from transactions on a regular basis. After about a month Candace J. had skimmed nearly $2,500. The district supervisor had suspected employee theft when an audit disclosed a steady discrepancy between sales and income. A store video camera had recorded several instances when Candace J. pocketed cash. She was indicted and subsequently convicted for stealing company assets.

Case 5.8   Victor R. worked on a construction crew for a large home-improvement business. Victor R. had a lot of conflict with the business owner, who often chastised Victor R. for the quality and pace of his work. The two frequently exchanged words.

After one heated argument the business owner fired Victor R. Upon hearing the news, Victor R. stormed out of the owner's office, muttering, "You'll be sorry you did this to me." Two nights later Victor R. broke into the company's garage and stole about $600 worth of tools and equipment. He was caught when one of his acquaintances, also a company employee, saw some of the stolen items in Victor R.'s car and reported the theft to the owner.

Case 5.9 Wayne G. had been employed at a jewelry manufacturer, as a machinist, for twelve years. Wayne G. was a dedicated, diligent, and conscientious employee. He had received several "employee of the month" awards.

A number of Wayne G.'s colleagues harassed him incessantly. Wayne G. was gay and some of his fellow employees scorned him for this. Wayne G. kept details of his lifestyle to himself but had a difficult time knowing how to respond to the steady stream of verbal harassment and taunts directed at him.

One afternoon Wayne G. decided he had had enough. When he went to work the following morning, he packed a handgun in his lunch box. At about 9:30 A.M. he pulled out the gun and shot and killed two fellow employees he considered most responsible for the harassment. Wayne G. pleaded guilty and received a fifty-year sentence.

CALIBRATION-RECALIBRATION

Sometimes crimes of revenge and retribution appear to have little rhyme or reason. In many instances, however, it is not hard to follow the bread crumbs and find what led to the offenses. Of course, no amount of detail or circumstantial evidence could possibly justify the crime, and we would not condone what happened, but some offenses are easier to understand and grasp than others. We would never encourage employees to steal from their employers, leave them threatening notes, or kill them. Yet when we examine the history and complex interior of the relationships that led to the crimes, we can sometimes—not always—appreciate what led to the vengeful and retributive acts.

Incarceration and incapacitation are necessary in many of these cases. Some perpetrators, although not all, are genuine public safety risks. However, many perpetrators of crimes of revenge and retribution are amenable to rehabilitation. Candace J., for example, expressed considerable remorse during my first interview with her:

I know it's no excuse, but I had given two long years of my life to that company [the corporate owner of the convenience store]. I was sure I was ready to be an assistant manager. I couldn't believe it when they told me I wasn't ready and needed to wait at least another six months. Thinking back on it, I just gave up. I threw in the towel. But I felt like I couldn't let the company get away with it. I just felt so angry and I couldn't let go of it. That's why I left those threatening notes and why I took the money. It's not like I was desperate for money. I just *had* to get back at the company. Now I realize how wrong that was, that I shouldn't have handled it that way. Look who lost in the end! But I know that's how I felt at the time.

Candace J. was eager to get on with her life and chart a new course. She was an earnest participant in the prison's "choosing new directions" program, which was designed to help inmates examine their mistakes in judgment and cultivate constructive problem-solving skills. Candace J. also took a parenting course sponsored by the state child welfare agency (action stage of change). Because she was going to be released from prison within about four months, Candace J. also prepared a comprehensive discharge plan that outlined the steps she planned to take to obtain a new residence, regain custody of her two children, continue counseling, and reestablish friendships and social support (preparation stage of change). Candace J. was also beginning to think about making restitution to the company for the money she stole, although she did not yet have a firm plan in mind (contemplation stage of change). Upon her release Candace J. did not pose a serious public safety threat and did not require home confinement or electronic monitoring.

Victor R. and Wayne G. presented different challenges. Victor R., who was fired from his construction job and then stole equipment from his boss, seemed unsure and ambivalent about committing himself to a genuine program of change. At one meeting Victor R. talked at length about his need to finish his GED (he had dropped out of school in the tenth grade) and enroll in a program at the prison designed for inmates with alcohol-related issues (contemplation stage of change). When we met again three months later, Victor D. showed me copies of the prison forms that he had completed to apply for the GED class and the alcoholism program (preparation stage). When I next saw Victor D., he had already begun, and then dropped out of, the GED class and was debating whether to continue in the alcoholism program. Victor D.'s long-standing learning disabilities made it difficult for him to succeed in an academic program.

"I was never good at school," Victor D. said. "Being back in that GED class reminded me of my horrible school experience. Man, it was painful. I just couldn't take it. And the alcoholism program . . . I went to three classes, which were okay, but then I got a good job offer as a porter over at high security. I really need the money, and I felt like I couldn't pass up the opportunity. I've been waiting for a job like that."

It was hard to assess whether Victor D. was ambivalent about addressing his alcohol-related issues and was merely using the job offer as a convenient way out of the program or whether he really felt in desperate need of money. In any case, my job was to encourage him to think through the relative costs and benefits of his decisions. At the end of our conversation I was guardedly hopeful that Victor D. would recommit himself to the GED class and alcoholism program.

I was less optimistic about Wayne G., who had killed two fellow employees at work. Wayne G. was reasonably well educated and certainly had the cognitive ability to understand the importance of counseling and address the issues that led him to resolve his workplace conflict in the violent way that he did. Intellectually, Wayne G. was able to articulate why it was important for him to engage in some in-depth exploration of the circumstances that led up to his crime (contemplation stage of change). Emotionally, however, Wayne G. seemed stuck, unable to move to any concrete rehabilitative steps. My sense was that Wayne G. was clinically depressed and that this was getting in the way. Depression in Wayne G.'s circumstances—facing a long prison sentence and confronting the guilt associated with murdering two people—is entirely understandable. I asked Wayne G. whether I could ask the prison psychiatrist to conduct an assessment to determine whether Wayne G. was suffering from depression or some other disorder that might be treated with psychotropic medication and perhaps counseling. Wayne G. agreed.

Authority Figure Revenge and Retribution

Crimes of revenge and retribution are sometimes directed at people who are in influential positions of authority in the perpetrator's life. Students sometimes become infuriated with teachers who assign a failing grade; criminals sometimes rail against the prosecutors, parole board members, or judges who sealed their fate; and inmates sometimes point threatening fingers at correctional officers who file disciplinary reports against them.

People who feel as if they have been harmed or railroaded by individuals in positions of authority sometimes have vengeful, even murderous, fantasies. Of course, most people do not act on their fantasies. But some do.

Case 5.10 Melody K., twenty-five, was serving a two-year sentence for possession of cocaine with intent to distribute. This was Melody K.'s second sentence for the same offense. She had been addicted to cocaine for five years.

Melody K. had difficulty getting along with one correctional officer in particular, Judy T. Melody K. complained that Judy T. was "on my case all the time" and that Judy T. had written her up for disciplinary infractions that she would not bother with for anyone else.

One afternoon Melody K. received a disciplinary report from Judy T. for contraband (having a pair of shoes that were not on Melody K.'s clothing list). When Melody K. started to argue, the two got into a shouting match. Melody K. grabbed Judy T. by the wrist and pushed her, at which point Judy T. summoned other officers for assistance. Melody K. was taken in handcuffs to the prison's segregation unit, where she was locked in a cell for twenty-three hours each day for thirty days as punishment for assaulting a correctional officer.

During her time in segregation Melody K. fussed and fumed about her alleged persecution by Judy T. Melody K. fantasized about what she might do to Judy T. to harm her. Three days after Melody K. was released from segregation she assaulted Judy T. with a prison-made knife [a shiv or shank in prison parlance]. Judy T. survived the stabbing with relatively minor injuries; Melody K. was convicted of assaulting a correctional officer with intent to murder and sentenced to an additional ten years.

Case 5.11   Sam M. was a pre-med student at a large state university. He was a serious student who was determined to get into medical school. Sam M. had few friends in college; he preferred to devote nearly all his time to studying.

Sam M. was shocked to learn that he had done poorly on the final exam in his organic chemistry course. He went to see his professor to find out what went wrong and to plead for an opportunity to take a makeup exam. The professor reviewed Sam M.'s exam with him but refused to allow him to retake the exam.

Sam M. was so distraught about his mediocre final grade that he fantasized about injuring the professor. Sam M. wrote a series of anonymous letters to the professor, threatening to harm him and members of his family. The professor contacted the campus police, who then turned the letters over to the state police. Sam M. was arrested and sentenced to home confinement for a year.

CALIBRATION-RECALIBRATION

Individuals who fantasize about harming people in positions of authority in their lives range from those who are deadly serious (literally) to those who merely flirt with threats. As we know from widespread and prominent media reports, some individuals carry out their fantasies in the most extreme form possible (shooting and killing teachers, judges, correctional officers). Some of these individuals suffer from major mental illness (chapter 8), but not all do.

Some offenders require little more than a slap on the wrist and a forceful message not to do it again, while others require long-term incarceration because of their obsessive determination to harm the object of their venomous wrath. Melody K., for example, spent weeks planning her assault on Judy T., the correctional officer. Melody K. was released from the prison's segregation unit and acted out her fantasy in rather short order. Melody K., who had a history of assaultive behavior, was able to articulate why she did what she did, but her monologue contained a number of key elements associated with offenders who manifest symptoms of antisocial personality disorder: "That bitch kept messin' with me and playing with my head. Damn, I don't know who she thinks she is. I had to do something. She just pushed and pushed and pushed, so I had to push back. What was I supposed to do, just smile and take her shit? That's not the way it works with me."

Melody K. clearly had not reached a point where she was willing or able to explore the nature and extent of her part in the drama (precontemplation stage of change). She may get there some day, but she was not there when I spoke with her. The contemplation, preparation, and action stages of change were far in the distance, out of sight. Incarceration for public safety and punitive purposes was appropriate. We needed to continue offering rehabilitation opportunities, but at that point we knew she was unlikely to take advantage of them.

Sam M., however, made impressive gains during his home confinement experience. He accepted the offer to consult with a therapist at the local community mental health center, and the therapist helped Sam M. begin to understand why he reacted as he did to the disappointing news about his organic chemistry grade, how he had isolated himself socially over a long period of time, and how he had developed some obsessive qualities. With his therapist's help Sam M. began to understand the connection between some of his behaviors and his relationship with his overly critical, demeaning parents (what mental health professionals call family-of-origin issues). Sam M. also found that a low dose of antidepressant medication prescribed by a psychiatrist at the mental health center helped enormously. Sam M. was in the action stage of change with respect to his mental health issues. He also broached the possibility, with his home-confinement officer, of participating in the court-sponsored victim-offender mediation program (contemplation stage of change with respect to restorative justice). Sam M. was eager to meet with his former professor and express his apology and remorse. The counselor began to explore how Sam M. and the professor might participate in the program.

Toward the end of his sentence Sam M. began investigating the possibility of entering the human service field rather than the medical field. He believed that his experiences and insights might be put to better use by helping other people who struggle in life. This plan also had the added benefit of defusing Sam M.'s preoccupation and obsession with a career in medicine.

• • •

Crimes of revenge and retribution are committed in a variety of different contexts. Many are triggered by domestic relationships and friendships that have soured such that one partner feels compelled to injure the other to settle a score. Other crimes are the outcome of workplace conflicts or disputes with people in positions of authority in the perpetrator's life.

Some offenders who commit crimes of revenge and retribution display classic symptoms of antisocial personality disorder, paranoid personality disorder, and narcissistic personality disorder. These offenders tend to be less responsive to rehabilitation programs and, typically, are not good candidates for restorative justice programs. Often they have a sense of entitlement about their crimes and are judgmental about their victims.

It is also true, however, that many offenders who commit crimes of revenge and retribution are solid prospects for rehabilitation and restorative justice programs. I have encountered many such offenders who truly grasp the dynamics in their lives and relationships that led them into revenge and retribution. Among the most difficult challenges in criminal justice is cultivating the astute judgment required to distinguish between these two extremes and among the finer shades of gray that lie amid them.

6

Crimes of Frolic

Although most crimes involve individual offenders, many crimes are committed by people who are involved in group mischief. Perhaps the most familiar group-related crimes are committed by gangs (chapter 3). Other crimes are committed by people who are not part of a formal gang but are involved in some kind of group that takes on a life of its own.

Many group crimes are related to phenomena that I have already addressed—greed, exploitation, opportunism, rage, revenge, and retribution. Many others, however, should be considered crimes of frolic, that is, crimes that result from group members' decision to have some fun, stir up some trouble, and so on. Frolic involves "playful behavior or action; prank" (*Random House* 1991). Of course, not all group frolic is innocent. Some results in serious crime and harm to others.

An essential ingredient in most crimes of frolic is group pressure and conformity. Scholars have studied the phenomena of group pressure, peer pressure, group influence, group psychology, and group conformity for decades (Asch 1951; Campbell 1980; Festinger, Schachter, and Bach 1950; Friedkin and Cook 1990; Janis 1972; Knight, Alpert, and Witt 1976; Sherif and Sherif 1964; Siegel and Siegel 1957). Taken as a whole, the research clearly documents the complex, powerful, and sometimes unpredictable influence that group dynamics have on individuals' decisions and behavior. Ample evidence demonstrates the influence of groups on individuals' participation in delinquent and criminal activity, drug use, alcohol use, sexual activity, and smoking (K. Maxwell 2002; Porter and Alison 2001; Warr 1993). Younger individuals seem to be especially vulnerable, impressionable, and more easily influenced.

Typical crimes of frolic committed by people in a group involve a perpetrator who has a mischievous idea and influences other group members (usually friends) to join in. Amir (1971), for example, summarizes five key stages that are usually present when a group of offenders participates in criminal activity[1]:

Initial idea. Someone in the group of friends and acquaintances broaches an idea for some kind of criminal mischief, such as vandalism, auto theft, and robberies.

Selection of target. Group members decide which property to vandalize, whose cars to steal, who might be robbed and in what communities or neighborhoods, or whom to assault.

Approach. Someone in the group initiates the first act of vandalism, theft of an auto, or robbery.

The crime. Other group members join in the criminal activity, with mutual encouragement and support.

After the crime. One or more group members takes responsibility for destroying the evidence, when possible.

Research shows that a group member can find it quite difficult to assert her or his independence and not go along with the group's wishes (Carpenter and Hollander 1982). The psychological forces involved in group pressure, influence, and conformity are powerful indeed.

Crimes of frolic occur in a variety of contexts and assume various forms. The most prominent themes involve thrill seeking, entertainment, and criminal behavior that occurs under the influence of alcohol and other drugs.

Thrill-Seeking Behavior

Some crimes of frolic occur when a group of people decides to stir up some thrilling, high-risk activity. The perpetrators do not decide explicitly to harm other people, but their high-risk behavior often results in serious injury.

Case 6.1 Anthony B. and three friends watched the Indianapolis 500 on television at his home. All four were car-racing enthusiasts. After the race the four decided to visit another friend across town. Before they left for the friend's home, Anthony B. proposed that they take two cars and reenact the Indianapolis 500 on an isolated stretch of highway leading to the friend's home. The two cars raced each other at speeds topping 85 miles an hour. Anthony B. lost control of the car that he was driving, crossed the median, and slammed head-on into an oncoming vehicle. Anthony B.'s spinal cord was damaged and his legs were paralyzed. The driver of the other car died as a result of the crash. Anthony B. was sentenced to six years in prison.

Case 6.2   Carl F. and Stuart C. met each other when both received appointments to the U.S. Naval Academy. Both young men struggled at the academy academically and were dismissed at the end of their first (plebe) year. Carl F. decided to move to Stuart C.'s home state. The two got an apartment together and spent most of their social time together.

One morning Carl F. and Stuart C. were lamenting their poor financial situation and disrupted academic careers. Carl F. dared Stuart C. to put on a disguise and rob the local small-town bank. By the end of the conversation, which had started out humorously, Carl F. and Stuart C. had agreed to follow through on the prank for, as Stuart C. put it, "the thrill of victory or the agony of defeat." They put on ski masks and walked into the bank, each armed with a fake pistol. Carl F. passed a note to a teller, who gave Carl F. about $1,700 in cash. Carl F. and Stuart C. ran from the bank in disbelief that they had actually been so brazen. A bank video camera filmed the two taking off their masks as they ran out of the bank. They were arrested and convicted of bank robbery.

CALIBRATION-RECALIBRATION

The two cases have a common profile: young men socialize in pairs or in a group; one suggests a high-risk, thrill-seeking activity; one individual takes the initiative to figure out the entertainment; and in the process they commit a serious crime that has tragic consequences. In Anthony B.'s case the youthful exuberance led to the death of a driver, permanent physical injury, and a lengthy prison sentence. In Carl F. and Stuart C.'s case two young men who were trying to get their lives back on track managed to convince each other to conduct what turned out to be a remarkably harebrained, bizarre, and self-destructive crime.

I find that most offenders who fit this profile—young, impressionable, and foolish—become good prospects for rehabilitation and restorative justice. Although some manifest serious impulse control symptoms that are not easily managed, most demonstrate considerable insight and remorse once the dust settles on their legal cases, and they settle in for the long haul that prison, parole, and probation require.

Anthony B., for example, was quite expressive about his predicament and showed clear signs that he was earnest about addressing issues in his life (action stage of change). He was also considering becoming involved in restorative justice activities (contemplation stage of change):

> This whole experience has taught me a lot about life in general and my life in particular—not that I wanted to learn it this way. Looking back on it, I realize now that I was wasting my life away. I'd hang out with my friends, go to work, and that was pretty much it. I didn't have much sense of direction, no serious relationship. I didn't realize how important my own family is and how much they care about me. I'll tell you, I sure realize it now. They've been unbelievably supportive. They visit me as much as they can and I know they'll be there for me when I get out. I just hope I don't let them down. I need them now more than ever.
>
> The worst part for me is knowing that my stupidity killed someone. Because of me, Mister _____ died and now his two young children have to grow up without a father. Sometimes thinking about this is just too much. Every single day I wish I had been the one to die in that accident instead of him.
>
> Talking to Meredith [a prison social worker] has really been good. Sometimes I just need to talk to someone and get it all out. Meredith knows how to listen, and she's really helped me to understand why I've made some of the lousy choices I've made and where I can go from here. I'm even thinking about meeting with Missus _____ [the victim's widow] as part of that mediation program they have here. I'm not sure what that would be like; I know it will be hard, but I think I can handle it. It's the least I can do, that is, if Missus _____ is willing to meet with me. I also want to join that program sponsored by MADD [Mothers Against Drunk Driving] where people like me speak to high school kids; I wasn't drunk when the accident happened, but I still have lots to say to those kids.

Carl F. was also impressive in our interview (I did not meet Stuart C.). He cried so hard during our first meeting, thinking about the disastrous decisions he had made in recent years and their tragic consequences, that we had to stop our conversation so that Carl F. could compose himself. These were not manipulative crocodile tears; they welled up suddenly and seemed to catch Carl F. off guard when the overwhelming and cumulative tension, angst, and guilt converged. Carl F. was able to articulate what was happening to him and put it in the context of the unexpected twists and turns his life had taken.

> You know, they say things happen for a reason, and I do my best to look at this mess that way. I'd like to believe that's the case. There I was, among

the best and the brightest at the Naval Academy. I knew I wasn't at the top of that talented heap, but I was pretty good. Hell, I was good enough to get into the academy, which is not easy to do.

I knew right off the bat—during plebe summer—that I was going to have a rough time. I was a pretty disciplined guy and I had done well in high school. But life at the academy just slapped me in the face. I had a difficult time settling in to the routine—the harassment, the rules and regulations, the constant demands and pressure. I thought I was doing pretty well, but I kept getting disciplined. I made it through the summer, but by November I was beginning to realize that the academy and I were not a great match. I was struggling academically and beginning to give up. My parents convinced me to stick with it; they brought me with them to this country when I was three, and my going to the academy was a dream come true for them. I didn't want to disappoint them.

At the end of the school year I was told I'd be dismissed from the academy for academic reasons. At that point I just lost it. I figured my life was over; I had let myself and my parents down. When I got home, Stuart C. and I started hanging out and crying on each other's shoulder. The same sort of thing happened to him. Looking back on it, our stupid decision to rob that bank was almost like a suicide wish. I think, deep down inside, I was hoping the cops would shoot and kill me.

Within six months of his incarceration Carl F. had enrolled in courses offered in the prison by a local community college and participated actively in a twelve-week program designed to help inmates chart new paths in life and develop the insights and skills needed to succeed (action stage of change). Toward the end of the program the instructor was so impressed with Carl F.'s performance that she asked him whether he would like to co-lead the next course. After serving about half his sentence, Carl F. was paroled to an extended period of electronic monitoring. He began working at a large pharmaceutical manufacturing plant as a technician and within eight months was promoted to a supervisory position.

Entertainment

I think it is important to distinguish between offenders whose modus operandi involves a pattern of thrill-seeking behavior and those who get into trouble in conjunction with more purely recreational and entertaining activities. With the first group, the thrill seekers, I am especially concerned about offenders' apparent wish and need for the kind of adrenalin rush that typically accompanies high-risk behaviors (such as drag racing and shooting rifle pellets at passers-by). These offenders often have chronic issues with impulse control, consistent with attention deficit disorder, and any meaningful responses (counseling, pharmacological, behavior management) must address these issues.

In contrast, I find that offenders whose crimes of frolic stem from poor judgment in the context of recreational pursuits and entertainment are more capable of self-control.

Case 6.3 Dan M. and his three friends had been hanging out together for about five years. They met in high school and continued to spend considerable time together, going to sporting events, playing cards, shooting pool, going to bars and nightclubs, and going out to eat. The group often played practical jokes and pranks on one another.

One evening Dan M. convinced the other group members to hike to a nearby highway overpass and take turns firing pellets from a powerful rifle at passing cars. After about twenty minutes of this activity, Dan M. fired a shot that hit a car in a rear tire, causing the driver to veer off the road and slam into a tree. The driver died in the accident. A neighbor had seen the young men shooting the rifle and notified the police. Dan M. and his friends were arrested, convicted of involuntary manslaughter, and sentenced to five years in prison.

Case 6.4 Amanda B. dropped out of school in the eleventh grade. She had a learning disability and found school frustrating. Amanda B.'s family life was chaotic; her father died of AIDS and her mother was a cocaine addict in recovery. Amanda B. had spent some time in three foster homes between the ages of seven and twelve, for varying lengths of time, when her mother was enrolled in drug rehabilitation programs.

Amanda B. spent much of her time hanging out with friends, either in an apartment that two of the friends shared or on a popular street adjacent to a university. One of her friends suggested to the group that they ride down to a nearby mall and, just for fun, see who could shoplift the most expensive items within an hour. Amanda B. committed her shoplifting in an upscale department store and was caught by a plainclothes security guard. As a first-time offender Amanda B. received probation. She was required to pay a fine and make restitution to the store for the stolen items that she damaged when she was caught by and scuffled with the security guard.

While on probation Amanda B. was arrested a second time for stealing. A passer-by notified police that Amanda B. and a friend, who had been hanging out on a street near the university, were stealing items from a merchant who was selling jewelry on the corner. When the police arrested Amanda B., they searched her and found stolen jewelry and a packet of cocaine. The judge canceled Amanda B.'s probation and sentenced her to six months in prison.

CALIBRATION-RECALIBRATION

Both Dan M.'s and Amanda B.'s cases highlight the importance of "recalibrating" when circumstances change in offenders' lives. Dan M., for example, was originally sentenced to five years in prison for involuntary manslaughter after he and his friends fired rifle pellets at cars traveling on the highway. The parole board denied Dan M.'s parole at his first two hearings. The board told him that to parole him would depreciate the seriousness of his offense. In addition, the board wanted Dan M. to complete a "choosing new directions" course and move from the medium-security prison in which he was housed to a minimum-security prison. The board also told Dan M. that it wanted him to spend some time in the prison's work-release program—to cultivate his vocational skills—before being released on parole.

The prison moved Dan M. to a lower security facility about three months later; soon after that, Dan M. started working at a health equipment manufacturer that participated in the prison's work-release program (Dan M. returned to the prison at the end of each workday). Six months later Dan M. was placed on electronic monitoring parole. After another six months, during which Dan M. continued his employment at the health equipment company without incident and met regularly with his parole officer, Dan M. was moved to regular parole.

About three months later a police officer stopped Dan M. after he ran a stop sign. When the police officer interviewed Dan M., he smelled alcohol. The officer tested Dan M.'s blood-alcohol-level at 0.09, slightly above the legal limit. Dan M. was charged with driving under the influence. Earlier that week Dan M. had also missed two meetings with his parole officer.

The parole board examined this problematic set of circumstances at Dan M.'s "violation hearing," an inquiry that is conducted whenever a parolee has been accused of violating the conditions of parole. The board had the option of revoking Dan M.'s parole and returning him to prison for the violation, rescinding the warrant (if evidence exonerated Dan M.), or re-releasing Dan M. on parole with stricter supervision and restrictions (recalibration).

After examining the evidence and interviewing Dan M., the board concluded that the combination of circumstances—the traffic violation, alcohol use, and missed appointments with the parole officer—raised a red flag that warranted recalibration of the conditions of Dan M.'s parole. The board did not believe that sending Dan M. back to prison would be productive. Until these recent incidents he had been doing well on parole; he had complied with all the conditions and met with his parole officer consistently. Dan M. himself seemed to understand the need for more structure and revised conditions:

> I was doing real well there for quite some time, doing all the right things, but I now realize I was starting to backslide. I think I was sort of rewarding myself for doing so well, and I thought I could get away with it. Now I see that I was starting to pick up some of my old habits. This has taught me that I can't let up even for a minute—I've got to work my program twenty-four–seven. I don't want to go back to where I was. I don't. I think it will probably be good for me to meet with Ron [Dan M.'s parole officer] more often. It's good that he's going to be watching me like a hawk.

The parole board decided to return Dan M. to electronic monitoring parole for a minimum of three months. The board agreed that at the end of that period it would consult with Dan M.'s parole officer, reassess the situation, and decide whether to lift the electronic monitoring.

Amanda B. presented a different recalibration challenge. She had violated her probation conditions and was convicted of two new offenses: theft and cocaine possession. Amanda B. appeared before the parole board one-third of the way through her new sentence and acknowledged that she had developed a serious cocaine problem. The board agreed that it would parole Amanda B. to a residential drug treatment program for women once she had completed a ten-week drug treatment program offered in the prison. Amanda B. completed the prison-based program successfully and was released to the residential program. She completed the six-month residential program and was then returned to probation supervision, where she has done well. Amanda B. has been working steadily at a clothing store and attending Narcotics Anonymous consistently.

Frolic Under the Influence

Although many crimes of frolic are not fueled by perpetrators' use of alcohol and other drugs, many are. In a significant percentage of cases involving frolic, police find evidence that offenders were under the influence of alcohol and other drugs. Usually, these offenders are not bona fide alcoholics or addicts (see chapter 7 for discussion of crimes of addiction); however, their use and abuse of substances is correlated with their criminal conduct. Here is a cross section of such cases:

Case 6.5   Burton L., twenty-one, and Laurie F., twenty, had been living together for two years. They had a two-year-old daughter. The couple first met at a local party.

Burton L. and Laurie F. occasionally used a drug known as GHB (gammahydroxy-butyrate), or "liquid X" (liquid ecstasy). GHB is a powerful hallucinogenic whose effects resemble those associated with acid. After using the drug one evening, Burton L. and Laurie F. drove to a fast-food restaurant with their child in the backseat. The couple panicked when they noticed that their child was having difficult breathing. They pulled off the road and called 911. The emergency medical crew notified police that the child had drunk from a small bottle that the couple had inadvertently left next to her on the backseat of the car. The bottle contained GHB. The child was admitted to the pediatric hospital with respiratory failure.

Case 6.6   One night Adam K. and two friends each consumed about a six-pack of beer and then drank several shots of whiskey. Toward the end of the evening Adam K. showed his friends his gun collection. He picked up one of his hunting rifles, pointed it playfully at one of his friends, and pulled the trigger, thinking that the rifle was not loaded. The rifle contained one round of ammunition; Adam K. shot his friend in the chest unintentionally, and the friend died instantly.

Case 6.7   Belinda T. was a recently divorced accountant at an insurance firm. One evening she went out to dinner with several friends. Belinda T. had two alcoholic drinks at the restaurant's bar before her friends arrived and had two more drinks during dinner.

After dinner Belinda T. suggested to her friends that they go to a local nightclub that was hosting a widely publicized singles night. Belinda T. drove her friends, but on the way she ran a red light and broadsided a car. The impact killed the driver of the other car and one of Belinda T.'s passengers.

Case 6.8   Will A., nineteen, and two friends got together on Halloween night. They smoked marijuana and "blunts" (a marijuana-and-tobacco cigar) and drank several beers each.

At about 1 A.M., Will A. suggested that the threesome head to a nearby cemetery. At the cemetery the three played hide-and-seek for some time and then decided to topple dozens of large grave markers. The three were arrested after being chased by a police officer. They were convicted of vandalism, placed on probation, and ordered to pay restitution for the $3,200 in damages that they had caused.

CALIBRATION-RECALIBRATION

When confronted with the facts, most of these offenders were willing and able to acknowledge the ways in which their recreational drug and alcohol use impaired their judgment and influenced their criminal behavior.

LAURIE F.: Honest to goodness, Burt [Burton L.] and I had no idea that bottle [of GHB, or liquid ecstasy] was even in the car, let alone next to the baby. I mean, no person in her right mind would do something like that. I guess we had no idea what was happening—we must have really been out of it. At the time it seemed like everyone we knew was using liquid X; we were just part of the crowd. I'm just so ashamed of myself; my baby didn't deserve that.

ADAM K.: It's hard for me to believe that I killed one of my best friends. Although my memory of that night is somewhat hazy, I clearly remember that all we meant to do was party hard. We used to do that every few weeks or so—you know, just kick back and get wasted [high on drugs and alcohol]. I've never been addicted to the stuff and I thought I could handle it. I must have been out of my mind to pick up that rifle and point it at my friend. No sane person would do that.

BELINDA T.: When I think back on that night—and believe me, that's not pleasant—I can remember how depressed I was. I had just gotten divorced, and while part of me was relieved to be out of that marriage, a big part of me was bummed out, really bummed out. I had never been much of a drinker, mostly because I can't hold my liquor well. But something happened to me that night that I can't really explain—like a rubber band in me just snapped and I let go. I just drank myself silly. To tell you the truth, I think I was just trying to numb the pain that I was experiencing. I feel sick that I destroyed two lives because of that.

Two of these offenders were somewhat less insightful, or at least less able to communicate whatever insight they may have had:

BURTON L: Me and Laurie just made one big mistake, you know? We had never did anything wrong like that before. Don't get me wrong, I know we screwed up. But it's not like we're real criminals, man. We're doin' our time and payin' the price. I feel bad about what happened; ain't no way nothin' like that's gonna happen again, you know what I'm sayin'? Everything's cool now.

WILL A.: Aw, I was just young and stupid. I mean, I'm still young but I don't think I'm as stupid as I was. Kids do things like that [the cemetery vandalism] all the time, especially after they've gotten a little buzz [gotten high on drugs]. Me and my boys just got caught. The judge really threw the book at us.

Many offenders who commit crimes of frolic while under the influence of alcohol and other drugs respond well to suggestions that they address their problems with substance use and abuse. Even those who do not consider themselves to be alcoholics or addicts often have the capacity to understand that it makes sense for them to learn about the destructiveness of alcohol and drugs and develop ways to control their use of these substances. Laurie F., Adam K., and Belinda T. all enrolled in the prison-sponsored alcohol and drug education program and completed it successfully. The formal staff reports on all three of these inmates showed that they participated actively and were serious students (action stage of change).

Burton L. and Will A., however, were not enthusiastic about participating in the program and were much more defensive about their alcohol- and drug-related problems. Burton A. adamantly refused to participate in any treatment programs and simply wanted to serve out his sentence: "Look, I made a mistake. I don't need nobody to tell me that. Ain't no good sittin' around all day with a bunch of drunks and addicts talkin' about it. I know what the deal is. I'll just do my time." Burton A. was at the precontemplation stage of change and showed no sign of progressing beyond it. Early release was out of the question.

Will A., who had been placed on probation initially, was subsequently arrested for possession of cocaine with intent to distribute. The new charges meant that his probation was revoked; Will A. also received a new two-year sentence. For him, it was necessary to shorten the leash and protect the public from his poor judgment (recalibration).

At his first parole hearing on his new sentence Will A. demonstrated little grasp of his issues with substance use and abuse (precontemplation stage of change):

QUESTION: I see here that you were on probation for a serious vandalism incident that occurred after you got high one night with a couple of your friends. Now you're doing this bid [serving this sentence] for cocaine possession. Do you see any pattern here with respect to your involvement with drugs?

ANSWER: It's no big thing.

QUESTION: Can you tell me a little about how often you were using drugs when you were on the street and what you were using?

ANSWER: Just weed [marijuana] most of the time. I started to get into a little bit of coke but not too much.

QUESTION: Do you think it would be a good idea to take the drug education class here, or do you think that wouldn't be useful to you?

ANSWER: Nah, I don't need it. Guys just sit in there and tell the teacher what she wants to hear. That'd be a waste of my time. I'd rather work in the kitchen.

Will A. epitomizes what I often see among youthful offenders—a tendency to minimize their problems and issues and a shortsighted reluctance to take assertive steps to address them. Will A. had been arrested three times as a juvenile, served time on probation, and spent two months at the state training school for offenses that included extortion (forcing other children to give him money), shoplifting, theft, and chronic truancy. He had been suspended from junior high and high school (twice each) for fighting. Will A. clearly was struggling to make the transition from adolescence to adulthood. The challenges that he faced were exacerbated by his history: he had been in and out of foster care and a group home for boys because of his parents' abusive and neglectful behavior and the sexual abuse that he had endured as a young boy. Sadly, his young life had been rife with chaos and lacked the nurturing and stability that every child needs.

Two prominent factors seem to be at play with cases such as Burton L.'s and Will A.'s. The first, as I noted earlier, is age. Crimes of frolic seem to be particularly prevalent among youthful offenders. As with many crimes, participation declines as age increases. Maturation is often as potent, or more potent, than formal interventions (although skillfully delivered programs and services certainly can make a difference).

The second key factor, which is correlated with maturation, is that many youthful offenders manifest symptoms of a mental health phenomenon that typically begins in childhood or adolescence and is a precursor of what in adults is known as antisocial personality disorder: conduct disorder. As with antisocial personality disorder, conduct disorder is difficult to treat. Offenders with this diagnosis often have difficulty with impulse control, are impressionable and easily influenced by others (a common feature in crimes of frolic), and show little evidence of remorse. Conduct disorder typically arises from destructive and chaotic family relationships and parent-child conflict and often is the by-product of inadequately managed attention deficit/hyperactivity disorder, posttraumatic stress, learning disorders, and affective disorders (such as depression and bipolar disorder).

According to the American Psychiatric Association, conduct disorder involves a consistent pattern of behavior in which the basic rights of others and widely accepted rules are violated (2000:93–94). These behaviors fall into four main groupings: aggressive conduct that causes or threatens physical harm to other people or animals; nonaggressive conduct that causes property loss or damage; deceitfulness or theft; and serious violations of rules. The problematic behavior causes clinically significant impairment in social, academic, or occupational functioning. The behavior pattern is usually present in a variety of settings such as home, school, or the community.

Children or adolescents with this disorder often initiate aggressive behavior and react aggressively to others. Typical behaviors include bullying, threatening, or intimidating behavior; initiating frequent physical fights; using a weapon that can cause serious physical harm (e.g., a bat, brick, broken bottle, knife, or gun); being physically cruel to people or animals; stealing while confronting a victim (e.g., mugging, purse snatching, extortion, or armed robbery); and forcing someone into sexual activity. Physical violence may take the form of rape, assault, or, in rare cases, homicide.

Individuals with conduct disorder may deliberately destroy others' property, for example, by setting fire with the intention of causing serious damage, smashing car windows, or vandalizing school property. They may also deceive others or break into someone else's house, building, or car; lie or break promises to obtain goods or favors or to avoid debts or obligations (e.g., "conning" other people); or steal items of some real value without confronting the victim (e.g., shoplifting, forgery). These individuals may also violate rules (e.g., school, parental). Children with this disorder often have a pattern, beginning before age thirteen, of staying out late at night despite parental rules to the contrary. They may run away from home overnight with some regularity and skip school repeatedly. Older individuals may be absent from work without good reason.

• • •

Crimes of frolic occur under a wide variety of circumstances and for a wide range of reasons. Immaturity and conduct disorder traits account for a significant portion of this pattern of offenses. In many instances individuals have a propensity for high-risk, thrill-seeking activities that provide them with an emotional or psychological "rush." In other cases the offenses are the product of individuals' pursuit of recreation and entertainment, often facilitated by the use of alcohol or other drugs.

Maturation, of course, is difficult to accelerate. Time marches at its own pace. Of course, mental health and social service professionals can do their best to hasten the process by offering opportunities for offenders to explore pertinent issues in their lives and achieve some measure of insight.

Offenders with significant impulse control challenges—for example, those likely to commit crimes of frolic involving high-risk, thrill-seeking behavior—are often less responsive to cognitive and "talking" therapies. Psychopharmacological intervention (principally the use of psychostimulants such as Ritalin and Adderall) is often helpful.

Finally, criminal justice professionals must be fully aware of the complex group dynamics often involved in crimes of frolic. Many offenders, particularly more youthful offenders, are highly susceptible to group influence and peer pressure. The dynamics are well known. Although destructive group identification and influence are hard to disrupt and replace, many creative ways have been identified to help offenders understand the potentially pernicious effects of their group-related mischief and to offer constructive alternatives (such as more positive and supervised after-school activities; structured sports activities; and enrichment programs in community and neighborhood centers where youths have contact with constructive role models and mentors). A comparatively modest investment of money to finance these activities may prevent the much greater expense required when police, courts, and corrections personnel are required to respond to crime.

7

Crimes of Addiction

People with addictions or whose offenses are related to addiction commit a substantial percentage of all crime. The most prominent crime-related addictions involve alcohol, other drugs (such as cocaine and heroin), and pathological gambling.

Addictions to substances (alcohol and other drugs) and gambling contribute to crime in three ways. First, some offenses are specifically defined as drug or gambling crimes, such as possession, distribution, manufacture, or cultivation of drugs (heroin, cocaine, methamphetamines, marijuana, and so on), or illegal gambling activities. Second, many crimes are related to drugs or gambling, for example, violent acts (such as murder, rape, domestic assault, robbery) that are committed by people who are under the influence. Also in this category is property crime (such as burglary, larceny, shoplifting, automobile theft) that is committed to obtain goods to sell (fence) for money to buy drugs, as well as crimes that occur as a result of "drug wars" or "gambling wars" (conflicts among groups vying for control of the drug trade or illicit gambling turf). Finally, many offenders are involved in a drug-using and/or gambling lifestyle in that they associate with people who commit crimes and teach crime-related skills (Ball et al. 1982; Goldstein 1985; Goldstein, Brownstein, and Ryan 1992; Harrison and Gfroerer 1992; MacCoun and Reuter 1998).

Widely cited statistics gathered in recent years by the U.S. Justice Department's Bureau of Justice Statistics are remarkably compelling and offer a powerful picture of the intimate relationship between drug and alcohol abuse and crime (U.S. Department of Justice 2000; Ditton 1999; Greenfeld 1998; Mumola 1998, 1999):

- Fifty-seven percent of state prisoners and 45 percent of federal prisoners surveyed reported using drugs in the month before their offense (up from 50 percent and 32 percent, respectively, in 1991).
- Nearly 75 percent of all prisoners can be characterized as having been involved with alcohol or drug abuse during the time leading up to their arrest.
- Four in 10 offenders report using alcohol at the time of their offense.
- Thirty-three percent of state prisoners and 22 percent of federal prisoners committed their offenses while under the influence of alcohol or other drugs (up from 31 percent and 17 percent, respectively, in 1991).
- One in 6 state and federal prisoners acknowledged committing the offense in order to get money for drugs.
- More than half of adult males arrested in a cross section of U.S. cities tested positive for drug use; one-third tested positive for cocaine in most of the sites.
- One-fourth of state prisoners and one-sixth of federal prisoners report symptoms consistent with alcohol or drug dependence.
- Half of mentally ill inmates in state prisons report being binge drinkers, 46 percent of this population report having been involved in physical fights while drunk, and 17 percent report having lost a job because of drinking.
- Forty-one percent of state prisoners and 30 percent of federal prisoners report drinking as much as one-fifth of a gallon of liquor in a single day (equivalent to twenty drinks, three 6-packs of beer, and three bottles of wine).
- Forty percent of state prisoners and 29 percent of federal prisoners report past alcohol-related domestic disputes.
- Two-thirds of violent crime victims who were attacked by an intimate (current or former spouse or boyfriend/girlfriend) report that alcohol was a factor.
- Four in 10 violent crimes involved alcohol (based on crime victim reports).
- Almost half of men and women on probation were under the influence at the time of their offense.
- Thirty-five percent of people on probation have consumed as much as one-fifth of a gallon of alcohol in a single day.
- Seventy percent of people on probation report past drug abuse; 31 percent report crack or cocaine use, 25 percent report use of stimulants, 20 percent report use of hallucinogens, 15 percent report use of barbiturates, and 8 percent report use of heroin.

Data on the prevalence and nature of pathological gambling, gathered from a wide variety of studies, are equally sobering (Blaszczynski and Silove 1995; Custer and Milt 1985; Dickerson and Baron 2000; National Research Council 1999; Shaffer et al. 1989; Volberg 1994). Recent estimates are that the lifetime prevalence of pathological gambling in the United States is 3.5 to 6.3 percent of the adult population and that at any one time 1.4 to 2.8 percent of the adult U.S. population suffers from the problem (Blume 1995; "Pathological Gambling" 1996).[1] The National Council on Compulsive Gambling estimates that the United States is home to three to ten million pathological gamblers. About two-thirds of pathological gamblers admit committing crimes—such as embezzling, stealing, and selling drugs—to finance gambling and to pay off gambling debts.

Evidence suggests that pathological gamblers are disproportionately young, poor, and poorly educated, attributes that are highly correlated with the offender population in general. In fact, studies estimate that 10 to 30 percent of the inmate population are pathological gamblers. Common psychological traits include a tendency toward boredom, chronic need for excitement, highly competitive nature, hair-trigger temper, poor impulse control, difficulty delaying gratification, and antisocial personality disorder ("Pathological Gambling" 1996). Significant percentages of pathological gamblers also manifest clinical symptoms of mood disorders (depression, bipolar disorder), anxiety disorders, substance abuse disorders, and antisocial personality disorder ("Study Finds Other Psychiatric Ills" 1999).

Professional literature on addictions distinguishes between substance dependence and substance abuse. Substance dependence is "a cluster of cognitive, behavioral, and physiological symptoms indicating that the individual continues use of the substance despite significant substance-related problems. There is a pattern of repeated self-administration that can result in tolerance, withdrawal, and compulsive drug-taking behavior" (American Psychiatric Association 2000:192). Common features include a need for markedly increased amounts of the substance to achieve intoxication or the desired effect; markedly diminished effect with continued use of the same amount of the substance; withdrawal symptoms; often taking the substance in larger amounts or for a longer period than was intended; a persistent desire or unsuccessful efforts to cut down or control substance use; spending a great deal of time in activities necessary to obtain the substance (e.g., visiting multiple doctors or driving long distances), use the substance, or recover from its effects; sacrificing important social, occupational, or recreational activities because of substance use; and continuing to use the substance despite awareness of a persistent or recurrent physical or psychological problem that is likely to have been caused or exacerbated by the substance (American Psychiatric Association 2000).

In contrast, substance abuse is "a maladaptive pattern of substance use manifested by recurrent and significant adverse consequences related to the repeated use of substances. . . . Unlike the criteria for Substance Dependence, the criteria for Substance Abuse do not include tolerance, withdrawal, or a pattern of compulsive use and instead include only the harmful consequences of repeated use" (American Psychiatric Association 2000:198). Common features of substance abuse include recurrent substance use resulting in a failure to fulfill major obligations and duties at work, school, or home; recurrent substance use in situations in which it is physically hazardous (e.g., driving an automobile or operating machinery); recurrent legal problems related to the substance use; and continued substance use despite having persistent or recurrent social or interpersonal problems caused or exacerbated by the substance use (American Psychiatric Association 2000:199).

Pathological gambling shares some of these characteristics, although the manifestation and context are obviously different. According to the widely accepted definition developed by the American Psychiatric Association (2000:671), pathological gambling entails persistent and recurrent maladaptive gambling behavior that disrupts personal, family, or vocational pursuits. Common features include preoccupation with gambling; need to gamble with increasing amounts of money in order to achieve the desired excitement; repeated unsuccessful attempts to control, cut back, or stop gambling; restless or irritable mood when attempting to cut down or stop gambling; a tendency to gamble as a way of escaping from problems or of relieving a dysphoric mood (feelings of helplessness, guilty, anxiety, depression); a tendency to return to gambling after losing money in an effort to recoup (known as "chasing losses"); lying to family members, therapist, or others to conceal the extent of involvement with gambling; committing illegal acts such as forgery, fraud, theft, or embezzlement to finance gambling; jeopardizing or losing a significant relationship, job, or educational or career opportunity because of gambling; and relying on others to provide money to relieve a desperate financial situation caused by gambling (American Psychiatric Association 2000:674).

Substance Abuse

As I noted earlier, crimes related to substance abuse can take several forms, including crimes that violate explicit drug laws (selling or manufacturing drugs, for example), crimes that people commit to obtain money to buy drugs (such as robbery, automobile theft, embezzlement), and crimes associated with a drug-involved lifestyle (such as vandalism and driving under the influence).

Case 7.1   Althea V. was a twenty-three-year-old mother of two young children. She was addicted to cocaine. In separate incidents Althea V. was arrested for prostitution and shoplifting. She explained that she prostituted herself and shoplifted because these were the most expedient ways for her to get money for drugs.

Case 7.2   Barry K. was a junior at a local college. He financed his education by selling methamphetamines ("speed") that he manufactured in his home laboratory.

Case 7.3   Lawrence M., thirty-seven, lived in a homeless shelter after he was evicted from his apartment for failing to pay the rent. He was a heroin addict; he lived off occasional odd jobs and by panhandling.

One afternoon Lawrence M. was desperate to buy a bag of heroin but did not have any money. He borrowed a gun from another resident at the homeless shelter and robbed a nearby convenience store.

Case 7.4   Tish B. was an attorney in the county's public defender's office, where she defended indigent criminal defendants. Tish B. had struggled since her college days with alcoholism.

Late one day Tish B. left the courthouse after losing a complex, stressful court case. On the way home Tish B. stopped at a liquor store and bought a bottle of vodka. When she got home, Tish B. lost control and drank most of the bottle. Soon after, Tish B. got in her car and drove to her sister's home for dinner. On the way Tish B. ignored a red light and killed a pedestrian who was crossing the street.

Case 7.5   Arnold F. was addicted to cocaine. For several months, until his arrest, Arnold F. sold cocaine to a growing list of customers in the area. He was arrested when he attempted to sell cocaine to an undercover police officer.

Case 7.6   Karen N. was a registered nurse who worked for a prominent home health care agency. Karen N. spent most of her time assisting terminally ill patients who were involved in the agency's hospice program.

The daughter of one of Karen N.'s patients noticed that some of her mother's narcotic pain medication, OxyContin, was missing. The daughter mentioned this to Karen N.'s supervisor one day when the supervisor was visiting. Karen N. eventually admitted that she was addicted to pain medication and had skimmed some of the patient's pills.

Case 7.7 Maurice B. worked in the shipping department of a large warehouse that supplied local outlets of a national electronics store. Maurice B. had recently started using heroin after being introduced to it by a woman he had begun to date. Soon Maurice B. was addicted. He was having difficulty supporting his heroin habit on his modest wages. He began to steal items from the warehouse inventory (stereos, computers, digital organizers, camcorders) to sell on the black market.

Case 7.8 Dale S. was arrested after turning himself in to police following the murder of his best friend, the friend's girlfriend, and the girlfriend's four-year-old daughter. Dale S. was playing cards with his friend one night while the girlfriend and her daughter were in an adjacent bedroom. Dale S. and his friend had ingested PCP (phencyclidine, or "angel dust"), smoked marijuana, taken a number of amphetamines, and drunk some beer.

During a break in their card game, Dale S. hit his friend in the head with a pistol, shot him dead, tied up the girlfriend and stabbed her to death, and murdered the four-year-old by slitting her throat with a knife.

CALIBRATION-RECALIBRATION

These cases represent a realistic cross section of crimes related to substance use and abuse. They involve crimes that violate drug laws, crimes committed to obtain money to buy drugs, and crimes associated with a drug-related lifestyle. Barry K. violated drug laws when he manufactured and sold methamphetamines, as did Tish B. when she drove her car under the influence of alcohol. Dale S. used a number of illegal drugs with his friend, and Karen N. violated drug-related statutes when she skimmed narcotics that belonged to her patient.

In contrast, Althea V. committed crimes that did not violate drug laws per se in order to finance her cocaine addiction. Her prostitution and shoplifting were a direct outgrowth of her substance dependence problem. Similarly, Lawrence M. robbed a convenience store to get money for drugs, Arnold F. sold cocaine to an undercover police officer to get money to support his addiction, and Maurice B. stole electronic products from his company to pay for heroin.

Barry K.'s and Dale S.'s are more unusual cases. Barry K. was not a drug user; for him, drug manufacturing and sales were simply a business enterprise and a profitable one at that. Dale S., who had no record of any violence, committed his heinous murders as a result of what evidence suggests was a drug-induced psychosis.

This remarkable diversity of circumstances suggests that criminal justice professionals must be thoughtful and selective with respect to their response to various drug- and alcohol-related offenses. The psychological, family, and community dynamics vary enormously, as do the etiological (causal) factors.

Clearly, criminal justice professionals must be very familiar with the nature of addictions, how they typically develop, and the state of the art with respect to rehabilitation and treatment. Scholars and practitioners generally agree that addictions often develop in stages and that the the various addictive substances have important similarities and differences. According to Jellinek's classic study of two thousand members of Alcoholics Anonymous (1952, 1960), drinkers progress through four phases: prealcoholic symptomatic phase, prodromal phase, crucial phase, and chronic phase. In the prealcoholic symptomatic phase drinkers experience relief from tension or stress. People who are predisposed toward alcoholism (whether by genetic endowment, cultural, personality, or other factors) typically will increase their alcohol consumption over time. During this period the drinker develops a physical tolerance to alcohol, requiring increasingly larger amounts to achieve the same sense of relief (McNeece and DiNitto 1998).

In the prodromal phase drinkers typically begin to have blackouts, experiencing some amnesia about what happened during the blackout. The drinker's need for alcohol tends to increase, and he or she may begin engaging in surreptitious, manipulative activities to hide and drink the alcohol.

In the next stage, the crucial phase, drinkers begin to lose control of their alcohol consumption. They have difficulty abstaining and find it hard to stop drinking once they have started. Problems with relationships at home and work often surface.

Finally, in the chronic phase drinkers remain intoxicated for extended periods of time. They obsess about drinking and often develop serious physical and emotional side effects.

Of course, drinkers' evolution from the first to last stage is not always this linear (Mann 1968; Vaillant 1995). Drinkers sometimes regress and progress over time.

Cocaine addiction also seems to develop in stages (McNeece and DiNitto 1998). According to Washton (1989), cocaine addicts generally progress through three stages: early, middle, and late. In the early stage the cocaine alters the individual's brain chemistry; addictive thinking begins; the individual begins to obsess about cocaine, have compulsive urges and cravings, withdraw from routine activities, and experience subtle physical and psychological changes (such as the jitters, irritability, and mood swings).

In the middle stage the developing cocaine addict experiences a loss of control of the use of the drug, cravings, an inability to stop using cocaine despite unpleasant consequences, denial about the implications of the drug use, increasing social isolation (from family and friends), increasing paranoid and panic symptoms, and impaired performance at work or in school.

Finally, in the late stage the cocaine addict fails in all efforts to stop using the drug and experiences severe financial problems, problems at work or in school, poor self-esteem, significant relationship problems, clinical depression, cocaine-induced psychosis, and sometimes death (McNeece and DiNitto 1998; Washton 1989).

Heroin addiction also has a unique trajectory. Results of interviews with heroin addicts suggest that typically they do not intend to become addicted and believe that they will be able avoid addiction (Duster 1970). Most heroin addicts report that their first use of the drug was unplanned. For example, first-timers may be offered heroin at a party and do not want to reject the invitation. These "preaddicts" gradually proceed with occasional recreational use until heroin dependence sets in. For some users dependence develops after just a couple of weeks of heavy, daily use; for others dependence occurs after a month or two (Krivanek 1989). Not all heroin users become addicted, although many do, and some are able to withdraw on their own (McNeece and DiNitto 1998).

Treatment of offenders who commit crimes associated with substance dependence and abuse needs to be tailored, keeping mind the uniqueness of offenders' addictions and their evolution. Many addicts manifest symptoms of antisocial personality disorder, in that they are manipulative, lie, and express little or no remorse for their actions. Offenders who are not addicts but are active, enterprising drug entrepreneurs often fall into this category.

Many addicts also have serious impulse control issues, which may explain why many addicts were drawn into drug use in the first place. They may have difficulty exercising independent judgment and are especially likely to fall victim to group pressure to use drugs.

The current conventional wisdom in the substance abuse field suggests that treatment of addictions must consider client characteristics, preferred therapist characteristics, the effectiveness of available intervention strategies, and prognosis (Seligman 1998). A high percentage of addicts have been abused or neglected by parents, caretakers, spouses, or partners. Approximately two-thirds of people with substance use disorders have another psychiatric diagnosis as well, such as depression, phobias, anxiety, and schizophrenia (so-called co-occurring disorders). For many of these individuals the substance use is a way of self-medicating, to help them cope with their coexisting psychiatric conditions. Unfortunately, the relationship between the substance and psychiatric disorder is often cyclical; the psychiatric stressors may lead to the use of substances, which exacerbates the psychiatric symptoms, and so on.

Professionals who treat substance users often encounter resistance, hostility, manipulativeness, and deception, although there are many exceptions (McNeece and DiNitto 1998; Seligman 1998). It is particularly helpful for professionals to have, or cultivate, skills designed to respond constructively to such clients in the criminal justice system, many of whom are "involuntary" (court-ordered) clients (Rooney 1992). Clinicians should also be familiar with the strengths and limitations of a wide variety of available treatments, including the use of an intervention (where two or more people concerned about the client's substance use meet with that person, usually along with a therapist, to present information about the ramifications of substance use and suggest that the client seek help); partial hospitalization; residential programs and therapeutic communities; pharmacotherapy (e.g., Antabuse, methadone, levo-alpha-acetylmethadol, buprenorphine, naltrexone, clonidine, antidepressants, anti-anxiety medication); psychoeducational groups; twelve-step programs (e.g., Alcoholics Anonymous, Narcotics Anonymous); self-help groups; couple's, family, and group therapy; and various forms of individual psychotherapy (e.g., cognitive-behavioral therapy, rational therapy, rational emotive therapy) (Fisher and Harrison 1997; Seligman 1998).

The diverse offenders whose cases I presented earlier provide useful illustrations of the need to tailor a rehabilitation approach. Three offenders—Barry K., Tish B., and Althea V.—were eager to participate in prison-sponsored programs. Barry K., the college student who manufactured methamphetamines from his home lab, immediately grasped the destructiveness of his large drug operation. He gave considerable credit for his insight to the drug education class that he had taken (action stage of change):

> When I was in the midst of my [drug manufacturing] operation, I wasn't thinking at all about anybody else. I'm embarrassed to admit it, but all I cared about then was all the money I was making. Talk about tunnel vision! When I was a kid my family was pretty poor. I just couldn't believe all the easy money I was earning by making and selling speed. At one level, I probably knew that I was causing all kinds of harm out there. But at another level, I managed to convince myself that these were victimless crimes.
>
> Being in the drug class has given me a whole different perspective. I had never really thought through how my drug business could be causing all kinds of crime out there. It's scary that a guy who has as much education as I have doesn't see that. I sure see it now.

Tish B., the attorney who killed a pedestrian while driving under the influence, knew that she needed more than a drug education class; she needed a comprehensive alcoholism treatment program and enrolled in one soon after she began serving her sentence (action stage of change):

> I'll never forget the conversation I had with my father when he first came to visit me after I was locked up. That was one of the worst—yet one of the most important—moments of my life. I was the kid he was always so proud of. I had gone to college and law school, and I was headed for a solid career. For years my father had warned me about drinking; he too is an alcoholic, and he was concerned that I had a genetic predisposition to alcoholism. I guess I was pretty pigheaded about it. In classic adolescent fashion I needed to rebel and prove that I was different from him. So I pushed the envelope and look where it got me.
>
> Anyway, when my father came to see me [at this point Tish B. started to sob], he didn't say, "I told you so." He just held me and cried with me. He told me that it looked like I had to learn about alcoholism the hard way, just like he had. He didn't tell me what I needed to do. At that moment I knew what I needed to do. The next day, for the first time in my life, I acknowledged that I'm an alcoholic. I immediately started to go to AA meetings here and I signed up for the alcoholism treatment group. I'm going to turn this thing around. I have too much going for me not to.

Althea V. faced a very different challenge. She had been addicted to cocaine for years, during which she earned money as a prostitute and as a habitual shoplifter. Althea V. had been arrested thirteen times, usually for solicitation (prostitution) or for possession of cocaine. She had been on probation three times and had served two short prison terms. Althea V. looked me in the eye and told me that she had finally "reached bottom" and was determined to turn her life around.

> I know inmates come in here all the time and tell you how much they're going to change this and that. You know and I know that many of 'em are just feeding you a line. And with my record, there ain't no reason why you should think I'm any different. But I'll tell y'all somethin.' This is it for me. I'm tired of this life. Yesterday, just before I came to see y'all, I talked to my counselor here and I told her that I want her to put me in the hardest program she got. Sure, I want parole. But I know I ain't gonna

do anybody no good unless I get my act together. My baby needs her mother. She don't need no foster care. I came here to tell you that I don't want you to give me parole right now. I wants to waive parole so I can do the [drug] program here. If it's all right with you, I'll write you when I be done with that and ask for a parole hearing then.

I had seen Althea V. during her other two prison sentences. This was the first time that I heard her acknowledge that she had a serious drug problem and talk explicitly about getting help (preparation stage of change).

Althea V. completed her drug treatment program and wrote asking for a new parole hearing. During the hearing Althea V. talked about how much she had learned in her treatment program: "My head was spinning after some of them classes. Until then I never realized that I might have used cocaine to help me cope with having been sexually molested by my stepfather and his brother when I was just a little kid. I kinda buried all that stuff, but I think the cocaine helped me bury it. It just felt so good to talk about what happened to me all them years ago."

Althea V.'s early trauma at the hands of her stepfather and his brother is an all-too-common scenario. A stunning proportion of female substance abusers report having been molested as children and adolescents. For many, the connection between their substance use and their victimization and subsequent posttraumatic stress is a direct one (Friedman 2000; Schiraldi 2000). Posttraumatic stress is

> the development of characteristic symptoms following exposure to an extreme traumatic stressor involving direct personal experience of an event that involves actual or threatened death or serious injury, or other threat to one's physical integrity; or witnessing an event that involves death, injury, or threat to the physical integrity of another person; or learning about unexpected or violent death, serious harm, or threat of death or injury experienced by a family member or other close associate.
>
> (American Psychiatric Association 2000:463)

For Althea V., any drug treatment she received had to include counseling that addressed her childhood victimization. Her painful trauma history appears to be intimately connected with her substance use.

Karen N., the nurse who skimmed her patient's narcotic pain medication, was an enigma. Intellectually, Karen N. certainly was able to understand the nature of her crime and substance abuse problem. According to her profile, Karen N. should have been a good rehabilitation prospect. During our interview, however, I saw little evidence of insight or commitment to change (pre-contemplation stage of change).

QUESTION: Ms. N., you've admitted that you took your patient's pills be-cause you had a drug problem, right?
ANSWER: Yes.
QUESTION: How long have you been addicted to pain medication?
ANSWER: About three years. It started after I had my second back operation.
I got hooked on the painkillers that my doctor prescribed.
QUESTION: Have you ever been in a treatment program for your addiction?
ANSWER: No.
QUESTION: May I ask why?
ANSWER: I don't really know.

Our conversation continued like this for some time. Karen N.'s respons-es were consistently brief, uninformative, and detached. Toward the end of the conversation it occurred to me that Karen N. might be clinically de-pressed. I asked her whether she felt depressed and she nodded her head yes. I then asked her whether she had ever talked with a doctor about her depres-sion and the possible use of antidepressants. Karen N. said that she had never had such a conversation but consented when I asked whether she would be willing to talk with a prison psychiatrist.

When I saw Karen N. three months later, she seemed to be a different per-son. The prison psychiatrist had diagnosed her with a major depressive disor-der and prescribed a widely used antidepressant. With the medication and cognitive-behavioral therapy, Karen N.'s mood had brightened dramatically, and she talked engagingly about her strong determination to enroll in the prison's drug treatment program (contemplation stage of change).

Unfortunately, neither Lawrence M., who was addicted to heroin and robbed a convenience store, nor Arnold F., who sold cocaine to an undercov-er police officer, was interested in discussing or enrolling in the prison's drug treatment program (precontemplation stage of change). They had both accu-mulated a significant number of disciplinary reports during their sentence and were unresponsive during our conversation. Both had been diagnosed by the prison psychologist with antisocial personality disorder, and both had a histo-ry of impulse control disorders (attention deficit/hyperactivity disorder). Con-tinued incarceration for public safety purposes was the only realistic option.

Dale S.'s case was particularly unusual. He had no history of violence and only minimal contact with the police before the evening when he brutally killed three people, including his best friend, his friend's girlfriend, and the girlfriend's four-year-old daughter. Dale S. had ingested a staggering amount of alcohol and powerful drugs, part of a pattern that Dale S. may have developed as a way to cope with a traumatic childhood filled with abuse, foster care, and residential placements. At his criminal court trial an expert witness for the defense, a psychiatrist with extensive experience in the substance abuse field, commented on Dale S.'s unusual clinical profile[2]:

PSYCHIATRIST: At the time I met him I was quite unprepared for the gentleman I did meet. He was very calm and very relaxed and smiling and was very pleasant, polite, and cooperative. He did not in any way refuse to answer questions and was very cooperative.

We were in a private room and talking and occasionally he might give a slight smile, which I think he was embarrassed by, because he could not remember all of the details or answer all of my questions, but he gave me a fairly complete story of the events that had happened—and two things happened during my interview with him that leave me quite impressed. Not only did he seem like a man who almost felt like "what am I doing in here?" but the appearance and the behavior [were] such that when they brought his tray in to eat, I noticed that the guards and attendants were quite concerned whether he had eaten.

DEFENSE ATTORNEY: During your conversation is it true that he received a telephone call stating that his wife was calling from the hospital and had just given birth to a child?

PSYCHIATRIST: Yes, and I sat back out of politeness and observed him, and I thought his facial expressions and the things he did were as routine and normal as I would expect, and from the questions he asked over the phone—they were quite within the realm of understanding and I thought he handled the call as I guess I would have if I had received the call—which is very hard for me to grasp.

DEFENSE ATTORNEY: I believe you stated in that report, that the decision you had to come to in your diagnosis was extremely hard for you to make, is that correct?

PSYCHIATRIST: Yes, sir.

DEFENSE ATTORNEY: Did you come to any diagnosis concerning Mr. S.'s reaction to drugs on the night of December the sixth, and I'll specifically direct your attention to page six of your report toward the bottom of that page, the last full paragraph.

PSYCHIATRIST: I can almost tell you without looking at it—I felt at the time I saw him and talked things over with him—I felt that within the range of what I would call normal was not happening.

This man was under the influence of heavy, continuous use of drugs—enough to maneuver and work with the drugs yet so completely under the influence of them that one felt it was almost on the border of psychotic behavior.

DEFENSE ATTORNEY: Did that come from his use of drugs just one night or did it come from a chronic buildup of the use of drugs?

PSYCHIATRIST: It would have to have been from a chronic buildup of the use of drugs. The sequence of events and the manner in which he discussed the things, it was as though it was in the realm of another world—as though he had done these things and had recalled them, but he could not explain them.

DEFENSE ATTORNEY: Let me direct your attention specifically to the last paragraph of your statement, starting on page six, and the sentence there indicates, and it starts like this . . . "It is to be noted that, under the influence of drugs, he is pushed apparently into the realm of near psychotic or schizophrenic-like behavior."

Doctor, could you explain that for the jury?

PSYCHIATRIST: Yes, I felt that this gentleman had obviously been using drugs so much and so continuously that my perception of his behavior was that it was under the influence of a constant, steady use, together with what was a very paranoid and suspicious nature.

At that time, as he described his actions and what took place, I thought he had, for that period of time—and I can't state how long before—actually lost what I would consider his touch with reality and was not totally aware or comprehending his actions in sequences or consequences.

Offenders whose crimes are directly influenced by their use of substances are usually diagnosed with what is known among mental health professionals as substance intoxication or substance-induced psychotic disorder. The distinction between the two is important. According to the American Psychiatric Association, substance intoxication entails the development of a reversible substance-specific syndrome because of the recent ingestion of (or exposure to) a substance, such as cocaine, heroin, or amphetamines (2000:199–200). The individual may manifest clinical symptoms such as belligerence, mood lability, cognitive impairment, impaired judgment, and impaired social or occupational functioning. These symptoms may result from the direct physiological effects of the substance on the central nervous system and develop during or shortly after use of the substance.

With substance intoxication the most common changes involve disturbances of perception, wakefulness, attention, thinking, judgment, psychomotor behavior, and interpersonal behavior. Individuals' actual symptoms vary, depending on which substance is involved, the dose, the duration or chronicity of dosing, the person's tolerance for the substance, the period of time since the last dose, the expectations of the person as to the substance's effects, and the environment or setting in which the substance is taken. People who are intoxicated for short periods of time (acute intoxication) may have different signs and symptoms from those individuals with more sustained or chronic intoxications. For example, moderate cocaine doses may initially produce gregariousness, but social withdrawal may develop if such doses are frequently repeated over days or weeks.

Many offenders experience substance intoxication. A much smaller percentage experience substance-induced psychotic disorder. The evidence in Dale S.'s case strongly suggests that the massive amounts of drugs that he used triggered a variety of psychotic symptoms that seriously impaired his judgment and led this otherwise nonviolent man to commit such violent acts. According to the American Psychiatric Association, substance-induced psychotic disorder entails prominent hallucinations or delusions that appear to be the direct physiological result of a substance (i.e., a drug of abuse or a medication) (2000:338).

A number of notorious cases involve offenders who murdered multiple victims in the midst of a psychotic episode comparable to Dale S.'s. Dorothy Lewis (1998) profiles a number of such cases in her *Guilty by Reason of Insanity: A Psychiatrist Explores the Minds of Killers*. Based on her broad and comprehensive survey of such cases, Lewis concludes:

> The nature of a person's offenses provides a window into his pathology. For example, overkill—the infliction of multiple gratuitous wounds on an already dead or dying victim . . . tells much about the attacker. These assailants just can't seem to stop. Psychotic murderers sometimes do this; their fury can reach extraordinary heights. Sometimes they respond to imagined threats to their own safety. Sometimes their "voices" tell them to keep going, to further mutilate the victim or violate the body. Sometimes they mistake their victims for other individuals in their lives—incestuous mothers, violent fathers, or taunting siblings. Manic states, too, have been associated with extremes of violence. And damage to certain parts of the brain can lead to paranoid misperceptions, impulsiveness, and extremes of emotion, especially rage. Once started on a course of action, brain-damaged killers sometimes cannot stop. Alcohol can loosen controls and may, in some people, trigger or exacerbate psychotic states. *Substances such as cocaine, LSD, and PCP have been reported to distort re-*

ality at times, increase paranoia, and precipitate extraordinary violence.
Jonathan [Jonathan Pincus, Lewis's professional colleague, a neurologist]
and I have found that, in instances of overkill, the offender usually was
psychotic, manic, or schizophrenic; had some type of brain dysfunction;
was under the influence of alcohol or drugs; or suffered from some combination of the above.   (Lewis 1998:97; emphasis added)

Settling on appropriate goals for an offender such as Dale S. is difficult.
In some states his crimes would lead to the death penalty. In fact, the state in
which Dale S. was convicted now has the death penalty for such crimes, although it did not when he was convicted. Dale S. was sentenced to life imprisonment without the possibility of parole for at least one hundred years.

Incarceration for public safety and punishment purposes is certainly warranted in such a case. The heinous nature of Dale S.'s crimes is without question. But what about rehabilitation and restorative justice? Dale S. was, in
fact, interested in exploring some of the issues in his life and his guilt around
the murders. He faithfully attended a group that I facilitated at the maximum-security penitentiary during the two years that I worked there. Interestingly, however, Dale S. was silent in the group most of the time. He chose
instead to write me letters about his thoughts and feelings. We exchanged regular correspondence for years, and this was the extent of Dale S.'s rehabilitative efforts ("thera-mail"?). Dale S. felt enormous guilt for his crimes, but he
was not in a position to participate in a victim-offender mediation program
(his direct victims were dead, and surviving family members had no interest
in meeting Dale S.) or perform community service in any form.

Although Dale S. will never be released from prison, he still felt the need
to explore therapeutic issues. He conveyed some of his sentiments succinctly
in the first letter that he wrote to me about his crimes, months after we had
begun corresponding about various issues in his life. Dale S.'s detailed description and recollection also provide a rare glimpse into the mind of an offender
who murdered three people soon after ingesting large amounts of drugs.

We have finally come to the part I've been dreading. No matter how
many times I think about that night I never quite accept that the person
doing the killing was me. There's no doubt it was me, but it's hell to live
with. I've been tripping [obsessing] the past two days trying to figure out
how to describe the murders to you. I really don't think I can. I don't
think there is any way I could make you feel and see what I did.

I guess I need to start with the purchase of the gun. I bought a .22 caliber pistol from a friend of mine maybe three or four weeks prior to the

murders. I bought it for squirrel hunting. Many times you'll shoot a squirrel and not kill it. I didn't like to see them suffer so I got the .22 to shoot them in the head with. My father-in-law showed me how to club them to death but that seemed worse than them suffering after being shot. We ate the dead squirrels. They are quite good.

On the night of the murders I went to my friend John's house and after that went to my friend Frank's house. Frank was my best friend. We had worked together on two different jobs. I really got into drugs more after meeting Frank. We did a lot of partying together. We also went camping, hunting, stuff like that. Frank was about 24 or 25.

Frank had some sort of nervous breakdown after he was married about a year. He was on a speed run and something snapped. He was admitted to a hospital nut ward for a while. He lost his memory for a short period of time.

Nan was Frank's girlfriend after his divorce from his first wife. Nan had a daughter, Annie. I did not know Nan well at all. She seemed like a nice person from the few times I was around her. Annie was a normal 4-year-old girl. Frank would baby-sit at times and I would drop in. We would play games with Annie until she wore us out. I could never purposely hurt a child, and I find Annie's death hard to cope with even after seven years.

I want you to have some idea as to my state of mind that night. Before arriving at Frank's I had taken eight to ten dime bags of PCP, I don't know how many minnie whites, I did one hit of acid, drank a few beers, and smoked many joints. I started at about 1:00 or 2:00 P.M. at a friend's house in Knoxville. It was around 11:30 P.M. or a quarter to midnight when I got to Frank's apartment. It had to be around that time because Nan got off work at midnight, and she got home soon after I got there. I wasn't paying much attention to the time, I guess. If I had realized it was so close to midnight I would have probably never gone to Frank's knowing Nan would be home. Not that she would say anything or get mad, but because it would have been bad manners. Frank and I were playing cards when Nan got home, or we were getting ready to, at least. Annie was still up so Nan went to put her to bed.

Frank and I did some more PCP while Nan put Annie to bed. We then went back to our card game. Nan didn't want to play and sat on the couch reading. Annie got out of bed and came into the living room to tell Nan something, and they both went into the bedroom.

Frank asked me if I wanted something to drink and went into the kitchen. I walked behind him and I pulled the pistol out and struck him on the head. <u>I have no idea why</u>. He turned around and I stepped back and shot him twice. Nan came running in to see what the noise was. She asked what had happened and I told her I just killed Frank. She asked why and I told her I didn't know.

The baby was crying and I remember telling Nan to put her to bed. Annie came in after Nan. Nan put Annie to bed and came back into the living room where I was. I made her strip and I tied her hands and feet. I then began to stab her. I don't remember how many times—10 or 12 maybe. It was sickening. Nan died. I then went and cut Annie's throat and that was even worse.

When I was doing all that it seemed as if someone else was doing it and making me watch. I was powerless to stop it from happening. I would not want to ever experience that again. I sometimes think of what I would do if I was forced into a kill or be killed situation in here. I have never really settled that question in my mind. Probably won't know unless it happens.

Well anyway, I left Frank's and went home. I went directly to the bathroom and took a bath and tried to wash the blood out of my clothes. I then went to bed and passed out. Carol [Dale S.'s wife] woke me up two or three hours later to take her to work. Lonna [Dale's young daughter] was out of school for some reason and I was to baby-sit. After dropping Carol off at work I went to a friend's house, put Lonna in her care, and passed out again. I woke up around 10:30 or 11:00 A.M. and took Lonna home to fix her something to eat. When the noon news came on they had the news of Frank's, Nan's, and Annie's deaths.

It didn't register at that time that I was responsible for the murders. In fact, it wasn't until two or three days later, after being questioned by the police, that I had any idea that I may have been a murderer. I began to get flashes of what had happened. I fought to block it all out, but I couldn't. This grew in time and left no doubt in my mind that I had done the killing. I went to my stepparents in Indiana to think things out; I told Carol I was going to look for a job. After about a week or so I went back home and turned myself in.

The honest truth is that I cannot give you any reason as to why I committed these murders. I do not know and I don't think I ever will. I remember no argument at all. I was not mad at Frank. He was my best friend.

Sit down and think of something that happened to someone else in your presence. The more you think about it the clearer the details are. That's the only way I can even come close to telling you how I felt after the murders. There was no way I could stop this terrible bastard from killing Frank, Nan, and Annie. It was like a movie almost. I'm out in the audience knowing what's about to happen, but what can you do from the audience? You have to sit and watch along with everyone else. Yes, I temporarily lost my mind. I have no doubt about that. It does not matter what others think. I know. I know I could never do anything so horrible under normal conditions.

It's hard for me to accept the fact that I did it. But I did, and I will have to live with it. I didn't want to kill anyone, didn't intend to, and realized I had done so only after it was done. I guess that's why I hate myself—because I lost control of myself while on drugs and killed three people. It's simple to say, well, I was on drugs and didn't know what I was doing. But then no one forced the drugs on me. I took them on my own free will. So who's to blame?

In important respects Dale S.'s case forces us to confront a number of fundamental questions about the purposes and goals of the criminal justice system. Unlike all the other offenders examined in this book, Dale S. will never be released from prison or from supervision in the criminal justice system. Lifelong incarceration is a given, both for punitive and public safety purposes. Whatever personal change efforts Dale S. engages in will be only for his satisfaction and development as a human being, not because they will enhance his functioning in the community. Interestingly, twenty years after Dale S. and I first met in the prison where he has now been incarcerated for more than a quarter century, Dale S. wrote to me about his efforts to give back to the community, a form of restorative justice: "I have changed jobs and now work in the Handicapped Center. The H.C. tapes books onto tapes for the blind. We also convert books to Braille and large print. I have worked on three or four children's books, some of the "Horrible Harry" series, and I am now working on a textbook. I like the work and it makes me feel like I'm finally helping someone."

Pathological Gambling

Access to legalized gambling has grown exponentially, in the form of casino betting (blackjack, roulette, poker, baccarat, slot machines, keno, craps, sports betting, and so on), state lotteries, and horse and dog tracks. State governments have expanded their reliance on the enormous revenue that legalized gambling generates.

Without question, police, courts, and corrections officials have felt the effects of increased gambling, both legal and illegal. And, of course, pathological gambling nearly always destroys the lives of the gambler and the gambler's family.

One of the most compelling, prototypical, and widely publicized illustrations of this tragic, and all-too-common, pattern involves the heartrending descent of Art Schlichter (MacGregor 2000). Schlichter played college football at Ohio State, where he was a star quarterback beginning in the late 1970s. He was featured on the cover of *Sports Illustrated* and was fourth in Heisman Trophy voting, the prominent award given to the nation's premiere college football player. In 1982 Schlichter was the number one pick in the National Football League (NFL) draft by the Baltimore Colts. Schlichter gambled away his $350,000 signing bonus, and in 1983 the NFL suspended him because of his gambling. Between 1987 and 1994 Schlichter was arrested four times on charges of bank fraud, unlawful gambling, and writing bad checks. In 1994 Schlichter was charged with federal and state crimes and in 1995 served a prison sentence in Terre Haute, Indiana. Schlichter was in a gambling treatment program in 1997 but was caught betting and sent back to prison. He filed for bankruptcy in 1998, listing $1 million in debt. In 2000 Schlichter was arrested and charged with money laundering and fraud, including the unauthorized use of his father's credit card to obtain $42,000 in cash.

No one familiar with Schlichter's case would deny that he is a textbook example of a pathological gambler. He claims that he started gambling as a child, betting small change on card games. Schlichter also bet heavily during his college days at Ohio State, at a local racetrack, and on various national sporting events (MacGregor 2000). A former colleague reports that when Schlichter was a quarterback with the Baltimore Colts, during football games he sometimes charted sporting events of games that he had bets on instead of charting the football plays that he was supposed to record. Media accounts describe how Schlichter would call a play in a huddle and then forget what play he had called when he got to the line of scrimmage because he was thinking about bets that he had placed. Schlichter hocked his wife's ring for money, wrote bad checks, borrowed money from friends, stole checks from employers and from his sister-in-law, and stole cash and credit cards from a good friend. As Schlichter himself said, "When you start stealing from your family and friends, you know it's only a matter of time before you're in jail or you put a gun to your head" (MacGregor 2000). A reporter who explored Schlichter's life in depth put it succinctly:

This is where a gambling addiction will take a man: He will steal from anyone, even his family. He will trash a promising professional football career and waste a powerful charisma that makes even victims want to believe in him after he has shattered their trust.

He will end up in a crowded jail cell, awaiting a trial that could put him in prison for 20 years.

Art Schlichter has done this to get money to feed the addiction that's controlling his life. He's so sick that he knows the wrong he does but does it anyway—crying to his therapist, wondering why he can't stop and whether he's losing his mind. (MacGregor 2000)

Pathological gambling has had a direct effect on a variety of crimes committed by people who are desperate for cash to pay off debts or to use for additional gambling. Various gambling-related offenses include embezzlement, fraud, forgery, counterfeiting, robbery, larceny, burglary, extortion, receiving stolen goods, murder, arson, identity theft, automobile theft, and drug trafficking.

Case 7.9 Tony Z. had been a correctional officer at a county jail for five years. He started the job after finishing two years of college.

On weekends and when he had other free time, Tony Z. visited a local casino with friends. Before long he was betting heavily on casino poker, baccarat, and blackjack. He also bet heavily on football, basketball, and baseball games. He became more and more obsessed with gambling and ended up losing $76,000.

Tony Z. was desperate to make up his losses. He forged his wife's signature on an equity loan on their house, and he depleted the couple's savings. At one point he was so desperate for money that he drove around a rural area in order to steal new credit cards from mailboxes.

Tony Z. was eventually arrested for bank fraud, stealing credit cards from mailboxes, and using credit cards fraudulently.

Case 7.10 Allison D. was the office manager in a small insurance firm. For several years she would spend one evening a week playing bingo at a local church. One of her girlfriends, whom she met at bingo, invited Allison D. to accompany her to a nearby casino to play slot machines. Shortly thereafter Allison D. became hooked on slot machines. Over two months she lost $3,200. To make up for her losses she began stealing cash payments that some of her employer's clients made for their insurance premiums. Her boss eventually noticed the discrepancy on the business's books, confronted her, and then called the police.

Case 7.11 Bobby S. regularly placed bets on various sporting events (especially professional and college football and basketball games) through a local bookie. During one particularly bad stretch in his betting, Bobby S. accumulated a $6,100 debt. For two weeks the bookie pressured Bobby S. daily to come up with the money. Bobby S. borrowed as much money as he could from several relatives and friends, but he was able to raise only $2,600. The bookie started to threaten Bobby S. and eventually told Bobby S. that his wife and kids could end up being hurt. In desperation Bobby S. robbed a credit union. The police arrested him two days later.

Professionals generally agree that pathological gamblers experience increasing tension or arousal before they gamble, and feelings of release or pleasure after they have gambled if they win their bet or guilt or remorse if they lose their bet. As with alcohol, cocaine, and heroin addiction, pathological gambling tends to develop in phases (Seligman 1998). In the first phase, winning, gamblers tend to be overconfident and expand their gambling activities. In the losing phase gamblers take undue risks and deplete their financial assets. In the final phase, desperation, gambling becomes frenzied and gamblers begin to borrow large sums of money, write bad checks, and engage in other money-related crimes (such as embezzlement, forgery, fraud, and drug trafficking).

Treatment for gambling generally mirrors approaches used with other addictions, especially alcohol and drugs. Here, too, common approaches include the use of an intervention; residential programs and therapeutic communities; pharmacotherapy (e.g., antidepressants, anti-anxiety medication); psychoeducational groups; twelve-step programs (e.g., Gamblers Anonymous); self-help groups; couple's, family, and group therapy; and various forms of individual psychotherapy (e.g., cognitive-behavioral therapy, rational therapy, rational emotive therapy).

As with alcoholics and drug addicts, many pathological gamblers do not seek help until they have hit bottom. Hitting bottom may be triggered by insurmountable debt, marital and relationship torment, or arrest for gambling-related crimes. Although some pathological gamblers seek treatment on their own, many are ordered to treatment by the court, as part of a probation plan, or by a parole board as a condition of early release from prison.

CALIBRATION-RECALIBRATION

As with all offenders, some pathological gamblers are better rehabilitation prospects than others. Allison D., who stole customers' cash payments at the insurance firm where she worked, was quite insightful, remorseful, and earnest about her recovery.

When I was arrested, I was incredibly angry. I had convinced myself that I was only "borrowing" the customers' cash payments; in my head I wasn't stealing. That just shows you how far gone I was. I was using that money to feed my gambling habit the way a heroin addict steals to buy bags of smack [heroin].

The truth is, I had never heard about gambling as an addiction. Well, maybe in places like Atlantic City and Las Vegas but certainly not around here. I thought I was just a two-bit gambler who couldn't possibly get in over her head. Boy, was I wrong! I got hooked fast, before I even realized what was happening.

We don't have a GA [Gamblers Anonymous] group here in the prison; there aren't enough people here to participate. But I go regularly to the AA [Alcoholics Anonymous] groups, 'cause they talk about a lot of the same issues. In some ways all addicts are the same, so I learn a lot from those discussions. You can bet—oops, wrong phrase—you can be sure I'll start going to GA meetings the day after I get out of this place. I promise you that. I have too much to lose by getting back into those slot machines. They were almost the death of me.

Allison D. was determined to address her issues immediately upon her release (contemplation stage with respect to joining a Gamblers Anonymous group) and had already taken partial steps by regularly attending Alcoholics Anonymous groups in the prison and by enrolling in the prison's mentor program, where she met regularly with a woman from the community who was helping her to focus on the major issues in her life, develop new insights and skills, and plan for her release (action stage). Allison D. had also taken the initiative to write to the director of the local victim-offender mediation program to discuss the possibility of meeting with her former employer; Allison D. told me that her former boss "was so good to me for so long. I can't believe I hurt him the way I did. He didn't deserve that; I really took advantage of him. I really want to tell him, to his face, how sorry I am, ask for forgiveness, and see if there might be some way for me to pay him back—what do you call that, restitution?"

I was much less encouraged about Tony Z. and Bobby S. Tony Z., the former correctional officer who committed bank fraud and stole credit cards, demonstrated reasonable insight during his first parole hearing. He acknowledged that he had a gambling problem and was taking steps to address it. He participated in an addictions group and was paroled about halfway through his sentence. However, five months after his release he was arrested again for both gambling and drug trafficking. At that point Tony Z. needed to be reincarcerated for public safety and punitive purposes (recalibration). At the parole violation hearing Tony Z. was sullen and virtually silent. He did not acknowledge the depth of his pathological gambling problem and did not offer a sound plan to address it (precontemplation stage). Tony Z. simply seemed resigned to his fate: completing his initial sentence without parole and returning to see the board once he became eligible on his new sentence.

Bobby S., who robbed a credit union in order to get money to pay a bookie, also did not display much insight. During his first year in prison Bobby S. was disciplined twice for gambling with other inmates and once for fighting about an unpaid gambling debt. When I met with him, Bobby S. seemed neither motivated nor remorseful.

QUESTION: My impression from the police and court documents I've reviewed is that you've had a pretty serious gambling problem. Is that right?

ANSWER: It depends what you mean by "serious."

QUESTION: Well, what's your opinion? Would you say your gambling problem is serious?

ANSWER: Nah, I was able to handle my gambling for a long, long time. Then I hit a bad spell and things kind of fell apart. What I did [robbing the credit union] wasn't such a bright idea; I know that. But you don't have to worry about me doing anything like that again.

QUESTION: Do you think you can handle any kind of gambling when you get out, or is it just too risky?

ANSWER: I'm not planning to get back into it [gambling] big time, the way I was. I may fool around a little bit, just for fun—just the legal stuff. I promise.

Bobby S. did not seem to think that he had a serious gambling problem, and he was not interested in pursuing any kind of insight-oriented rehabilitation or therapeutic program (precontemplation stage). His comment about maybe gambling "a little bit" after his release from prison is analogous to an alcoholic who believes that he or she can be a social drinker without risking serious relapse. Bobby S. seemed resistant to each and every suggestion that prison staff and the parole board made about courses of action. At least at that point, continued incarceration for Bobby S. was the only realistic option, with sustained, periodic encouragement along the way to address his gambling and addiction issues. Close supervision by parole or probation staff after

Bobby S.'s release would be critically important. Bobby S. had characteristics common to people with antisocial personality disorder, which made him a serious relapse risk.

• • •

Criminals with one or more addictions constitute a significant portion of the offender population. Alcohol and drugs—their manufacture, sale, or use—are connected in one way or another to an enormous percentage of the crimes that are committed. In addition to crimes that violate explicit drug laws, addicts commit many additional crimes in order to obtain money to procure drugs or commit crimes while under the influence of drugs or alcohol.

The rapid expansion of legalized gambling has also had a profound effect on crime rates. Casino gambling and various forms of sports betting are responsible for a considerable amount of crime committed by people who are pathological gamblers.

Any comprehensive crime-prevention strategy *must* acknowledge and address issues related to addiction. To do otherwise is to ignore the elephant that fills the room.

8

Crimes of Mental Illness

A number of major mental illnesses—such as schizophrenia, depression, bipolar disorder, anxiety disorders, and mental retardation—are associated with a significant portion of crime (Guy et al. 1985; Powell, Holt, and Fondacaro 1997; Steadman et al. 1989; and Teplin 1990).

Here is what a recent federal study found about the prevalence of mental illness among offenders (Ditton 1999). This study considered an inmate mentally ill if he or she reported a current mental or emotional condition or an overnight stay in a mental health or treatment program.

- State and federal prisons and local jails hold 283,800 mentally ill offenders, and 547,800 mentally ill offenders are on probation.
- Seven percent of federal prison inmates are mentally ill.
- Sixteen percent of inmates in state prisons, local jails, or on probation report a mental condition or have stayed overnight in a psychiatric hospital, unit, or treatment program.
- Twenty percent of violent offenders manifest symptoms of mental illness.
- Twenty-nine percent of white female inmates in state prisons are mentally ill.
- Forty percent of white female inmates younger than twenty-five are mentally ill.
- Twenty percent of black female inmates are mentally ill.
- Twenty-two percent of Hispanic female inmates are mentally ill.

Biological Correlates of Mental Illness

In contrast to a number of archaic theories of crime causation, which focused on the clinical significance of factors such as offenders' head circumference and body types, contemporary research suggests a profound connection between biological factors and the criminal behavior of many mentally ill offenders. These influences include genetic factors, neurochemical and hormonal factors, and neuropsychological and brain dysfunction (Farrington 1998).

There is growing evidence that genetic factors may account for a significant portion of criminal behavior. This evidence is based on various studies comparing the offense patterns of identical twins and fraternal twins, comparing children who were separated at birth from their biological parents and raised by adoptive parents, and comparing identical twins reared together and identical twins reared apart. Based on her comprehensive review of the research record on the relationship between biological factors and criminal behavior, Fishbein concludes that "the bulk of genetic research on antisocial behavior indicates that traits predisposing to antisociality which may be inherited are behavioral, temperamental, and personality dispositions, and include irritability, proneness to anger, high activity levels, low arousal levels, dominance, mania, impulsivity, sensation-seeking, hyperemotionality, extraversion, depressed mood, and negative affect" (1998:94–95).

Research also suggests that a close connection exists between neurotransmitters, particularly serotonin levels, and criminal behavior. Neurotransmitters are chemicals stored in brain cells that carry information between these cells. We have empirical evidence that institutionalized antisocial and violent patients have low brain serotonin levels and high blood serotonin levels, even after controlling for factors such as socioeconomic status, intelligence, smoking, drinking, and drug use (Farrington 1998; Fishbein 1998; Mednick, Moffitt, and Stack 1987). Also, high levels of the hormone testosterone tend to be associated with violence.

Neuropsychological and brain dysfunction studies also offer some tentative evidence of a relationship between brain mechanisms that control behavior and high-risk behavior. Researchers argue that a relationship exists between impaired frontal lobes and criminal behavior. Evidence suggests that the frontal lobes are the site of the brain's "executive functions," involving abstract reasoning, anticipation, planning, sustaining attention, concentration, and inhibiting inappropriate behavior (Farrington 1998; Moffitt 1993).

Lewis (1998), a psychiatrist specializing in the assessment and treatment of violent offenders, offers compelling commentary about the relationship between brain dysfunction and extraordinarily violent crimes:

Two doctors up at Harvard—a neurosurgeon and a psychiatrist—had reported finding abnormal electrical activity in the brains of some of their episodically violent patients. Vernon Mark, the neurosurgeon, and Frank Ervin, the psychiatrist, had inserted electrodes deep into the brains of these aggressive individuals. They found that these patients had episodes of violence that coincided with abnormal electrical discharges, localized in the most ancient structures of their brains. We humans share these brain structures with alligators and other primitive, unfriendly creatures. At the onset of these episodes, patients experienced auras—that is, weird feelings. Some complained of odd perceptions and sensations. Others described being assailed by vile odors. In other patients, the sweet smell of perfume presaged an episode. Some patients saw blinding light. Others experience nausea and vague abdominal pains. Some felt dizzy. And some patients reported feeling as though they were reliving past events. (Lewis 1998:44–45)

Several psychiatric disorders are most likely to appear in an offender population: schizophrenia and other psychotic disorders, mood disorders (especially, major depression and bipolar disorder), anxiety disorders (especially posttraumatic stress disorder, generalized anxiety disorder, substance-induced anxiety disorder), paraphilias (sexual disorders such as pedophilia), and mild mental retardation. Occasionally, one also encounters offenders diagnosed with a dissociative disorder (particularly dissociative identity disorder).

Schizophrenia and Psychotic Disorders

A significant percentage of offenders with major mental illness have been diagnosed with schizophrenia or another psychotic disorder (although relatively few people with these disorders commit serious crimes). The term *psychotic* usually refers to the presence of delusions (distorted thinking or cognition) or prominent hallucinations (hearing voices, for example). Such offenders often engage in behavior—such as disorderly conduct and assault—that is clearly a function of their mental illness.

Schizophrenia, the most prominent form of psychosis, entails some combination of delusions, hallucinations, disorganized speech (incoherence), and grossly disorganized or catatonic behavior involving significant psychomotor disturbance (such as excessive motor activity, mutism, peculiar voluntary movements). The various subtypes within the broad disorder of schizophrenia include paranoid type (for example, persecutory delusions where an offender assaults or kills someone whom he or she imagines is "out to get" him or her), disorganized type (where the key features are disorganized speech and behavior and flat or inappropriate affect), and catatonic type (where the key feature is some significant psychomotor disturbance) (American Psychiatric Association 2000).

Most offenders with schizophrenia have little understanding that they have a psychotic illness; the lack of insight is a function of the illness itself and exacerbates noncompliance with treatment, relapse rates, probation and parole violations, and disciplinary problems in prison settings. Offenders with schizophrenia also have a much higher risk of suicide and a much higher incidence of assaultive and violent behavior. Approximately 10 percent of people with schizophrenia commit suicide, and 20 to 40 percent make at least one attempt. Special risk factors associated with suicide fit the profile of a significant number of offenders: male, forty-five or younger, feelings of hopelessness, a history of unemployment, and depressive symptoms. Major predictors of violence among people with schizophrenia are also highly correlated with the offender population: male, young, past history of violence, noncompliance with antipsychotic medication, and excessive substance abuse (American Psychiatric Association 2000; Kales, Stefanis, and Talbott 1990; Tsuang and Faraone 1997; Seligman 1998).

The evidence that schizophrenia has significant biological determinants and bases is substantial. Individuals with schizophrenia have unusually enlarged lateral ventricles, decreased brain tissue, decreased volume in the temporal lobe, decreased thalamic volume, increased incidence of large cavum septum pellucidi (space between the two leaflets of the septum pellucidum—a thin layer of nervous tissue that separates the two lateral ventricles of the brain—which may indicate prenatal midline developmental brain abnormality), and decreased cerebral blood flow and metabolism (American Psychiatric Association 2000:304–5; Seligman 1998).

The onset of schizophrenia typically occurs between the late teens and the midthirties (for men typical onset is between eighteen and twenty-five years, and for women between twenty-five and their midthirties). The lifetime course of the illness varies considerably; some individuals experience alternating periods of remission and exacerbation, while others manifest symptoms more chronically. Complete remission is unusual (American Psychiatric Association 2000; Henrichs 2001; Tsuang and Faraone 1997; Seligman 1998).

Case 8.1 Arlindo P. has a history of mental illness. He was diagnosed with schizophrenia at sixteen and hospitalized on several occasions. Arlindo P. functions well when he takes his prescribed neuroleptic (antipsychotic) medication.

Arlindo P. became addicted to cocaine and stopped going to the local community mental health center for his medication. His schizophrenia symptoms, which involved paranoid delusions, returned. One evening Arlindo P. stabbed his roommate and injured him seriously; after his arrest Arlindo P. told police and his lawyer that he believed his roommate was a terrorist agent who was going to poison his food and water.

Case 8.2 Paula Z. was twenty-two when she was diagnosed with schizophrenia. She lived in a supervised apartment complex and received mental health services from the nearby community mental health center.

One afternoon Paula Z. had an argument with the group home manager and left the facility. She was missing for three weeks; during that time Paula Z. lived on the street or stayed with a friend who once lived at the group home. Paula Z. did not take her neuroleptic medication during this period and her psychiatric symptoms reappeared. Paula Z. was arrested for shoplifting.

CALIBRATION-RECALIBRATION

Treatment of schizophrenia has changed dramatically over the years. Contemporary approaches typically include a combination of neuroleptic medication, which is often highly effective; social skills training; psychotherapy (especially cognitive-behavioral therapy); and family intervention. Neuroleptic drugs can effectively alleviate the core psychotic symptoms that some offenders experience, such as delusions and hallucinations.

Offenders living in the community whose difficulties stem from their schizophrenia, such as Arlindo P. and Paula Z., must maintain close connections with community-based mental health services to minimize the likelihood of re-offending. Although such offenders seldom return to "normal" functioning, comprehensive and sustained community mental health services—both outpatient and residential—are often effective and enable the offenders to function well in supervised settings. Factors that appear to reduce the likelihood of recidivism include having a positive work history, average or above average intelligence, being married, abrupt onset of clinical symptoms (as opposed to a chronic history), midlife onset of symptoms, absence of psychotic assaultiveness, depression, family history of depression and mania, positive and supportive environment in the community, and absence of a family history of schizophrenia (Kales, Stefanis, and Talbott 1990; Seligman 1998).

When offenders relapse, strengthening the community-based mental health services is often effective and, when the courts permit, is often a more constructive response than incarceration. Because complete remission of symptoms is unusual (American Psychiatric Association 2000:309; Henrichs 2001), offenders with schizophrenia who are under supervision require comprehensive treatment, supportive services, and close monitoring and supervision.

Mood Disorders

Mood disorders, as the term suggests, entail a serious disturbance in the individual's basic mood. The mood disorders that appear to be linked most closely to criminal conduct are major depression and bipolar disorder.

Major depression (as opposed to the less severe form of depression, dysthymia) typically entails a sustained period of some combination of depressed mood most of the day, nearly every day; markedly diminished interest or pleasure in all, or almost all, activities most of the day, nearly every day; significant weight loss when not dieting or weight gain, or decrease or increase in appetite nearly every day; insomnia or hypersomnia (excessive need to sleep) nearly every day; psychomotor agitation or retardation nearly every day; fatigue or loss of energy nearly every day; feelings of worthlessness or excessive or inappropriate guilt nearly every day; diminished ability to think or concentrate, or indecisiveness, nearly every day; and recurrent thoughts of death, recurrent suicidal ideation without a specific plan, or a suicide attempt or a specific plan for committing suicide (American Psychiatric Association 2000:356; Mondimore 1995; A. Schwartz and Schwartz 1993).

Current estimates are that nearly 15 percent of individuals with major depressive disorder commit suicide. Statistically, women are much more likely to be diagnosed with major depressive disorder; estimates of the lifetime risk for the disorder for women range from 10 to 25 percent, whereas for men the estimates range from 5 to 12 percent. The average age of onset is in the midtwenties, which is the age group of a significant portion of the offender population. Hence women offenders are a particularly high-risk group for major depressive order (American Psychiatric Association 2000).

Case 8.3 Lisa S. was the office manager at a large restaurant. She was having major marital problems and was heading toward a divorce. Lisa S. and her husband separated and she moved into her own apartment. She was having great difficulty managing her budget and expenses. In addition, her mother, to whom she was very close, had died recently.

Lisa S. was finding it more and more difficult to get through the day without crying and feeling overwhelmed with despair. She had recurring thoughts of suicide and began drinking heavily. Lisa S. began embezzling money from the restaurant where she worked. The business's bookkeeper had difficulty reconciling the financial records and suspected that someone was taking cash. The restaurant's owner notified the police, who were able to trace the embezzlement to Lisa S.

Case 8.4 Tom Z. was serving a six-year sentence after being convicted of death resulting from driving dangerously. Tom Z. was driving home late one night when his car struck two teenagers who were changing a tire in the highway's breakdown lane.

For about a year before the accident Tom Z. had been seeing a psychiatrist for the treatment of clinical depression. Two days before the accident Tom Z. had started taking new antidepressant medication. Tom Z. claimed that the new medication made him drowsy and that this contributed to the accident. Tom Z. also reported that his incarceration exacerbated his symptoms of depression and that he was having suicidal thoughts.

Bipolar disorder usually entails some combination of depressive episodes and manic episodes. A manic episode involves an abnormally and persistently elevated, expansive, and irritable mood over a period of time, with symptoms such as grandiosity; reduced need for sleep; increased talkativeness; racing thoughts; distractibility; increased activity; and excessive pleasure seeking (for example, excessive spending) (American Psychiatric Association 2000:388; Fawcett, Golden, and Rosenfeld 2000; Seligman 1998:174). According to Seligman (1998):

> A Manic Episode, like an episode of Major Depression, is typically quite severe and causes impairment in social and occupational functioning. People experiencing this phase of a Bipolar Disorder tend to view themselves as powerful and destined for great success. They disregard the potential risks of their behavior, as well as the feelings of others, and they may become hostile and threatening if challenged. Their judgment and impulse control are poor, and they typically are hyperactive and distractible. Their speech tends to be loud, pressured, and intrusive. Approximately 75 percent of people in Manic Episodes have delusions or hallucinations (usually mood-congruent), which may lead clinicians to misdiagnose them as having Schizophrenia.

Completed suicides occur in approximately 10 to 15 percent of individuals with bipolar disorder. The literature holds many documented cases of child and spousal abuse, and other forms of violence, during severe manic episodes or during episodes with psychotic features (American Psychiatric Association 2000:384). A significant percentage of offenders with bipolar disorder also have problems with alcohol and other drug dependence and abuse (Fawcett, Golden, and Rosenfeld 2000). Studies comparing groups of individuals with bipolar disorder with groups with major depressive disorder or groups without any mood disorder tend to show increased rates of right-hemisphere lesions, bilateral subcortical (beneath the cerebral cortex) lesions, or periventricular (involving the gray matter of the hypothalamus) lesions in those with bipolar disorder (American Psychiatric Association 2000). The incidence of bipolar disorder appears to be nearly the same in men and women. Estimates of lifetime prevalence of the disorder are 0.4 to 1.6 percent of the population. The average age of onset for both men and women is about twenty.

Symptoms of bipolar disorder were clearly evident in the case of a middle-aged man who assaulted his girlfriend:

Case 8.5 Erwin M. was a colonel in the Marine Corps. When he was thirty-seven, Erwin M. began to experience symptoms of bipolar disorder. He eventually received a medical discharge from the Marine Corps because of his psychiatric illness.

One evening Erwin M. entered into a manic phase of his bipolar illness. He went without slept for nearly three days; he stayed up all night completing a "master plan" to start a real estate business. Edwin M. called several friends at odd hours to tell them about his new venture and to recruit investors. He tried to keep his friends on the phone for unusually long periods of time. He spent his days spending extraordinarily large sums of money on clothing, furniture, and supplies for his new business. He also visited with his girlfriend to tell her that he wanted to leave the relationship. During that visit Edwin M. became enraged with his girlfriend and punched her repeatedly. He was charged with felony assault.

One particularly dramatic case involving bipolar disorder involved a psychiatrist in training who was convicted of second-degree murder (Saltzman 1996). A jury concluded that Dr. David Barrett, a psychiatrist in training at Brown University, was guilty of killing Joseph A. Silvia, even though psychiatrists for both the prosecution and the defense agreed that Barrett suffered from bipolar disorder.

Barrett was a graduate of the University of Pennsylvania and University of Vermont Medical School. He had argued with a convenience store clerk and then with a friend of the clerk's, who had told Barrett not to bother the clerk.

During the dispute with the clerk's friend, Barrett pulled out a .38-caliber revolver and fired shots that killed the clerk's friend.

Much of the criminal court trial focused on Barrett's history of mental illness and on whether his bipolar disorder was responsible for his behavior. Barrett saw at least seven psychiatrists from the age of ten until weeks before the murder. His father testified that nine different family members, spanning three generations, had been diagnosed with bipolar disorder. Barrett himself testified that his thinking had been quite disorganized because he had not been taking medication for his bipolar disorder. He reported that his severe mood swings had stabilized since the shooting because he had resumed taking his medication. A psychiatrist and a psychologist who worked for the state prison system testified that Barrett was delusional when they saw him. The prison psychiatrist testified that Barrett "told me he could command the loyalty of other inmates to rise, and they would rise and hang the corrections officers up by their heels" (Saltzman 1996:A1). Several of Barrett's friends testified that

> he had become increasingly grandiose and combative in the months before the shooting, with one saying that he had nearly picked a fight with a bodybuilder at another gas station. A former resident of the Brown University psychiatry program was one of several people who expressed concerns about Barrett to supervisors, which led Brown to put Barrett on a mandatory medical leave days before the shooting. (Saltzman 1996:A1)

CALIBRATION-RECALIBRATION

Substantial research evidence suggests that major depression is best treated with a combination of antidepressant medication (tricyclic antidepressants, monoamine oxidase inhibitors, and serotonin reuptake inhibitors) and psychotherapy (such as cognitive-behavioral and family therapy). In some instances electroconvulsive therapy has been used with offenders who do not respond well to antidepressant medication (Grinspoon and Bakalar 1996; Mondimore 1995). For offenders living in the community, brief hospitalization, day treatment programs, and residential crisis centers are often appropriate.

Hospitalization of offenders with bipolar disorder who are living in the community may be necessary (if they are prison inmates, they may need to be transferred to a psychiatric unit within the prison or to a psychiatric hospital or forensic unit until they are stabilized on medication); during a manic phase these individuals' aggressive and self-destructive behavior may need to be contained.

Medication is the primary form of treatment for bipolar disorder. Typical drug regimes include lithium to help control the manic symptoms along with antipsychotic, antidepressant, or anticonvulsant medications. Medication is usually supplemented by psychotherapy (Fawcett, Golden, and Rosenfeld 2000; Seligman 1998). Offenders with bipolar disorder often have difficulty complying with medication protocols for a long period of time. Hence close supervision and monitoring are essential.

Anxiety Disorders

As a group, offenders suffering with anxiety disorders have difficulty managing stress in their lives. Among offenders, two anxiety disorders are particularly prominent: generalized anxiety disorder and posttraumatic stress disorder. Individuals with generalized anxiety disorder experience excessive amounts of anxiety and worry over a long period of time (Craske 1999; Knapp and VandeCreek 1994; Richards, Musser, and Gershon 1999). These offenders find it difficult to control their anxiety and worry, which can lead to conflict with other people, poor decision making, serious impairment, and criminal conduct. These individuals typically have some combination of symptoms of edginess or restlessness; tire easily; have difficulty concentrating; are irritable; suffer muscle tension; have difficulty relaxing; fear rejection; are apprehensive about losing control; are unable to control their thinking; are confused; and have difficulty sleeping. For the typical offender with generalized anxiety disorder, "the intensity, duration, or frequency of the anxiety and worry is far out of proportion to the actual likelihood or impact of the feared event" (American Psychiatric Association 2000:473). This disorder is diagnosed somewhat more frequently in women than in men.

Case 8.6 Wanda G. was on probation for possession of cocaine. As part of her probation, she was required to attend counseling sessions at the local community mental health center to help her with her drug addiction and her anxiety symptoms. She had been diagnosed with generalized anxiety disorder. She told her social worker that she had a great deal of difficulty completing tasks at her new job at a cable company, was not sleeping well, worried constantly about violating conditions of her probation, and felt irritable much of the time. Wanda G. claimed that the anti-anxiety medication she was on was not helping her much.

> Wanda G. got into a series of arguments with her boss at work. Wanda G. told her probation officer that her boss was criticizing the quality of her work. Eventually, Wanda G. was fired from her job. She did not report this news to her probation officer. She relapsed and used cocaine.

Posttraumatic stress disorder (PTSD) is a common phenomenon among offenders. A large percentage of offenders have been victims of child abuse, sexual assault, domestic violence, abandonment, and other traumatic events. Their trauma histories are often a contributing factor in their criminal behavior. For example, women who were sexually assaulted as children—which includes a significant percentage of female offenders—sometimes turn to drugs and alcohol to numb the pain and help them cope with the trauma (see chapter 7). Over time their alcohol and drug dependence and use may lead to crime to support their addiction (for example, shoplifting, robbery, prostitution), or they may commit crimes while under the influence.

According to the American Psychiatric Association, trauma survivors who have PTSD respond to traumatic events with intense fear, helplessness, or horror (2000:467). These individuals usually have difficulty concentrating and behave irritably and angrily. These behaviors can lead to interpersonal and domestic conflict and violence, which may lead to arrest and involvement in the criminal justice system; prison inmates with PTSD often have significant disciplinary problems. People who have PTSD are also at high risk of alcohol and substance dependence and abuse, which may exacerbate their poor judgment and unlawful behavior.

Case 8.7   Rhonda V., thirty-two, was sexually abused as a child. Her stepfather performed oral sex on, and had intercourse with, her beginning when she was eleven. The sexual abuse continued until Rhonda V. was fourteen, when her mother and stepfather divorced.

Rhonda V. never told her mother or any other adult about the sexual abuse. For years she kept the details to herself. When she was eighteen, she was diagnosed with depression and attempted to commit suicide. Shortly after her hospitalization Rhonda V. began using cocaine and soon became addicted. Eventually, she was arrested for dealing cocaine. According to Rhonda V., "The high I got from cocaine seemed like the best medicine in the world. It worked better than every depression drug the doctors gave me. It got to the point that I had to get high so I could stop thinking about what my stepfather did to me all those years. To tell you the truth, during those years I didn't care whether I became an addict. What mattered is that I didn't feel the pain. Now I'm thinking differently. I really want to get my kids back [the state child welfare agency placed Rhonda V.'s two children in foster care]. I know I've got to stick with treatment if I'm gonna get my boys back."

CALIBRATION-RECALIBRATION

Ideally, treatment for PTSD should begin soon after the traumatic experience (Scrignar 1996; Seligman 1998). Unfortunately, for most offenders the trauma precedes their arrest by many years. Nonetheless, many offenders can benefit from widely used interventions designed for PTSD survivors. Among the more popular interventions are group therapy and support groups for people who have experienced similar forms of trauma (for example, sexual abuse, domestic violence, witnessing the murder of a parent). Various types of cognitive-behavioral therapy can be effective. For survivors of sexual abuse, for example, a common approach entails helping victims to relive their trauma (by gathering information about the trauma, recalling their responses to the trauma, and discussing the trauma's meaning) and to develop new coping and problem-solving skills. Various forms of anxiety-management training, stress inoculation training, and eye movement desensitization can also be helpful (Knapp and VandeCreek 1994; Richards, Musser, and Gershon 1999; Seligman 1998).

Paraphilias

Individuals who commit sex-related offenses constitute a significant portion of the offender population. Some sex offenders do not manifest symptoms of mental illness, for example, under-the-influence opportunists who simply take advantage of someone sexually. However, many sex offenders have been diagnosed with a serious psychiatric disorder: paraphilia. Paraphilias involve "recurrent, intense sexually arousing fantasies, sexual urges, or behaviors generally involving 1) nonhuman objects, 2) the suffering or humiliation of oneself or one's partner, or 3) children or other nonconsenting persons" (American Psychiatric Association 2000:566). Several prominent paraphilias do not typically lead to arrest, conviction, and a prison sentence (fetishism, exhibitionism, sexual masochism), although several do. The most common paraphilia found in the offender population is pedophilia.

Pedophilia involves sexual activity with a prepubescent child (generally thirteen or younger). Offenders with pedophilia usually report an attraction to children of a particular age range. Some offenders prefer males, some prefer females, and some have no preference. Offenders attracted to females generally prefer younger victims (eight to ten years old), whereas those attracted to males usually prefer older children. Some offenders are attracted only to children (exclusive type), whereas others are attracted to adults as well (nonexclusive type) (American Psychiatric Association 2000; Feierman 1990; Schwarz and Cellini 1995, 1997, 1999).

Offenders with pedophilia engage in a variety of behaviors; they may limit themselves to undressing a child and only looking, or they may expose themselves, masturbate in the child's presence, fondle the child, perform fellatio or cunnilingus on the child, or penetrate the child's mouth, vagina, or anus with their fingers, foreign objects, or penis. Offenders will often try to convince the child that the activities are for educational purposes or accuse the child of being sexually provocative. Victims may include the offender's children by birth, adoptive children, foster children, stepchildren, relatives' children, or children from outside the family (for example, neighborhood children). It is not unusual for offenders to threaten children if they disclose the sexual abuse (Feierman 1990; B. Schwartz and Cellini 1995, 1997, 1999).

In one notorious case a man who went to graduate school to become a clinical social worker sexually abused two minors:

> A social worker who at one time counseled abused children was sentenced yesterday to serve 20 years in prison for sexually assaulting two minors.
>
> Lawrence F. Coleman, 41, of 1540 Douglas Ave., North Providence was sentenced by Judge John F. Sheehan. The judge imposed a 30-year sentence but suspended 10 years.
>
> The victims, who are now adults, were not in any counseling program with Coleman.
>
> One of the victims addressed the court before sentencing. Her voice choked with emotion, she said that the sexual assaults had devastated her and given her low self-esteem. . . .
>
> In January Coleman was arraigned on 10 counts of first degree sexual assault before Superior Court Judge John P. Bourcier. He [Coleman] was freed on $100,000 surety bail. In March he pleaded guilty before Judge Sheehan, who kept bail at the same amount.
>
> Coleman earned a degree in clinical psychology from Rhode Island College in 1981 and another in social work from Boston University in 1984.
>
> He worked as a counselor at a health center in Greenville, counseling children who were victims of physical and sexual abuse. (Crombie 1989:B3)

Some offenders engage in elaborate machinations in order to gain access to children. They may work hard to win the trust of the child's parent, marrying a woman with an attractive child, trading children with other offenders with pedophilia, or arranging to care for foster children (Feierman 1990).

Pedophilia usually begins in adolescence, although the exceptions are many. The recidivism rate is high, especially for offenders who prefer male victims. Many offenders report that they are not distressed about their sexual activities, although many others report extreme guilt, shame, and humiliation. Clinical depression is a common correlate. The vast majority of offenders are male, and the symptoms tend to be chronic and lifelong (American Psychiatric Association 2000; B. Schwartz and Cellini 1995, 1997, 1999; Seligman 1998).

Case 8.8 Bert I., forty-three, was an official in the state child welfare agency. He was responsible for inspecting group homes that provide services to abused and neglected children.

Bert I. was arrested by state police after the proprietor of a motel suspected that Bert I. was abusing minors at the motel. After obtaining a search warrant, state police forced their way into Bert I.'s motel room and found him engaging in sexual activity, and using cocaine, with a twelve-year-old boy who was in the legal custody of the state child welfare agency. Bert I. was sentenced to seven years in prison.

Case 8.9 Herman C., fifty-seven, was married to his third wife, Alice U., thirty-eight. Alice U. had a twelve-year-old daughter, Chelsea. Alice U. typically worked an evening shift at a local hospital, leaving Herman C. alone with Chelsea.

About a year after Herman C. and Alice U. were married, he started to sneak into Chelsea's bedroom at night while Alice U. was at work. At first he only stroked Chelsea's arms and legs while she slept. Over time he began to fondle Chelsea's breasts. Eventually, Herman C. coaxed Chelsea into performing fellatio and having intercourse. He coerced Chelsea into having sexual relations over a four-year period and threatened to harm her if she told her mother.

Case 8.10 Stephen L., twenty-eight, worked in a comics store. He frequently spent his evenings looking at pornographic photographs of young children posted on the Internet.

One afternoon he walked through a large park, looking for young children who were playing alone. Stephen L. approached an eleven-year-old boy and invited him to go to a "secret hideout." He brought the boy to his apartment, showed the boy pornographic videos, performed fellatio on the boy, had the boy perform fellatio on him, and engaged in mutual masturbation. Over a period of six months Stephen L.

recruited a number of other young victims. One victim reported the sexual assault to his father, who notified police. Stephen L. was arrested, convicted, and sentenced to twelve years in prison.

Case 8.11 Mario D. was the special education director of an urban school district. His marriage was failing and he faced mounting pressure at work.

Mario D. contacted a number of young special education students and their mothers and, using a false name and identity, solicited them to pose nude for photographs and to perform sexual acts on videotape. One mother reported Mario D. to the police. He pleaded guilty in criminal court and was sentenced to three years in prison. At his sentencing Mario D. acknowledged that he had suffered for years with a sexual disorder that requires treatment.

CALIBRATION-RECALIBRATION

The treatment of sex offenders has matured tremendously in recent years. Through ambitious research on a wide range of treatment innovations, scholars and practitioners are reaching consensus about the most constructive approach to this daunting challenge. Put simply, the most realistic goal with sex offenders is risk management; cure, in the strict sense of the term, is not likely with most offenders. Some sex offenders are likely to recidivate no matter how comprehensive and sophisticated the treatment programs and supervision are. Some recidivists will harm victims violently, some will commit new sex offenses, and some will recidivate by committing other crimes that are not sexual. In one compelling study of a sample of rapists and child molesters assessed at a maximum-security psychiatric facility (Quinsey 1998), 28 percent were later convicted of a new sex offense, 40 percent were arrested or returned for a violent or sexual offense, and 57 percent were arrested or returned for any offense (the percentages reflect several ways of grouping the same sample).

Research suggests that certain sex offenders are more likely to recidivate than others. Key risk factors include the number of previous sex offenses, gender of the victim, relationship of the victim to the offender, offender's marital status, and offender's age. Homosexual child molesters have the highest recidivism rates and incest offenders (primarily father-daughter incest) the lowest (Quinsey 1998; B. Schwartz and Cellini 1995, 1997, 1999).

Treatment and supervision resources need to focus on higher-risk offenders. Three approaches are prominent. The first is pharmacological, in which offenders are given drugs—antiandrogens (such as medroxyprogesterone acetate or DepoProvera)—to reduce their sexual arousability and the frequency of sexual fantasies. The second approach is psychotherapeutic, or evocative, where the focus is on enhancing offenders' empathy for their victims, identifying triggers for the undesirable behaviors, and developing a sense of responsibility for their offenses. Finally, the cognitive-behavioral approach seeks to address offenders' skill deficits (for example, relationship and interpersonal skills); change their ways of thinking (cognitions) that are believed to be related to sexual offending; reduce the stress that triggers offending; introduce aversives that pair paraphilic urges and fantasies with negative experiences such as electric shocks or noxious odors; and alter deviant patterns of sexual arousal or preference (Feierman 1990; Flora 2001; Seligman 1998). In general, insight-oriented, nondirective, and nonconfrontational approaches to sex offender treatment have not been effective and may even exacerbate the risk of recidivism. Better results have been achieved with programs that promote anticrime attitudes among offenders and help them develop more refined problem-solving and self-management skills. Quinsey argues that his comprehensive review of research on sex offender treatment demonstrates that "there is no identifiable "gold standard" treatment that could be adopted for use without further evaluation" (1998:415).

Professionals who specialize in the treatment of sex offenders generally agree that high-quality supervision, sometimes in the form of electronic monitoring, and skill development, are essential to prevent re-offending:

> Based on the correctional treatment literature, characteristics of programs that have some hope of success in reducing recidivism include the following: a skill-based training approach; the modeling of prosocial behaviors and attitudes; a directive but nonpunitive orientation; a focus on modifying antecedents to criminal behavior; a supervised community component in order to assess and teach the offender relevant skills; and a high-risk clientele.
>
> Characteristics of programs that are likely to be ineffective or associated with increased recidivism include these: confrontation without skill building; a nondirective approach; a punitive orientation; a focus on irrelevant (noncriminogenic) factors (e.g., building an offender's self-esteem without modifying his procriminal attitudes; Wormith 1984); and the use of highly sophisticated verbal therapies, such as insight-oriented psychotherapy. (Quinsey 1998:417)

Mental Retardation

Some offenders get into difficulty because of their limited intelligence and cognitive ability. Because they function at a relatively low level, these offenders are particularly impressionable and vulnerable to pressure from individuals and groups. They are sometimes known as "naive" offenders.

Technically, these offenders are typically diagnosed as having mental retardation and related developmental disabilities. The diagnosis of mental retardation applies when an individual has an intelligence quotient (IQ) of approximately 70 or below, as measured by standardized tests such as Wechsler Intelligence Scales and the Stanford-Binet (American Psychiatric Association 2000; Beirne-Smith, Patton, and Ittenbach 2001; Jongsma and Slaggert 2000). Offenders diagnosed with mental retardation typically manifest deficits or impairments in adaptive functioning (the individual's ability to meet the standards expected for his or her age) related to communication, self-care, home living, social and interpersonal skills, use of community resources, self-direction, functional academic skills, work, leisure, health, and safety.

In the offender population one is most likely to encounter individuals with mild mental retardation, as opposed to individuals with moderate, severe, and profound mental retardation. Mild mental retardation is roughly equivalent to what was once referred to as the educational category of "educable," which constitutes about 85 percent of individuals who are diagnosed with mental retardation. By their late teenage years these individuals usually acquire academic skills up to approximately the sixth-grade level. As adults they usually develop sufficient social and vocational skills to support themselves, although they may need supervision, guidance, and assistance (American Psychiatric Association 2000; Beirne-Smith, Patton, and Ittenbach 2001; Jacobson and Mulick 1996; Jongsma and Slaggert 2000).

Case 8.12 Jimmy K., twenty-five, was arrested by local police after a neighbor saw him and several other young men setting fires in a park. The group burned down a large storage shed.

Jimmy K. dropped out of school in the ninth grade. He spent most of his school years in special education classes and received supportive or resource services. Jimmy K. struggled academically and socially; he had an IQ of 60. He had few friends and always got excited when others invited him to join them in activities. One of Jimmy K.'s teenage neighbors had invited Jimmy K. to join the group that was headed to the park to set fires.

Case 8.13 Marla F., thirty-one, spent most of her childhood in foster homes and group homes. Her single mother abandoned her when she was six. According to child welfare records, both mother and daughter had been diagnosed with mild mental retardation.

Marla F. had been living in a supervised apartment funded by a state agency. She also worked at a local nursery, caring for plants and flowers. At the nursery Marla F. met another young woman with mild developmental disabilities. Both were arrested for using cocaine and trying to sell the drug to an undercover police officer.

CALIBRATION-RECALIBRATION

Offenders diagnosed with mild mental retardation are often cooperative, congenial, and eager to comply with treatment recommendations and supervision. Their earnestness sometimes exceeds their ability to comply with rules, regulations, and treatment protocols. Hence close supervision, monitoring, supportive services, and comprehensive case management are important (Beirne-Smith, Patton, and Ittenbach 2001; Jacobson and Mulick 1996).

Treatment of offenders with mild mental retardation typically focuses explicitly on practical, basic problem-solving skills. Emphasis is usually on helping these offenders to identify their problems, generate alternative solutions, evaluate their options, and implement steps designed to address problems (Seligman 1998). Individual, family, and group counseling can be quite effective. Individual counseling often uses standard behavioral interventions to help offenders develop basic skills related to, for example, taking a bus, shopping, budgeting, working, and maintaining relationships. With some individuals psychotropic medication may be appropriate to address problems related to aggression, agitation, and hyperactivity associated with mental retardation.

Comprehensive case management is key. Jimmy K., for example, spent a short time in prison and then was paroled to electronic monitoring. He functioned at a fairly high level, which enabled Jimmy K. to comply with a number of parole requirements, such as contacting his parole counselor regularly, working, and attending group therapy sessions at a community mental health center. Jimmy K. occasionally violated his curfew requirement, usually because of his confusion about schedules and time management. His parole counselor helped Jimmy K. develop a rigid schedule to minimize misunderstanding; the counselor was reluctant to return Jimmy K. to prison for violating curfew, especially in light of his disability.

Marla F., who was convicted of drug possession and distribution, posed more of a challenge. In principle every offender who is convicted of a drug-related offense should be required to participate in some kind of drug education or drug treatment program. During her prison stay Marla F. was unable to participate meaningfully in the institution's drug treatment program. Marla F. had difficulty following group discussions and was reluctant to share her experiences or opinions with others in the group. Marla F. had only a limited ability to understand instructional information about drug dependence and abuse. The prison social services staff eventually assigned a substance abuse specialist to work with Marla F. individually. Although this strategy was unprecedented in this particular prison system, it was the only realistic way to help Marla F. address her substance abuse issues at a level commensurate with her ability to understand. The parole board and staff needed to revise their expectations, considering the extent and nature of Marla F.'s disability. She was paroled to a highly structured, outpatient drug treatment program.

Dissociative Disorders

Occasionally, offenders present with what are known as dissociative disorders, which entail "a disruption in the usually integrated functions of consciousness, memory, identity, or perception" (American Psychiatric Association 2000:519). The range of dissociative disorders is broad. They can take the form of problems with memory (dissociative amnesia); sudden and unexpected travel away from home or work, accompanied by an inability to recall one's past and confusion about personal identity or the assumption of a new identity (dissociative fugue); a persistent or recurring feeling of being detached from one's mental processes or body (depersonalization disorder); and the presence of two or more distinct identities or personality states that recurrently take control of the one's behavior, accompanied by an inability to recall important personal information that is too extensive to be explained by ordinary forgetfulness (dissociative identity disorder, formerly known as multiple personality disorder) (American Psychiatric Association 2000; Kluft and Fine 1993; Piper 1996; Ross 1996).

Cases involving dissociative identity disorder are perhaps the most common dissociative disorder among offenders, although it is rare. Offenders who are able to convince a judge or jury of their dissociative identity disorder at the time of the crime may be found not guilty by reason of insanity and committed to a psychiatric hospital for treatment. Others mount the insanity defense but fail to win a verdict in their favor; they may be sent to prison, where, ideally, their symptoms are treated to the greatest extent possible.

Offenders who are diagnosed with dissociative identity disorder cope with the presence of two or more distinct identities or personalities that take control of their behavior (Haddock 2001; Spira and Yalom 1996). According to the American Psychiatric Association, dissociative identity disorder reflects a failure to integrate various aspects of identity, memory, and consciousness (2000:526). Individuals with this disorder experience each personality as if it has a distinct personal history, self-image, identity, and name. Typically, the sufferer has a primary identity that carries the individual's given name and is passive, dependent, guilty, and depressed. The "alternate" identities usually have different names and characteristics that are quite different from the primary identity's. The individual may assume unique identities in specific circumstances; these identities, or personalities, may differ in reported age and gender, vocabulary, general knowledge, or mood. The individual may experience the alternate identities as taking control in sequence, at each other's expense; the identities may deny knowledge of one another, be critical of one another, or appear to be in open conflict. At times one or more powerful identities may allocate time to the others. Aggressive or hostile identities may interrupt activities or place the others in uncomfortable situations.

Offenders who have been diagnosed with dissociative identity disorder frequently report histories of severe physical and sexual abuse, particularly during childhood. They often report symptoms similar to posttraumatic stress disorder (for example, nightmares, flashbacks, and startle responses). Some individuals engage in self-mutilation, suicide attempts, and violent behavior. Research studies show that the disorder is diagnosed three to nine times more often in adult females than in adult males (American Psychiatric Association 2000; Piper 1996; Ross 1996; Seligman 1998).

One of the best-known criminal cases involving dissociative identity disorder is chronicled in Daniel Keyes's *The Minds of Billy Milligan* (1982). Milligan was charged with kidnapping and raping three women. He was acquitted based on the defense that he suffered from what was then known as multiple personality disorder. Evidence and testimony showed that Milligan had twenty-four distinct personalities, including Philip, a petty criminal; Kevin, a drug dealer and robber; April, who wanted to kill Billy Milligan's stepfather; Adalana, who was a shy, lonely lesbian who "used" Billy Milligan's body to rape women; and David, an eight-year-old child. Keyes introduces his observations by describing his first encounters with Billy Milligan:

> When I talked with him alone during visiting hours in his room at the mental hospital, I discovered that Billy, as he came to be called, was very different from the poised young man I'd first met. He now spoke hesitantly, his knees jiggling nervously. His memory was poor, with long periods blanked out by amnesia. He could generalize about those portions of his past that he vaguely recalled, his voice often quavering at painful memories, but he could not provide many details. After trying, vainly, to draw out his experiences, I was ready to give up.

Then one day something startling happened.

Billy Milligan fused completely for the first time, revealing a new individual, an amalgam of all his personalities. The fused Milligan had a clear, almost total recall of all the personalities from their creation—all their thoughts, actions, relationships, tragic experiences and comic adventures.

(1982:viii)

CALIBRATION-RECALIBRATION

Offenders who successfully show that they suffer from dissociative identity disorder may be found not guilty by reason of insanity and hospitalized in a psychiatric facility or, if found guilty, hospitalized in the psychiatric unit of a prison (at least until they are stabilized on medication, at which point they may be returned to the general inmate population).

For offenders who receive treatment, a major goal is to try to help them "integrate" their various personalities. This is generally a long, slow process facilitated by therapists who have specialized training. Therapists also try to help clients improve their overall functioning, resolve important issues in their lives, enhance social relationships and interpersonal skills, and manage their day-to-day lives (Haddock 2001; Seligman 1998; Spira and Yalom 1996). Treatment of posttraumatic stress symptoms is often important, as well. Overall, a significant number of offenders with dissociative identity disorder improve over time with competent, sustained treatment (Kluft and Fine 1993; Ross 1996; Seligman 1998).

Many offenders suffer from a major mental illness. The most common forms of mental illness found in the offender population are schizophrenia and other psychotic disorders, mood disorders (major depression and bipolar disorder), anxiety disorders (panic disorder, posttraumatic stress disorder, generalized anxiety disorder, posttraumatic stress disorder, substance-induced anxiety disorder), paraphilias (sexual disorders, especially pedophilia), and mental retardation. Occasionally, one also encounters offenders diagnosed with a dissociative disorder (particularly dissociative identity disorder).

It is particularly important for criminal justice professionals who work with mentally ill offenders to understand what we know about the biological bases of mental illness, the ways in which mental illness can lead to criminal activity, and various treatment options, including psychopharmacology; individual, family, and group counseling; and options for residential care. Professionals should be especially earnest about arranging for comprehensive supervision and case management of offenders with major mental illness. Close monitoring is the most effective way to enhance these offenders' compliance with treatment and to prevent recidivism.

9

Final Lessons

The premise of my typology of criminal circumstances is that meaningful attempts to address the crime problem must take into consideration the diverse circumstances in offenders' lives that contribute to their criminal conduct. The vast majority of criminal acts arise from offenders' sense of desperation (financial and interpersonal); greed, exploitation, and opportunism; rage; wish for revenge and retribution; eagerness for frolic and entertainment; addictions to alcohol, other drugs, and/or gambling; and mental illness and mental retardation.

Recognition of the circumstances that lead some people to commit crimes should fuel more than intellectual curiosity. It should also be relevant. We can in fact use the typology of criminal circumstances to prevent and control crime.

Crime Prevention

Constructing a blueprint for crime prevention is about as easy as coming up with a blueprint for cancer prevention. No simple solution will suffice because of the many variables and diverse causes. Any realistic and comprehensive approach must acknowledge the daunting task and the myriad variables and factors that we know contribute to the problem.

Also, any worthwhile crime prevention strategy must address both "micro" and "macro" issues. Clearly, many people have mental health–, relationship–, and addiction-related problems that require attention if we are to prevent these problems from leading to crime. This retail approach to crime prevention is absolutely essential. At the same time focusing only on at-risk individuals would be shortsighted. Much of the challenge requires action at a broader societal, structural, or wholesale level with respect to pertinent public policy debates, economic issues, community dynamics, racism, and so on (Shireman and Reamer 1986). With respect to the micro and macro issues, the typology of criminal circumstances provides a useful framework for intervention.

Crimes of Desperation

Clearly, poverty and many individuals' lack of financial resources are at the root of most crimes of desperation, such as theft, embezzlement, shoplifting, and fraud. Of course, no one can provide a magic solution that would give every human adequate means. If only life were so simple.

In a capitalist nation we must recognize that one price that we pay for a free-market economy is that some people will have difficulty participating in the labor market and benefiting from economic growth. Whether poverty is a function of culture, discrimination, economic conditions, or poor education, some individuals are going to struggle economically and reach a point of desperation that leads them to commit crimes. At the broadest level economic and tax reforms designed to redistribute income; high caliber, egalitarian educational and vocational programs; and antipoverty and antidiscrimination programs and policies have the potential to prevent crimes of desperation.

At the individual level programs and services designed to identify individuals at risk and strengthen their ability to compete in the marketplace, by enhancing their educational and vocational skills, are essential. This is not a complicated concept, although implementation often is difficult to achieve. I have encountered countless instances where meaningful education and vocational training have helped a potential offender in chronically desperate circumstances move from the high-risk to the low-risk column. Early and meaningful intervention with schoolage youth is absolutely essential.

Of course, not all crimes of desperation result from financial difficulties. Some owe more to interpersonal factors, where individuals feel caught up in personal circumstances, such as a marital or work-related conflict, that lead them to conclude that they have no choice but to commit a crime. Sadly, in its movies, television shows, and popular press, our culture celebrates, glorifies, and markets violent responses to interpersonal conflict. It should be no great surprise that so many offenders conclude that violence is the appropriate response to disagreement and dispute. Here our task is to educate and train people to resolve problems in their lives constructively, without resorting to crime. Beginning with schoolage children, educators must ensure that people understand that committing crimes such as assault or fraud in order to wiggle out of seemingly desperate circumstances is often counterproductive and self-destructive. Widespread instruction, in schools and by media outlets, in practical problem-solving skills in crisis circumstances could do much to show people that they do have alternatives to crime.

Crimes of Greed, Exploitation, and Opportunism

Crimes of greed, exploitation, and opportunism are among the most intractable, challenging crimes to prevent. Practically speaking, it is difficult to construct comprehensive strategies to make people less greedy, exploitative, and opportunistic. Some people are saddled with characteristics of antisocial personality disorder that are not easily undone. In addition to whatever congenital inclinations that some people may have in this direction or their exposure to poor role models, capitalist cultures tend to exacerbate the problem. Much of our culture communicates the concept that "he who dies with the most toys wins," that the route to happiness and fulfillment is paved in material possessions. Some individuals have such a deep-seated need to acquire toys that they resort to crimes to get them. The intersection of antisocial personality traits and the acquisitive messages embedded in capitalism can be quite toxic.

At an individual level programs designed to confront and challenge criminal thinking and values, and provide reasonable and appealing alternatives, make the most sense. At the societal level we can try to shift the culture's values away from a sense of materialistic entitlement and toward more equitable distribution and communal sharing of resources (Reamer 1993, 1999). This would require a fundamental shift in the broader society's core values—no easy task but one worth pursuing in the context of family life, schools, religious institutions, and the workplace. Ideally, major media outlets—especially the television, music, movie, and news industries—would embark on deliberate and concerted attempts to convey more constructive messages about common human needs and mutual aid. Schools also should make a concerted effort to teach students how to be critical consumers of media messages. These may seem to be hackneyed recommendations, but they are essential.

Crimes of Rage

Crimes of rage—whether they are committed against family members, friends, or strangers—are often committed by people with poor impulse control. Programs and services designed to help at-risk individuals manage their impulses (for example, anger-management programs and domestic violence prevention programs) make the most sense. In some instances psychotropic medication can be a useful adjunct for individuals with biochemical complications that exacerbate their lack of impulse control.

Crimes of Revenge and Retribution

By definition, crimes of revenge and retribution are based on calculated, planned, and vengeful efforts to harm others. Here the challenge has less to do with impulse control and more to do with antisocial personality traits, criminal thinking, and criminal values. The most constructive efforts are those that challenge these attributes and instincts. Counseling programs are a start, but it is also important to avoid popularizing criminal values and thinking in television shows and movies.

Crimes of Frolic

The variable that correlates most highly with crimes of frolic is immaturity. No quick fix exists for this. During the slow process of maturation that ultimately leads most people away from crimes of frolic, programs that challenge criminal thinking and that help younger offenders cultivate insight, empathy, and interpersonal, problem-solving, educational, and vocational skills are most appropriate.

Crimes of Addiction

Without a doubt, programs and policies designed to address alcohol and drug dependence and abuse must be a top priority. In light of the indisputable correlation between the majority of crime and drug and alcohol abuse, we will make no significant progress unless we reduce the availability of addictive drugs, treat addicts and alcoholics ambitiously and competently, and provide meaningful lifestyle and vocational alternatives to drug dealers and abusers. Effective efforts in this arena will have the greatest effect on crime.

We have growing evidence that thoughtfully designed treatment for substance abuse is less expensive than imprisonment and that it reduces recidivism rates. In 1999 approximately 6.3 million adults were under the supervision of corrections personnel, who oversaw their incarceration, parole, or probation. Drug offenders accounted for 21 percent of the states' prison population and 59 percent of the federal prison population; these figures do not include inmates whose crimes were related to drug or alcohol use but who were not convicted of drug-related crimes (Office of National Drug Control

Policy 2001). The National Center on Addiction and Substance Abuse (1998) estimates that of the $38 billion spent on corrections in 1996, more than $30 billion paid for incarcerating inmates who had a history of drug and/or alcohol abuse, were convicted of drug and/or alcohol violations, were using drugs and/or alcohol at the time of their crimes, or had committed their crimes to get money to buy drugs. State corrections officials estimate that 70 to 85 percent of inmates need some level of substance abuse treatment (U.S. General Accounting Office 1991).

The average cost per year to incarcerate an inmate in the United States during this period (1997–98) was approximately $21,000 (the federal average was about $24,000, and the state average was about $20,000), according to the Office of National Drug Control Policy (2001). The National Treatment Improvement Evaluation Study, sponsored by the Substance Abuse and Mental Health Services Administration (1999), reports that the average cost per treatment between 1993 and 1995 was $2,941 and that the average treatment benefit to society was $9,177 per client. This resulted in an average savings of $3 for every dollar spent: every dollar spent on treatment saved society $3 by reducing costs associated with crime—from police to courts to victim compensation to corrections—as well as reduced health care costs and increased earnings by those treated.

Community-based drug and alcohol treatment that is provided to offenders whose cases were handled by a drug court also appears to be cost effective. For example, the drug court operating in Washington, D.C., reports that referring an offender to a treatment program court saves the district $4,065 to $8,845 in incarceration costs and substantially reduces prosecution costs (U.S. Department of Justice 1997). Moreover, a number of studies suggest that drug court participants have lower recidivism rates than comparable drug-involved offenders who go through the regular courts (Office of National Drug Control Policy 2001).

Although compulsive and pathological gambling is not as pervasive, it is a growing and increasingly significant crime-related problem. A comprehensive crime-prevention strategy cannot ignore the expanding reach of gambling and its effect on the crime rate. The evidence is clear and convincing.

Crimes of Mental Illness

Comprehensive mental health services—especially community-based services—are an essential ingredient in a crime-prevention strategy. Major mental illness and mental retardation are significant correlates of the crime problem. Inadequate funding and inferior mental health services add up to a ticking crime bomb. Individuals who suffer from schizophrenia and other psychotic disorders, depression, bipolar disorder, major anxiety and posttraumatic stress, paraphilias, mental retardation, and dissociative disorders sometimes have little, if any, control over their behavior. While most of these individuals do not commit crimes, some do as a direct or indirect result of their psychiatric disability. The combination of assertive supervision, case management, coordination of services, therapeutic programs, and psychotropic medication greatly enhances crime prevention.[1] Mental illness must be diagnosed and treated in childhood, when such symptoms appear, before grossly dysfunctional, destructive, and lifelong behavior patterns are established. In principle, schools can serve as early detection and referral resources for children and their families.

Responding to Crime

No matter how skilled and thoughtful our preventative efforts, some people will commit crimes. We can do our best to reduce the magnitude of the problem, but we will never reduce the incidence to zero.

Among the most significant challenges before us are those related to reforms of the criminal justice system. Historically, criminal justice professionals, legislators, and other public officials have approached crime control rather simplistically: upon conviction, criminals are placed on probation, incarcerated, or paroled. Over time, we have refined and expanded our approach to include a number of creative alternatives, such as diversion programs, restorative justice programs, electronic monitoring, and so forth.

Earlier I introduced the concepts of calibration and recalibration. The overall task is to identify appropriate goals for each offender in light of the individual's crime, the circumstances that led to the crime, criminal history, insight, remorse, dangerousness, family and community support, and rehabilitation prospects (especially the offender's stage of change: precontemplation, contemplation, preparation, action, maintenance). For the typical offender realistic goals include incarceration for public safety purposes, punishment, rehabilitation, and restorative justice. Once goals are established and pursued, periodic recalibration is often necessary in order to keep the offender on track. Recalibration should occur when an offender's life circumstances change significantly (for example, the offender loses a job, separates from a partner, is evicted) or "red flags" emerge (for example, the offender misses an appointment with a probation or parole counselor, expresses concern about relapsing with illegal drugs, violates curfew while on electronic monitoring, or is arrested on a new charge).

Such changes in life circumstances and red flags trigger a new decision point in the risk-management process and provide an opportunity for recalibration and updated risk assessment (Kemshall 2000).

Recalibration should be based on a comprehensive assessment of the offender's current life circumstances. This can be facilitated by use of one or more widely accepted, standardized risk-assessment tools and instruments. One popular instrument is the Level of Service Inventory–Revised (LSI-R) (Andrews and Bonta 1995, 1998; Simourd and Malcolm 1998). This instrument includes fifty-four items that measure ten components of offender risk:

- Criminal history—the nature and extent of the offender's criminal background (for example, number of previous offenses, types of offenses)
- Education and employment—highest level of education, education history, employment history
- Financial resources—sources of income and financial status and stressors
- Family and marital relationships—current family constellation and connections, family history, marital status and history, key relationships and stressors
- Accommodations—housing status and options
- Leisure and recreation—lifestyle choices and patterns related to spending leisure and recreational time
- Companions—nature and extent of social contacts, friends, acquaintances
- Alcohol and drug problems—history and current status of drug and alcohol dependence and abuse
- Emotional and personal—psychiatric status and history, current emotional and personal issues (for example, depression, relationship conflict, impulse control issues)
- Attitudes and orientation—nature of offender's attitudes toward the law, orientation toward criminal thinking and values

A second example of a standardized risk-management tool is the client management classification (CMC) system (Lerner, Arling, and Baird 1986). The CMC is divided into four sections (Harris 1994). An attitude section includes forty-five items concerning the offender's attitude toward the offense, his or her offense pattern, school adjustment, vocational and residential adjustment, family functioning, interpersonal relations, emotions, plans, and perceived problems. The second section focuses on the offender's history, emphasizing his or her legal involvement, medical history, academic achievement, family history, and marital status. The third section focuses on the offender's behavior, including his or her general demeanor, dress, affect, cooperation, and so on. The final section summarizes the criminal justice professional's impressions and provides an opportunity to rate the offender on seven key factors (for example, vocational and educational deficits, criminal value orientation). A major value of such tools is that they facilitate a multifaceted, farsighted view of the whole person within a broad social context. This opens many avenues for diverse, constructive interventions.

At every decision point and calibration-recalibration opportunity, criminal justice professionals should approach each offender with a clear continuum of options in mind, considering (1) factors included in the typology of criminal circumstances (that is, the extent to which the offender presents with issues of desperation; greed, exploitation, and opportunism; rage; revenge and retribution; frolic; addiction; and mental illness or retardation); (2) the potential goals of incarceration for public safety purposes, punishment, rehabilitation, and restorative justice; and (3) the offender's stage of change (precontemplation, contemplation, preparation, action, maintenance).

In some instances an offender's difficulty complying with expectations warrants increased sanctions and supervision; for example, a period of electronic monitoring may be appropriate for a parolee who is having difficulty complying with a treatment program's requirements or who changes residence without permission, whereas a probationer who relapses on drugs may be referred to a residential drug treatment program. In other instances supervision and restrictions may be relaxed to reward offenders who are compliant and doing well (for example, an incarcerated offender may be released on parole to an alcohol treatment program, or a compliant and responsible parolee may be excused from electronic monitoring).

Ideally, every incarcerated offender would be supervised for a reasonable period following release from jail or prison. Allowing offenders to leave prison without any parole or probation supervision serves no one's interests; in most cases leaving prison "cold turkey," with no supervision, is a recipe for failure. No inmate should leave prison without a comprehensive discharge plan that includes thoughtful details related to the inmate's housing, employment, family, mental health, rehabilitation, and other social service needs. The discharge plan, which should be formulated and implemented soon after the offender's incarceration, should be based on systematic and periodic reviews of the inmate's records and interviews with the inmate, family members, potential employers, landlords, and other individuals who are central to the inmate's life. Comprehensive wraparound services—services that address the significant issues in offenders' lives and that involve those most intimately involved in offenders' lives—can do much to reduce the likelihood of recidivism. Sadly, a significant number of inmates are released from prison without such a plan. Imagine walking out of prison after several years of incarceration, with lean family and community connections, empty pockets, a minimum-wage job, and a significant history of mental illness and substance abuse. No wonder nearly half of all released prisoners are rearrested within three years (Reid 1999).

The menu of options for initial calibration, which is rank-ordered from least to most restrictive, includes

> Probation—minimal supervision with referral for appropriate social, mental health, educational, and vocational services
>
> Intensive supervision—probation with more frequent contacts and restrictions (for example, travel and curfew restrictions)
>
> Specialized caseloads—supervision of offenders with common issues, needs, and profiles (for example, sex offenders, compulsive gamblers, offenders who are drug dependent or violent)
>
> Curfew restrictions—requiring offenders to report to their place of residence by a certain time; restricting travel
>
> Electronic monitoring—requiring offenders to wear a locked electronic transmitter that permits their probation and parole supervisors to monitor their whereabouts
>
> Residential programs—residential treatment programs for specialized groups of offenders, for example, sex offenders, offenders who are drug and alcohol dependent, offenders with significant psychiatric disorders
>
> Prison/jail—incarceration in local or county jails, state or federal prisons

If circumstances suggest that a change in sanctions is necessary (either an increase or decrease in supervision and restrictions), criminal justice professionals can select from a wide range of available institutional and community-based sanctions (Carter and Ley 2001:62–63):

> 1. Counseling or reprimand. This is the most common response to minor offenses and minor probation and parole violations. It involves confronting the offender with the apparent violation, listening to his or her side of the story, and delivering a stern admonition or warning.
> 2. Increased reporting requirements. For the probationer or parolee who commits minor violations, such as not keeping appointments or finding full-time employment, the supervising counselor can incre e the frequency of his or her reporting requirements.

3. Loss of travel or other privileges. Supervising counselors can withhold permission for the offender to leave the city, county, or state. They can also impose a curfew.

4. Increased drug and alcohol testing. This is the most common response for the offender who tests positive for drugs or alcohol. The supervising counselor can either increase the frequency of random drug tests or place the offender on a more frequent, fixed testing schedule.

5. Treatment and education referrals. Supervisors should refer offenders to appropriate treatment and rehabilitation programs (usually alcohol, drug, and mental health programs) whenever the need arises. They should also refer offenders for educational and vocational education programs to enhance their knowledge and skills.

6. Restructuring payments. Offenders' payment plans (e.g., restitution, victim compensation, fines, probation fees, child support) may require adjustment when parolees lose a job, become disabled, or have their employment hours reduced.

7. Extension of supervision. In some jurisdictions staff may petition the court to extend supervision of the client who has not complied with all conditions.

8. Community service. This is an appropriate sanction to use as punishment, to hold the offender accountable, or as a restorative justice option.

9. Electronic monitoring. This option is appropriate for offenders who require close supervision but not incarceration.

10. Drug and alcohol treatment. Supervisors should refer offenders with significant drug or alcohol problems to appropriate outpatient and residential programs.

11. Intensive probation and parole supervision. Some offenders do not require incarceration but do require strict supervision. Intensive supervision entails frequent contacts, strict schedules, and close monitoring. This may be combined with other sanctions (for example, frequent drug testing, electronic monitoring).

12. Incarceration. Offenders who commit serious crimes, consistently violate probation or parole conditions, or commit new crimes while on probation or parole may require incarceration for punitive and public safety purposes. Some jurisdictions have introduced daytime incarceration centers (offenders return home at the end of each day, a system that provides close supervision without the cost of twenty-four-hour institutional care).

Criminal justice professionals should always keep in mind that options available at the time of calibration and recalibration exist on a continuum from less to more restrictive. Supervisors should impose sanctions incrementally, based on the relevant goals, the offender's stage of change, and the offender's risk-assessment profile. The use of intermediate sanctions—those sanctions between "the harshness of prison and the laxity of regular probation" (Reitz 1998:557)—should be a guiding principle at every decision point. Common intermediate sanctions include intensive supervision, house arrest and electronic monitoring, drug and alcohol treatment programs, day reporting centers, community service, and monetary penalties and fines (Burke 2001a, 2001b; Byrne, Lurigio, and Petersilia 1992; A. Klein 1997; Langan 1994; Petersilia 1998).

Substantial empirical evidence demonstrates that "recidivism rates (for new crimes) of offenders sentenced to well-managed intermediate sanctions do not differ significantly from those of comparable offenders receiving other sentences" (Tonry 1998:685). However, if offenders referred to intermediate sanction programs are not screened carefully, risk to the public and costs can increase as a result of the referral of inappropriate offenders. Typically, programs that offer intermediate sanctions are designed neither for offenders who pose a serious threat to public safety (for example, offenders convicted of violent crimes) nor for offenders who pose little threat to public safety and who require minimal supervision (for example, people convicted of failure to pay child support or traffic fines). Based on his comprehensive survey of intermediate sanction programs, Tonry concludes that,

1. For offenders who do not present unacceptable risks of violence, well-managed intermediate sanctions offer a cost-effective way to keep them in the community with no greater risk of criminality in the future.
2. Intermediate sanctions can be misused when judges have complete discretion at the time of sentencing—clear sentencing guidelines and benchmarks may reduce judges' inappropriate use of intermediate sanctions.
3. Intermediate sanctions may offer promise as a way to get and keep offenders in drug and other treatment programs
4. Community service and monetary penalties remain woefully underdeveloped in the United States; Americans could learn much from the experiences of European countries, which have been much more ambitious in their use of various forms of community and individual restitution (for example, requiring offenders to work in community-based programs for people with disabilities, to help maintain public buildings and property, and to pay restitution to crime victims).

5. Intermediate sanctions are unlikely to come into widespread use as prison alternatives unless sentencing theories and policies become more expansive and move away from oversimplified ideas about proportionality in punishment. (1998:704)

The linchpin in successful work with offenders—at the time of calibration and recalibration—is understanding and appreciating each offender's readiness for change and enhancing the conditions that will promote individual change. Extensive empirical research on the stages-of-change model suggests that ten key variables influence the processes of change (Prochaska, Norcross, and DiClemente 1995; Prochaska and Velicer 1997; Velicer et al. 1998). The first five are classified as experiential processes and are used primarily in the earlier stages of change (precontemplation, contemplation, and preparation). The last five are called behavioral processes and are used primarily in the later stages (action and maintenance).

1. Consciousness raising involves increasing the awareness of offenders about the causes, consequences, and cures for a particular problem behavior. Interventions that can increase awareness include feedback, education, confrontation, and interpretation. For example, it is important for perpetrators of domestic violence to learn about the dynamics that trigger their behavior and the effect that it has on their victims. Similarly, offenders involved in white-collar crime should be confronted with the consequences of their actions and be helped to appreciate the repercussions of their offenses.

2. "Dramatic relief" produces increased emotional experiences, followed by reduced affect (emotional experience), if the offender can take appropriate action. Psychodrama, role playing, grieving, and personal testimonies are examples of techniques that can move people emotionally. These techniques are particularly appropriate for offenders convicted of crimes of violence and crimes involving one or more forms of addiction.

3. Environmental re-evaluation combines both affective (emotional) and cognitive assessments of how the presence or absence of a personal habit or behavior affects one's social environment. It can also include the awareness that one can serve as a positive or negative role model for others. Empathy training and family interventions can lead to such reassessments. This form of assessment is particularly appropriate for offenders who have some capacity for insight and personal reflection. For example, offenders convicted of breaking and entering, drunk driving, embezzlement, or automobile theft can be helped to

empathize with their victims and to begin to understand how their behavior influences other people in their lives (their children, for example). Some offenders—especially those with symptoms of antisocial personality disorder and narcissism—may have difficulty carrying out this kind of self-assessment.

4. Social liberation requires an increase in social opportunities or alternatives, especially for people who are economically disadvantaged or oppressed. Advocacy, empowerment procedures, and appropriate policies can produce increased opportunities (related to, for example, job and educational training and opportunities, mental health services, and services and housing for abused women). This process is especially useful for perpetrators of crimes of desperation, for whom meaningful jobs and educational opportunities provide genuine alternatives to criminal conduct.

5. Self-re-evaluation combines both cognitive and affective assessments of one's self-image with and without a particular unhealthy habit or behavior, such as one's image as a criminal or abusive person. Values clarification and healthy role models can be effective. Once again, this process is particularly useful with offenders who have the ability to reflect on their own conduct and its effect on others. It is less useful with offenders who are narcissistic and antisocial.

6. Stimulus control removes cues for unhealthy habits and behaviors and adds prompts for more constructive, healthier alternatives. This process is particularly important for the large number of offenders who have an addiction to alcohol, drugs, or gambling. Avoidance (for example, staying away from bars, neighborhoods with a lot of drug activity, gambling casinos, and acquaintances who are addicts) and self-help groups can provide stimuli that support change and reduce risks for relapse.

7. Helping relationships combine caring, trust, openness, and acceptance as well as support for the constructive, healthy behavior change. Rapport building, a therapeutic alliance, access to counselors, and buddy systems can be valuable sources of social support. This is an essential component of nearly every successful effort with offenders.

8. Counterconditioning requires the learning of healthier behaviors that can substitute for problem behaviors (such as domestic violence, drug and alcohol use, shoplifting). Relaxation techniques can counter the stress and conflict that some offenders experience in their intimate relationships; assertion can counter peer pressure (for example, related to crimes of frolic or gang activity); and constructive social activity (sports and other recreational activities) can counter alcohol and drug use.

9. Reinforcement management provides consequences for taking steps in a particular direction. While reinforcement management can include the use of punishments (for example, the use of electronic monitoring or incarceration), people who are changing rely on rewards much more than punishments. Concrete rewards (such as the removal of electronic monitoring and later curfews for individuals on probation or parole); positive recognition by individuals (for example, a probation officer, parole officer, or judge) and groups (members of support and therapy groups); and positive self-statements are ways to increase reinforcement and the probability that the offender will repeat positive, law-abiding behaviors.

10. Self-liberation is both the belief that one can change and the commitment and recommitment to act on that belief. Personal resolutions and public testimonies (for example, before family, friends, and support group members) can promote self-liberation or "willpower" related to problematic behaviors such as drug and alcohol use, gambling, and domestic violence.

The task facing criminal justice professionals in their efforts to promote and facilitate change—both individual change and reforms in the criminal justice system and broader society—is substantial. We have learned a great deal over the centuries about the nature of criminal behavior and its causes. We have replaced antiquated theories with an impressive collection of insightful perspectives on etiology that take into account far more than offenders' free will and body types. Especially in recent years we have expanded our understanding of the potentially powerful influence of diverse psychological, familial, economic, community, cultural, biological, and organizational factors. We have also greatly enhanced our repertoire of necessary and constructive responses to crime, including the traditional use of imprisonment, probation, and parole and more innovative options such as day reporting centers, electronic monitoring, mediation, restitution, and community service.

The enduring challenge is to pursue crime prevention and control thoughtfully, in the truest sense of the term, and in a principled fashion. We must dispense with our instinct to always respond to crime impulsively and severely. Instead we must intervene with constant consideration and balancing of the fundamental goals of incarceration for public safety, punishment, rehabilitation, and restorative justice; offenders' stage of change; and a deep-seated sense of fairness. In the end justice will be served only when our prevention of, and response to, crime is proportionate and just.

1. First Lessons

1. As a member of the Rhode Island Parole Board, I have met with many crime victims. The board formally and routinely invites all crime victims to meet with the board to discuss the circumstances of their victimization and their feelings about whether the inmate should be paroled.

I based my extensive review of cases on widely accepted qualitative research methods. These steps involve (1) logging data about the criminal offense and the circumstances leading up to it (e.g., drug addiction, domestic dispute, mental illness, debt), (2) developing a code book, (3) conducting first-level coding, based on identifying initial conceptual units and placing them into categories, (4) conducting second-level coding, during which I created broader conceptual categories, and (5) looking for meaning and relationships in the data (see Holosko 2001; Reamer 1998; Sherman and Reid 1994; Unrau and Coleman 1997).

2. For discussion of grounded theory and its relationship to qualitative research, see B. Glaser and Strauss (1967) and Strauss and Corbin (1990).

3. Many competent discussions are available for curious readers: Barkan (2000); Bernard, Vold, and Snipes (2002); Crutchfield, Kurbrin, and Bridges (2000); Gottfredson and Hirschi (1990); Hagan (1990); Reid (1999); Schmalleger (2001); Sheley (2000); Siegel (2000); Wilson and Petersilia (1995).

4. The free will–determinism debate actually has ancient philosophical roots. Empedocles and Heraclitus, for example, are early sources of pre-Socratic thought on the meaning of determinism in nature and the idea of natural law. Ideas about determinism—especially the influence of divine will—became prominent later, in the fourth century B.C., promoted by the Stoics, the Greek school of philosophy founded by Zeno. The origins of modern-world debate about free will and determinism ordinarily are traced to the work of the eighteenth-century French astronomer Pierre-Simon Laplace. For a more complete discussion, see Dworkin (1970), Feinberg (1970), Hospers (1966), Nagel (1970), Smart (1970), and Taylor (1963).

5. A prominent biblical reference to retribution appears in Deuteronomy 13:11. Stoning is the most common form of capital punishment in the Bible. People who witnessed

the offender's crime were the first to cast stones, followed by the rest of the people. "Punishment by stoning enabled the entire public to participate and thereby express its outrage against the crime" (Lieber 2001:1070). In a modern-day version of public shaming we sometimes see the calculated orchestration of what is known in law enforcement circles as the "perp walk," where newly arrested, high-profile suspects are paraded in handcuffs in front of a phalanx of newspaper photographers and television camera people (tipped to be there by prosecutors or police) as a way to humiliate the accused wrongdoers and publicize their alleged misdeeds and culpability. This public relations strategy, which has retributivist overtones, is quite deliberate (Fineman and Isikoff 2002).

6. Day reporting centers are offices staffed by corrections, probation, or parole staffers to whom an offender must report every day.

2. Crimes of Desperation

1. In fact, Mollicone was already involved to some extent in the action stage. During his prison stay he had become actively involved in a structured program in which a small number of inmates met in the prison with groups of students in order to discuss what the inmates had learned about their poor decisions in life.

4. Crimes of Rage

1. Attention deficit/hyperactivity disorder is often correlated with other diagnoses, such as depression, bipolar disorder, anxiety disorders, conduct disorders, various learning disabilities, and substance dependence and abuse.

5. Crimes of Revenge and Retribution

1. Paranoid personality disorder must be distinguished from other, more severe, psychiatric disorders: delusional disorder (persecutory type) and schizophrenia (paranoid type). I will discuss these more serious disorders in chapter 8.

6. Crimes of Frolic

1. Amir's research focused on perpetrators of gang rape. His comments about stages in groups' behavior seem relevant to crimes of frolic as well.

7. Crimes of Addiction

1. Lifetime prevalence refers to the percentage of the population that is diagnosed at some point during their lifetime.

2. The dialogue that follows is excerpted from actual courtroom transcripts, edited lightly for clarity and to preserve anonymity.

9. Final Lessons

1. A growing body of empirical evidence shows that community-based mental health treatment can offer a clinically effective and cost-effective alternative to institutional care for people with chronic mental illness (see Essock, Frisman, and Kontos 1998; Rosenheck and Neale 1998; Rosenheck, Neale, and Frisman 1995; Spiegel 1999).

Abadinsky, Howard. 1985. *Organized Crime.* 2d ed. Chicago: Nelson-Hall.

Abrahamsen, David. 1960. *The Psychology of Crime.* New York: Columbia University Press.

Abrams, Karen M. and Gail Erlick Robinson. 2002. "Occupational Effects of Stalking." *Canadian Journal of Psychiatry* 47(5): 468–72.

Alarid, Leanne Fiftal, James W. Marquart, Velmer S. Burston Jr., Francis T. Cullen, and Steven J. Cuvelier. 1996. "Women's Roles in Serious Offenses: A Study of Adult Felons." *Justice Quarterly* 13: 431–54.

Albanese, Jay S. 1989. *Organized Crime in America.* 2d ed. Cincinnati, Ohio: Anderson.

American Psychiatric Association. 2000. *DSM-IV-TR: Diagnostic and Statistical Manual of Mental Disorders.* 4th ed. Washington, D.C.: Author.

Amir, Menachem. 1971. *Patterns in Forcible Rape.* Chicago: University of Chicago Press.

Andrews, D. A. and James Bonta. 1995. *The Level of Service Inventory–Revised.* Toronto: Multi-Health Systems.

———. 1998. *The Psychology of Criminal Conduct.* 2d ed. Cincinnati, Ohio: Anderson.

Asch, Solomon E. 1951. "Effects of Group Pressures Upon the Modification and Distortion of Judgment." In Harold Guetzkow, ed., *Groups, Leadership, and Man,* 177–90. Pittsburgh: Carnegie Press.

Ball, John, Lawrence Rosen, John Flueck, and David N. Narco. 1982. "Lifetime Criminality of Heroin Addicts in the United States." *Journal of Drug Issues* 12:225–39.

Barkan, Steven. 2000. *Criminology: A Sociological Understanding.* Englewood Cliffs, N.J.: Prentice Hall.

Barkley, Russell A. and Kevin R. Murphy. 1998. *Attention-Deficit Hyperactivity Disorder.* New York: Guilford.

Beccaria, Cesare. 1963. *On Crimes and Punishments.* Translated by Henry Paolucci. 1764. Reprint, Indianapolis, Ind.: Bobbs-Merrill.

Beck, Allen J. and Paige M. Harrison. 2001. "Prisoners in 2000." *Bureau of Justice Statistics Bulletin,* August, pp. 1–66.

Becker, Howard S. 1963. *Outsiders: Studies in the Sociology of Deviance.* New York: Free Press.

————, ed. 1964. *The Other Side: Perspectives on Deviance.* New York: Free Press.

Beirne-Smith, Mary, James R. Patton, and Richard F. Ittenbach. 2001. *Mental Retardation.* Englewood Cliffs, N.J.: Prentice Hall.

Belknap, Joanne. 1996. *Invisible Woman: Gender, Crime, and Justice.* Belmont, Calif.: Wadsworth.

Bentham, Jeremy. 1973. *An Introduction to the Principles of Morals and Legislation.* 1789. Reprint, New York: Anchor.

Bequai, August. 1979. *Organized Crime: The Fifth Estate.* Lexington, Mass.: D. C. Heath.

Bernard, Thomas J., George B. Vold, and Jeffrey B. Snipes. 2002. *Theoretical Criminology.* 2d ed. New York: Oxford University Press.

Bies, Robert J. and Thomas M. Tripp. 1996. "Beyond Distrust: 'Getting Even' and the Need for Revenge." In Roderick M. Kramer and Tom T. Tyler, eds., *Trust in Organizations: Frontiers of Theory and Research,* 246–60. Thousand Oaks, Calif.: Sage.

Bies, Robert J., Thomas M. Tripp, and Roderick M. Kramer. 1997. "At the Breaking Point: Cognitive and Social Dynamics of Revenge in Organizations." In Robert A. Giacalone and Jerald Greenberg, eds., *Antisocial Behavior in Organizations,* 18–36. Thousand Oaks, Calif.: Sage.

Blaszczynski, Alex and Derrick Silove. 1995. "Cognitive and Behavioral Therapies for Pathological Gambling." *Journal of Gambling Studies* 11:195–220.

Bloch, Herbert A. and Gilbert Geis. 1970. *Man, Crime, and Society.* 2d ed. New York: Random House.

Blume, Sheila. 1995. "Pathological Gambling." *British Medical Journal* 311:522–23.

Bonger, Willem. 1969. *Criminality and Economic Conditions.* 1910. Reprint, Bloomington, Ind.: Indiana University Press.

Bradford, John M. 1982. "Arson: A Clinical Study." *Canadian Journal of Psychiatry* 27(3): 188–93.

Braithwaite, John. 1998. "Restorative Justice." In Michael Tonry, ed., *The Handbook of Crime and Punishment,* 323–44. New York: Oxford University Press.

Brewer, Ann M. 2000. "Road Rage: What, Who, When, Where, and How?" *Transport Reviews* 20(1): 49–64.

Brissett-Chapman, Sheryl. 1995. "Child Abuse and Neglect: Direct Practice." In Richard L. Edwards, ed., *Encyclopedia of Social Work,* 19th ed., 1:353–66. Washington, D.C.: National Association of Social Workers.

Burgess, Ernest W. 1925. "The Growth of the City." In Robert E. Park, Ernest W. Burgess, and Robert D. McKenzie, eds., *The City,* 47–62. Chicago: University of Chicago Press.

Burke, Peggy. 2001a. "Beyond the Continuum of Sanctions: A Menu of Outcome-Based Interventions." In Madeline M. Carter, ed., *Responding to Parole and Probation Violations,* 77–81. Silver Spring, Md.: Center for Effective Public Policy.

————. 2001b. "Probation and Parole Violations: An Overview of Critical Issues." In Madeline M. Carter, ed., *Responding to Parole and Probation Violations,* 5–12. Silver Spring, Md.: Center for Effective Public Policy.

Byrne, James M., Arthur J. Lurigio, and Joan Petersilia, eds. 1992. *Smart Sentencing: The Emergence of Intermediate Sanctions.* Newbury Park, Calif.: Sage.

Callahan, Sidney. 1997. "Oh, Behave!" *Commonweal* 126(22): 8–9.

Campbell, Bruce A. 1980. "A Theoretical Approach to Peer Influence in Adolescent Socialization." *American Journal of Political Science* 24(2): 324–44.

Carpenter, William A. and Edwin P. Hollander. 1982. "Overcoming Hurdles to Independence in Groups." *Journal of Social Psychology* 117:237–41.

Carter, Madeline M. and Ann Ley. 2001. "Making It Work: Developing Tools to Carry Out the Policy." In Madeline M. Carter, ed., *Responding to Parole and Probation Violations,* 51–71. Silver Spring, Md.: Center for Effective Public Policy.

Chambliss, William J. 1975. "Toward a Political Economy of Crime." *Theory and Society* 2:152–53.

Chesney-Lind, Meda. 1989. "Girls' Crime and Woman's Place: Toward a Feminist Model of Female Delinquency." *Crime and Delinquency* 35(1): 5–29.

Clinard, Marshall B. and Richard Quinney. 1973. *Criminal Behavior Systems: A Typology.* 2d ed. New York: Holt, Rinehart and Winston.

Clinard, Marshall B., Richard Quinney, and John Wildeman. 1994. *Criminal Behavior Systems: A Typology.* 3d ed. Cincinnati, Ohio: Anderson.

Cloward, Richard and Lloyd Ohlin. 1960. *Delinquency and Opportunity: A Theory of Delinquent Gangs.* New York: Free Press.

Cohen, Albert K. 1955. *Delinquent Boys.* New York: Free Press.

Craske, Michelle G. 1999. *Anxiety Disorders: Psychological Approaches to Theory and Treatment.* Boulder, Colo.: Westview.

Crombie, Dave. 1989. "Social Worker Sentenced in Assaults." *Providence (Rhode Island) Journal-Bulletin,* April 20, p. B3.

Crutchfield, Robert D., Charles Kubrin, and George S. Bridges, eds. 2000. *Crime.* Thousand Oaks, Calif.: Pine Forge Press.

Custer, Robert L. and Harry Milt. 1985. *When Luck Runs Out: Help for Compulsive Gamblers and their Families.* New York: Warner Brothers.

Daly, Kathleen. 1994. *Gender, Crime, and Punishment.* New Haven, Conn.: Yale University Press.

———. 1998. "Gender, Crime, and Criminology." In Michael Tonry, ed., *The Handbook of Crime and Punishment,* 85–108. New York: Oxford University Press.

Darwin, Charles. 1963. *On the Origin of the Species by Means of Natural Selection.* 1859. Reprint, New York: Heritage.

Davis, Liane V. 1995. "Domestic Violence." In Richard L. Edwards, ed., *Encyclopedia of Social Work,* 19th ed., 1:780–89. Washington, D.C.: National Association of Social Workers.

Deffenbacher, Jerry, Maureen E. Huff, Rebekah S. Lynch, Eugene R. Oetting, and Natalie Salvatore. 2000. "Characteristics and Treatment of High-Anger Drivers." *Journal of Counseling Psychology* 47(1): 5–17.

Denno, Deborah W. 1994. "Gender, Crime, and the Criminal Law Defenses." *Journal of Criminal Law and Criminology* 85:80–180.

Dickerson, Mary and Ellen Baron. 2000. "Contemporary Issues and Future Directions for Research into Pathological Gambling." *Addiction* 95(8): 1145–59.

Ditton, Paula M. 1999. *Mental Health and Treatment of Inmates and Probationers.* Washington, D.C.: U.S. Department of Justice, Bureau of Justice Statistics.

Douglas, Scott C. and Mark J. Martinko. 2001. "Exploring the Role of Individual Differences in the Prediction of Workplace Aggression." *Journal of Applied Psychology* 86(4): 547–59.

Dugdale, Robert. 1877. *The Jukes: A Study in Crime, Pauperism, and Heredity.* New York: Putnam.

Dukes, Richard L., Stephanie L. Clayton, Lessie T. Jenkins, Thomas L. Miller, and Susan E. Rodgers. 2001. "Effects of Aggressive Driving and Driver Characteristics on Road Rage." *Social Science Journal* 38(2): 323–31.

Durkheim, Emile. 1951. *Suicide*. New York: Free Press.

———. 1964. *The Division of Labor in Society*. New York: Free Press.

Duster, Troy. 1970. *The Legislation of Morality*. New York: Free Press.

Dworkin, Gerald, ed. 1970. *Determinism, Free Will, and Moral Responsibility*. Englewood Cliffs, N.J.: Prentice-Hall.

Edelhertz, Herbert. 1970. *The Nature, Impact, and Prosecution of White-Collar Crime*. Report prepared for the National Institute of Law Enforcement and Criminal Justice. Washington, D.C.: U.S. Government Printing Office.

Ellison, Patricia A., John McGovern, Herbert L. Petri, and Michael H. Figler. 1995. "Anonymity and Aggressive Driving Behavior: A Field Study." *Journal of Social Behavior and Personality* 10:265–72.

Ellison, Phyllis Anne Teeter and Sam Goldstein. 2002. "Poor Self-Control and How It Impacts Relationships." *Attention!* April, pp. 19–23.

Essock, Susan M., Linda K. Frisman, and Nina J. Kontos. 1998. "Cost Effectiveness of Assertive Community Treatment Teams." *American Journal of Orthopsychiatry* 68(2): 179–90.

Everett, Craig A. and Sandra Volgy Everett. 1999. *Family Therapy for ADHD*. New York: Guilford.

Ezorsky, Gertrude, ed. 1972. *Philosophical Perspectives on Punishment*. Albany: State University of New York Press.

Farrington, David P. 1998. "Individual Differences and Offending." In Michael Tonry, ed., *The Handbook of Crime and Punishment*, 241–68. New York: Oxford University Press.

Fawcett, Jan, Bernard Golden, and Nancy Rosenfeld. 2000. *New Hope for People with Bipolar Disorder*. Roseville, Calif.: Prima.

Feierman, Jay R. 1990. *Pedophilia: Biosocial Dimensions*. New York: Springer-Verlag.

Feinberg, Joel. 1965. "The Expressive Function of Punishment." *Monist* 49:397–408.

———. 1970. *Doing and Deserving: Essays on the Theory of Responsibility*. Princeton, N.J.: Princeton University Press.

Festinger, Leon, Stanley Schachter, and Kurt Bach. 1950. *Social Pressures in Informal Groups*. New York: Harper.

Fineman, Howard, and Michael Isikoff. 2002. "Laying Down the Law." *Newsweek*, August 5, pp. 20–23.

Finkelhor, David and Kersti Yilo. 1985. *License to Rape: Sexual Abuse of Wives*. New York: Holt, Rinehart and Winston.

Fishbein, Diana H. 1998. "Biological Perspectives in Criminology." In Stuart Henry and Werner Einstadter, eds., *The Criminology Theory Reader*, 92–109. New York: New York University Press.

Fisher, Gary L. and Thomas C. Harrison. 1997. *Substance Abuse*. Needham Heights, Mass.: Allyn and Bacon.

Flora, Rudy. 2001. *How to Work with Sex Offenders: A Handbook for Criminal Justice, Human Service, and Mental Health Professionals*. New York: Haworth.

Fong, G., D. Frost, and S. Stansfeld. 2001. "Road Rage: A Psychiatric Phenomenon?" *Social Psychiatry and Psychiatric Epidemiology* 36(6): 277–86.

Forst, B., W. Rhodes, J. Dimm, A. Gelman, and B. Mullin. 1982. *Targeting Federal Resources on Recidivism: Final Report of the Federal Career Criminal Research Project.* Washington, D.C.: U.S. Department of Justice, National Institute of Justice.

Friedkin, Noah E. and Karen S. Cook. 1990. "Peer Group Influence." *Sociological Methods and Research* 19(1): 122–43.

Friedman, Matthew. 2000. *Post-traumatic Stress Disorders: The Latest Assessment and Treatment Strategies.* Kansas City, Mo.: Compact Clinicals.

Gabel, Katherine and Denise Johnston. 1995. "Female Criminal Offenders." In Richard L. Edwards, ed., *Encyclopedia of Social Work,* 19th ed., 2:1013–27. Washington, D.C.: National Association of Social Workers.

Galaway, Burt and Joe Hudson, eds. 1996. *Restorative Justice: International Perspectives.* Monsey, N.Y.: Criminal Justice Press.

Gelles, Richard J. 1998. "Family Violence." In Michael Tonry, ed., *The Handbook of Crime and Punishment,* 178–206. New York: Oxford University Press.

Gelles, Richard J. and Murray Straus. 1987. "Is Violence Towards Children Increasing? A Comparison of 1975 and 1985 National Survey Rates." *Journal of Interpersonal Violence* 2:212–22.

———. 1988. *Intimate Violence.* New York: Simon and Schuster.

Gibbons, Don C. 1982. *Society, Crime, and Criminal Behavior.* 4th ed. Englewood Cliffs, N.J.: Prentice-Hall.

Gilfus, Mary E. 1992. "From Victims to Survivors to Offenders: Women's Routes of Entry and Immersion into Street Crime." *Women and Criminal Justice* 4:63–89.

Glaser, Barney and Anselm Strauss. 1967. *The Discovery of Grounded Theory: Strategies for Qualitative Research.* Chicago: Aldine de Gruyter.

Glaser, Daniel. 1978. *Crime in Our Changing Society.* New York: Holt, Rinehart and Winston.

Glueck, Sheldon and Eleanor Glueck. 1956. *Physique and Delinquency.* New York: Harper and Row.

Goddard, Henry H. 1912. *The Kallikak Family.* New York: Macmillan.

Goldstein, Paul. 1985. "The Drug/Violence Nexus: A Tripartite Concept Framework." *Journal of Drug Issues* 14:493–506.

Goldstein, Paul, Henry Brownstein, and Patrick Ryan. 1992. "Drug-Related Homicide in New York: 1984 and 1988." *Crime and Delinquency* 38(4): 459–76.

Goring, Charles. 1913. *The English Convict.* London: His Majesty's Stationery Office.

Gottfredson, Michael R. and Travis Hirschi. 1990. *A General Theory of Crime.* Stanford, Calif.: Stanford University Press.

Greenfeld, Lawrence A. 1998. *Alcohol and Crime.* Washington, D.C.: U.S. Department of Justice, Bureau of Justice Statistics..

Greenwood, Peter W. 1982. *Selective Incapacitation.* Santa Monica, Calif.: Rand.

Grinspoon, Lester and James B. Bakalar. 1996. *Depression and Other Mood Disorders.* Rev. ed. Boston: Harvard Mental Health Letter.

Groth, Nicholas and H. Jean Birnbaum. 1979. *Men Who Rape: The Psychology of the Offender.* New York: Plenum.

Guy, Edward, Jerome Platt, Israel Zwerling, and Samuel Bullock. 1985. "Mental Health Status of Prisoners in an Urban Jail." *Criminal Justice and Behavior* 12(1): 29–53.

Haddock, Deborah Bray. 2001. *The Dissociative Identity Disorder Source Book.* Columbus, Ohio: McGraw-Hill.

Hagan, Frank E. 1990. *Introduction to Criminology.* 2d ed. Chicago: Nelson-Hall.

Hallowell, Edward M. and John J. Ratey. 1995. *Driven to Distraction: Recognizing and Coping with Attention Deficit Disorder from Childhood Through Adulthood.* New York: Simon and Schuster.

Harris, Patricia M. 1994. "Client Management Classification and Prediction of Probation Outcome." *Crime and Delinquency* 40(2): 154–74.

Harrison, Lana and Joseph Gfroerer. 1992. "The Intersection of Drug Use and Criminal Behavior: Results from the National Household Survey on Drug Abuse." *Crime and Delinquency* 38(4): 422–43.

Heinrichs, R. Walter. 2001. *In Search of Madness: Schizophrenia and Neuroscience.* New York: Oxford University Press.

Hirschi, Travis. 1969. *Causes of Delinquency.* Berkeley: University of California Press.

Holosko, Michael J. 2001. "Overview of Qualitative Research Methods." In Bruce Thyer, ed., *The Handbook of Social Work Research Methods,* 263–72. Thousand Oaks, Calif.: Sage.

Hospers, John. 1966. "What Means This Freedom?" In Bernard Berofsky, ed., *Free Will and Determinism,* 6, 40. New York: Harper and Row.

Jacobs, James B. and Christopher Panarella. 1998. "Organized Crime." In Michael Tonry, ed., *The Handbook of Crime and Punishment,* 159–77. New York: Oxford University Press.

Jacobson, John W. and James A. Mulick. 1996. *Manual of Diagnosis and Professional Practice in Mental Retardation.* Washington, D.C.: American Psychological Association.

Janis, Irving. 1972. *Victims of Groupthink.* Boston: Houghton-Mifflin.

Jellinek, Elvin M. 1952. "Phases of Alcohol Addiction." *Quarterly Journal of Studies of Alcohol* 13:673–84.

———. 1960. *The Disease Concept of Alcoholism.* New Haven, Conn.: Hillhouse Press.

Jongsma, Arthur E. and Kellye Slaggert, eds. 2000. *The Mental Retardation and Developmental Disability Treatment Planner.* New York: John Wiley and Sons.

Kales, Anthony, Costas N. Stefanis, John A. Talbott, eds. 1990. *Recent Advances in Schizophrenia.* New York: Springer-Verlag.

Kant, Immanuel. 1887. *The Philosophy of Law.* Translated by W. Hastie. Edinburgh: T. T. Clark.

Kelly, Kate and Peggy Ramundo. 1995. *You Mean I'm Not Lazy, Stupid, or Crazy?! A Self-Help Book for Adults with Attention Deficit Disorder.* New York: Simon and Schuster.

Kemshall, Hazel. 2000. "Researching Risk in the Probation Service." *Social Policy and Administration* 34(4): 465–77.

Keyes, Daniel. 1982. *The Minds of Billy Milligan.* New York: Bantam.

Kim, Sung Hee and Richard H. Smith. 1993. "Revenge and Conflict Escalation." *Negotiation Journal* 9(1): 37–43.

Kirk, Laura M. 1999. "No Parole for DiPrete: Ex-governor Must Serve Full Term, Board Decides." *Providence (Rhode Island) Journal,* May 25, p. A-1.

Klein, Andrew R. 1997. *Alternative Sentencing, Intermediate Sanctions, and Probation.* Cincinnati, Ohio: Anderson.

Klein, Malcolm. 1971. *Street Gangs and Street Workers.* Englewood Cliffs, N.J.: Prentice-Hall.

———. 1998. "Street Gangs." In Michael Tonry, ed., *The Handbook of Crime and Punishment,* 111–32. New York: Oxford University Press.

Kluft, Richard P. and Catherine G. Fine, eds. 1993. *Clinical Perspectives on Multiple Personality Disorder.* Washington, D.C.: American Psychiatric Press.

Knapp, Samuel and Leon VandeCreek. 1994. *Anxiety Disorders: A Scientific Approach for Selecting the Most Effective Treatment.* Sarasota, Fla.: Professional Resource Press.

Knight, E. Leon, Mark I. Alpert, and Robert Witt. 1976. "Variation in Group Conformity Influence." *Journal of Social Psychology* 98:137–38.

Kretschmer, Ernst. 1926. *Physique and Character.* Translated by W. J. H. Sprott. New York: Harcourt, Brace.

Krivanek, Jara. 1989. *Addictions.* Sydney: Allen and Unwin.

Langan, Patrick. 1994. "Between Prison and Probation: Intermediate Sanctions." *Science* 264:791–93.

Lauritsen, Janet L. and Robert J. Sampson. 1998. "Minorities, Crime, and Criminal Justice." In Michael Tonry, ed., *The Handbook of Crime and Punishment,* 58–84. New York: Oxford University Press.

Lemert, Edwin M. 1951. *Social Pathology.* New York: McGraw-Hill.

———. 1967. *Human Deviance: Social Problems and Social Control.* New York: Prentice-Hall.

Lerner, Kenneth, Gary Arling, and S. Christopher Baird. 1986. "Client Management Classification Strategies for Case Supervision." *Crime and Delinquency* 32(3): 254–71.

Lewis, Dorothy Otnow. 1998. *Guilty by Reason of Insanity: A Psychiatrist Explores the Minds of Killers.* New York: Fawcett Columbine.

Lieber, David L., ed. 2001. *Etz Hayim: Torah and Commentary.* New York: Rabbinical Assembly.

Lombroso, Cesare. 1911. *Crimes: Its Causes and Remedies.* Boston: Little, Brown.

MacCoun, Robert and Peter Reuter. 1998. "Drug Control." In Michael Tonry, ed., *The Handbook of Crime and Punishment,* 207–38. New York: Oxford University Press.

MacGregor, Scott. 2000. "Art Schlichter: Bad Bets and Wasted Talent; Gambling Addiction Leads Quarterback to a Cell." *Cincinnati Enquirer.* July 2. http://www.enquirer.com/editions/2000/07/02/spt_art_schlichter_bad.html (August 15, 2002).

MacKay, Scott. 1998. "The DiPrete Case: A History of Public Malfeasance from Almeida to Zanni." *Providence (Rhode Island) Journal,* December 12, p. A-1.

Maier, Anne McDonald. 1992. *Mother Love, Deadly Love: The Texas Cheerleader Murder Plot.* New York: Carol Publishing.

Mann, Marty. 1968. *New Primer on Alcoholism.* 2d ed. New York: Holt, Rinehart and Winston.

Marks, Malcolm J. 1988. "Remorse, Revenge, and Forgiveness." *Psychotherapy Patient* 5(1–2): 317–30.

Matza, David. 1964. *Delinquency and Drift.* New York: Wiley.

Maxwell, Gabrielle M. and Allison Morris. 1992. *Family Participation, Cultural Diversity, and Victim Involvement in Youth Justice: A New Zealand Experiment.* Wellington, N.Z.: Victoria University of Wellington, Institute of Criminology.

———. 1993. *Family, Victims, and Culture: Youth Justice in New Zealand.* Wellington, N.Z.: Victoria University of Wellington, Institute of Criminology.

Maxwell, Kimberly. 2002. "Friends: The Role of Peer Influence Across Adolescent Risk Behaviors." *Journal of Youth and Adolescence* 31(4): 267–78.

McCullough, Michael E., C. Garth Bellah, Shelley Dean Kilpatrick, and Judith L. Johnson. 2001. "Vengefulness: Relationships with Forgiveness, Rumination, Well-being and the Big Five." *Personality and Social Psychology Bulletin* 27(5): 601–10.

McGaghy, Charles. 1976. "Child Molesters: A Study of Their Careers as Deviants." In Marshall B. Clinard and Richard Quinney, eds., *Criminal Behavior Systems,* 75–88. New York: Holt, Rinehart and Winston.

McNeece, C. Aaron and Diana M. DiNitto. 1998. *Chemical Dependency: A Systems Approach.* Boston: Allyn and Bacon.

Mednick, Sarnoff A., Terrie E. Moffitt, and Susan A. Stack. 1987. *The Causes of Crime: New Biological Approaches.* New York: Cambridge University Press.

Merton, Robert K. 1957. *Social Theory and Social Structure.* New York: Free Press.

Miller, Eleanor. 1986. *Street Woman.* Philadelphia: Temple University Press.

Miller, Walter. 1958. "Lower Class Cultures as a Generating Milieu of Gang Delinquency." *Journal of Social Issues* 14:5–19.

Moffitt, Terrie E. 1993. " 'Life-course-persistent' and 'Adolescence Limited' Antisocial Behavior: A Developmental Taxonomy." *Psychological Review* 100:674–701.

Mondimore, Francis Mark. 1995. *Depression: The Mood Disease.* Rev. ed. Baltimore, Md.: Johns Hopkins University Press.

Mooney, Tom. 2002. "Now Free, Mollicone Must Lecture on His Misdeeds." *Providence (Rhode Island) Journal,* July 25, pp. A-1, A-13.

Mumola, Christopher J. 1998. *Substance Abuse and Treatment of Adults on Probation, 1995.* Washington, D.C.: U.S. Department of Justice, Bureau of Justice Statistics.

———. 1999. *Substance Abuse and Treatment, State and Federal Prisoners, 1997.* Washington, D.C.: U.S. Department of Justice, Bureau of Justice Statistics.

Nagel, Ernest. 1970. "Determinism in History." In Dworkin, *Determinism, Free Will, and Moral Responsibility,* 49–81.

Nagin, Daniel S. 1998. "Deterrence and Incapacitation." In Michael Tonry, ed., *The Handbook of Crime and Punishment,* 345–68. New York: Oxford University Press.

National Center on Addiction and Substance Abuse at Columbia University. 1998. "Behind Bars: Substance Abuse and America's Prison Population." Report.

National Center on Child Abuse and Neglect. 1996. *Third National Study of the Incidence of Child Abuse and Neglect: 1993.* Washington, D.C.: U.S. Department of Health and Human Services.

National Center on Elder Abuse. 1998. *National Elder Abuse Incidence Study: Final Report.* Washington, D.C.: U.S. Department of Health and Human Services, Administration for Children and Families and Administration on Aging.

National Clearinghouse on Child Abuse and Neglect Information. 2002. *National Child Abuse and Neglect Data System (NCANDS): Summary of Key Findings from Calendar Year 2000.* http://www.calib.com/nccanch/pubs/factsheets/canstats.cfm (August 7, 2002).

National Institute for Occupational Safety and Health. 1996. *Violence in the Workplace.* Washington, D.C.: Author.

National Research Council. 1999. *Pathological Gambling: A Critical Review.* Washington, D.C.: National Academy Press.

Needels, Karen. 1996. "Go Directly to Jail and Do Not Collect? A Long-Term Study of Recidivism and Employment Patterns Among Prison Releasees." *Journal of Research in Crime and Delinquency* 33:471–96.

Nugent, William R., Mark S. Umbreit, Lizabeth Winamaki, and Jeff Paddock. 2001. "Participation in Victim-Offender Mediation and Re-Offense: Successful Replications?" *Journal of Research on Social Work Practice* 11(1): 5–23.

O'Brien, Shirley. 1986. *Why They Did It: Stories of Eight Convicted Child Molesters.* Springfield, Ill.: Charles C. Thomas.

Office of National Drug Control Policy. Executive Office of the President. 2001. "Drug Treatment in the Criminal Justice System." In *Drug Policy Information Clearinghouse Fact Sheet.* Washington, D.C.: Drug Policy Information Clearinghouse.

Park, Robert E. 1952. *Human Communities.* Glencoe, Ill.: Free Press.

"Pathological Gambling." 1996. *Harvard Mental Health Letter* 12(7):1–5.

Petersilia, Joan. 1998. "Probation and Parole." In Michael Tonry, ed., *The Handbook of Crime and Punishment,* 563–88. New York: Oxford University Press.

Petersilia, Joan and Peter Greenwood. 1978. "Mandatory Prison Sentences: Their Projected Effects on Crime and Prison Populations." *Journal of Criminal Law and Criminology* 69:604–15.

Peterson, Mark A. and Harriet B. Braiker. 1980. *Doing Crime: A Survey of California Prison Inmates.* Santa Monica, Calif.: Rand.

Pettiway, Leon E. 1987. "Arson for Revenge: The Role of Environmental Situation, Age, Sex, and Race." *Journal of Quantitative Criminology* 3(2): 169–84.

Piehl, Anne M. 1998. "Economic Conditions, Work, and Crime." In Michael Tonry, ed., *The Handbook of Crime and Punishment,* 302–19. New York: Oxford University Press.

Pillemer, Karl and David Finkelhor. 1988. "The Prevalence of Elder Abuse: A Random Sample Survey." *Gerontologist* 28:51–57.

Piper, August. 1996. *Hoax and Reality: The Bizarre World of Multiple Personality Disorder.* Northvale, N.J.: Jason Aronson.

Platt, Anthony. 1974. "Prospects for a Radical Criminology in the United States." *Crime and Social Justice* 1:2–10.

Porter, Louise E. and Laurence J. Alison. 2001. "A Partially Ordered Scale of Influence in Violent Group Behavior: An Example from Gang Rape." *Small Group Research* 32(4): 475–97.

Powell, Thomas A., John C. Holt, and Karen M. Fondacaro. 1997. "The Prevalence of Mental Illness Among Inmates in a Rural State." *Law and Human Behavior* 21(4): 427–38.

Prochaska, James O. 1994. "Strong and Weak Principles for Progressing from Precontemplation to Action on the Basis of Twelve Problem Behaviors." *Health Psychology* 13:47–51.

Prochaska, James O. and Wayne F. Velicer. 1997. "The Transtheoretical Model of Health Behavior Change." *American Journal of Health Promotion* 12:38–48.

Prochaska, James O., John C. Norcross, and Carlos C. DiClemente. 1995. *Changing for Good.* New York: William Morrow.

Quinney, Richard. 1970. *The Social Reality of Crime.* Boston: Little, Brown.

———. 1974. *Critique of Legal Order: Crime Control in Capitalist Society.* Boston: Little, Brown.

———. 1977. *Class, State, and Crime: On the Theory and Practice of Criminal Justice.* New York: David McKay.

———. 1979. *Criminology.* 2d ed. New York: McGraw-Hill.

Quinsey, Vernon L. 1998. "Treatment of Sex Offenders." In Michael Tonry, ed., *The Handbook of Crime and Punishment,* 403–25. New York: Oxford University Press.

Random House Webster's College Dictionary. 1991. New York: Random House.

Rathbone, Daniel B. and George C. Huckabee. 1999. *Controlling Road Rage: A Literature Review and Pilot Study.* Washington, D.C.: AAA Foundation for Traffic Safety.

Reamer, Frederic G. 1993. *The Philosophical Foundations of Social Work.* New York: Columbia University Press.

———. 1998. *Social Work Research and Evaluation Skills.* New York: Columbia University Press.

———. 1999. *Social Work Values and Ethics.* 2d ed. New York: Columbia University Press.

Reckless, Walter C. 1961. *The Crime Problem.* 3d ed. New York: Appleton-Century-Crofts.

Reid, Sue Titus. 1999. *Crime and Criminology.* New York: McGraw-Hill.

Reitz, Kevin R. 1998. "Sentencing." In Michael Tonry, ed., *The Handbook of Crime and Punishment,* 542–62. New York: Oxford University Press.

Rennison, Callie. 2000. *Criminal Victimization 1999: Changes, 1998–99, with Trends, 1993–99.* Washington, D.C.: U.S. Department of Justice, Bureau of Justice Statistics.

Richards, Stephanie S., William S. Musser, and Samuel Gershon. 1999. *Maintenance Pharmacotherapies for Neuropsychiatric Disorders.* Philadelphia: Brunner/Mazel.

Roberts, Albert R., ed. 2002. *Handbook of Domestic Violence Intervention Strategies: Policies, Programs, and Legal Remedies.* New York: Oxford University Press.

Robin, Arthur L. 2000. *ADHD in Adolescents: Diagnosis and Treatment.* New York: Guilford.

Rooney, Ronald H. 1992. *Strategies for Work with Involuntary Clients.* New York: Columbia University Press.

Rosenheck, Robert A. and Michael S. Neale. 1998. "Cost-effectiveness of Intense Psychiatric Community Care for High Users of Inpatient Psychiatric Services." *Archives of General Psychiatry* 55(5): 459–66.

Rosenheck, Robert A., Michael S. Neale, and Linda K. Frisman. 1995. "Issues in Estimating the Cost of Innovative Mental Health Programs." *Psychiatric Quarterly* 66(1): 9–31.

Ross, Colin A. 1996. *Dissociative Identity Disorder: Diagnosis, Clinical Features, and Treatment of Multiple Personality.* New York: John Wiley and Sons.

Russell, Dianne. 1984. *Sexual Exploitation: Rape, Child Sexual Abuse, and Workplace Harassment.* Newbury Park, Calif.: Sage.

Saltzman, Jonathan. 1996. "Jury Finds Barrett Guilty, Psychiatrist-in-Training Convicted of Second-degree Murder." *Providence (Rhode Island) Journal-Bulletin,* November 6, p. A-1.

Samenow, Stanton. 1998. *Straight Talk About Criminals: Understanding and Treating Antisocial Individuals.* Northvale, N.J.: Jason Aronson.

Sampson, Robert J. and John H. Laub. 1993. *Crime in the Making.* Cambridge, Mass.: Harvard University Press.

Schafer, Stephen. 1976. *Introduction to Criminology.* Reston, Va.: Reston Publishing.

Schiraldi, Glenn R. 2000. *The Post-Traumatic Disorder Sourcebook.* New York: McGraw-Hill.

Schmalleger, Frank M. 2001. *Criminology Today.* Englewood Cliffs, N.J.: Prentice Hall.

Schrag, Clarence. 1971. *Crime and Justice: American Style.* Washington, D.C.: U.S. Government Printing Office.

Schur, Edwin M. 1969. "Reactions to Deviance: A Critical Assessment." *American Journal of Sociology* 75:309–22.

———. 1971. *Labeling Deviant Behavior.* New York: Harper and Row.

Schwartz, Arthur and Ruth M. Schwartz. 1993. *Depression: Theories and Treatment*. New York: Columbia University Press.

Schwartz, Barbara K. and Henry R. Cellini, eds. 1995. *The Sex Offender: Corrections, Treatment, and Legal Practice*. Vol. 1. Kingston, N.J.: Civic Research Institute.

———. 1997. *The Sex Offender: New Insights, Treatment Interventions, and Legal Developments*. Vol. 2. Kingston, N.J.: Civic Research Institute.

———. 1999. *The Sex Offender: Theoretical Advances, Treating Special Populations, and Legal Developments*, Vol. 3. Kingston, N.J.: Civic Research Institute.

Scrignar, Chester B. 1996. *Posttraumatic Stress Disorder: Diagnosis, Treatment, and Legal Issues*. 3d ed. New Orleans: Bruno Press.

Seligman, Linda. 1998. *Selecting Effective Treatments: A Comprehensive, Systematic Guide to Treating Mental Disorders*. San Francisco: Jossey-Bass.

Seton, Paul H. 2001. "On the Importance of Getting Even: A Study of the Origins and Intentions of Revenge." *Smith College Studies in Social Work* 72(1): 77–97.

Shaffer, Howard J., Sharon A. Stein, Blase Gambino, and Thomas N. Cummings, eds. 1989. *Compulsive Gambling: Theory, Research, and Practice*. Lexington, Mass.: Lexington Books.

Shaw, Clifford R. and Henry D. McKay. 1942. *Juvenile Delinquency and Urban Areas*. Chicago: University of Chicago Press.

Sheley, Joseph F. 2000. *Criminology: A Contemporary Handbook*. 3d ed. Belmont, Calif.: Wadsworth.

Sheridan, Lorraine and Graham M. Davies. 2001. "Stalking: The Elusive Crime." *Legal and Criminological Psychology* 6:133–47.

Sherif, Muzafer and Carolyn W. Sherif. 1964. *Reference Groups*. New York: Harper and Row.

Sherman, Edmund and William J. Reid. 1994. *Qualitative Research in Social Work*. New York: Columbia University Press.

Shinnar, Shlomo and Reuel Shinnar. 1975. "The Effects of the Criminal Justice System on the Control of Crime: A Quantitative Approach." *Law and Society Review* 9:581–611.

Shireman, Charles H. and Frederic G. Reamer. 1986. *Rehabilitating Juvenile Justice*. New York: Columbia University Press.

Shover, Neal. 1998. "White-Collar Crime." In Michael Tonry, ed., *The Handbook of Crime and Punishment*, 133–58. New York: Oxford University Press.

Siegel, Alberta Engall and Sidney Siegel. 1957. "Reference Groups, Membership Groups, and Attitude Change." *Journal of Abnormal and Social Psychology* 55:360–64.

Siegel, Larry J. 2000. *Criminology*. Belmont, Calif.: Wadsworth.

Simon, Rita and Jean Landis. 1991. *The Crimes Women Commit, the Punishments They Receive*. Lexington, Mass.: Lexington Books.

Simourd, David J. and P. Bruce Malcolm. 1998. "Reliability and Validity of the Level of Service Inventory–Revised Among Federally Incarcerated Sex Offenders." *Journal of Interpersonal Violence* 13(2): 261–75.

Smart, J.J.C. 1970. "Free Will, Praise, and Blame." In Dworkin, *Determinism, Free Will, and Moral Responsibility*, 196–213.

Spergel, Irving. 1964. *Racketville, Slumtown, Haulburg: An Exploratory Study of Delinquent Subcultures*. Chicago: University of Chicago Press.

———. 1995. *The Youth Gang Problem: A Community Approach*. New York: Oxford University Press.

Spiegel, David, ed. 1999. *Efficacy and Cost-Effectiveness of Psychotherapy.* Washington, D.C.: American Psychiatric Press.

Spira, James L. and Irvin D. Yalom. 1996. *Treating Dissociative Identity Disorder.* New York: Jossey-Bass.

Steadman, Henry, Stanley Fabisiak, Joel Dvoskin, and Edward Holohean. 1989. "A Survey of Mental Disability Among State Prison Inmates." *Hospital and Community Psychiatry* 38(1): 1086–90.

Steffensmeier, Darrell and Emilie Allan. 1996. "Gender and Crime: Toward a Gendered Theory of Female Offending." *Annual Review of Sociology* 22:459–87.

Straus, Murray and Richard J. Gelles. 1986. "Societal Change and Change in Family Violence from 1975 to 1985 as Revealed in Two National Surveys." *Journal of Marriage and the Family* 48:465–479.

Strauss, Anselm and Juliet Corbin. 1990. *Basics of Qualitative Research: Grounded Theory Procedures and Techniques.* Newbury Park, Calif.: Sage.

Stuckless, Noreen and Richard Goranson. 1994. "A Selected Bibliography of Literature on Revenge." *Psychological Reports* 75(2): 803–11.

"Study Finds Other Psychiatric Ills Accompany Pathological Gambling." 1999. *Outcomes and Accountability Alert* 4(8): 4–5.

Substance Abuse and Mental Health Services Administration. Center for Substance Abuse Treatment. National Evaluation Data Services. 1999. *The Cost and Benefits of Substance Abuse Treatment: Findings from the National Treatment Improvement Evaluation Study.* Rockville, Md.: Substance Abuse and Mental Health Services Administration, U.S. Department of Health and Human Services.

Sullivan, Mercer. 1989. *Getting Paid.* Ithaca, N.Y.: Cornell University Press.

Sutherland, Edwin H. 1940. "White-Collar Criminality." *American Sociological Review* 5:1–11.

———. 1947. *Principles of Criminology.* 4th ed. Philadelphia: Lippincott.

Tannenbaum, Frank. 1938. *Crime and the Community.* Boston: Ginn.

Tatara, Toshio. 1995. "Elder Abuse." In Richard L. Edwards, ed., *Encyclopedia of Social Work,* 19th ed., 1:834–42. Washington, D.C.: National Association of Social Workers.

Taylor, R. 1963. *Metaphysics.* Englewood Cliffs, N.J.: Prentice-Hall.

Teplin, Linda A. 1990. "The Prevalence of Severe Mental Disorder Among Male Urban Jail Detainees: Comparison with the Epidemiologic Catchment Area Program." *American Journal of Public Health* 80(6): 663–69.

Terris, William and John Jones. 1982. "Psychological Factors Related to Employees' Theft in the Convenience Store Industry." *Psychological Reports* 51(3): 1219–38.

Thrasher, Frederick M. 1927. *The Gang: A Study of 1,133 Gangs in Chicago.* Chicago: University of Chicago Press.

Tonry, Michael. 1998. "Intermediate Sanctions." In Michael Tonry, ed., *The Handbook of Crime and Punishment,* 683–711. New York: Oxford University Press.

Tsuang, Ming T. and Stephen V. Faraone. 1997. *Schizophrenia: The Facts.* New York: Oxford University Press.

Umbreit, Mark S. 1997. "Restorative Justice: What Works?" *ICCA Journal on Community Corrections* 7(4): 21–23.

———. 2001. *The Handbook on Victim-Offender Mediation: An Essential Guide for Practice and Research.* San Francisco: Jossey-Bass.

U.S. Advisory Board on Child Abuse and Neglect. 1995. *A Nation's Shame: Fatal Child Abuse and Neglect in the United States.* Washington, D.C.: U.S. Department of Health and Human Services.

U.S. Department of Justice. Bureau of Justice Statistics. 1994. *Domestic Violence: Violence Between Intimates.* Washington, D.C.: U.S. Department of Justice.

———. 2000. *Arrestee Drug Abuse Monitoring (ADAM) Program: 1999 Annual Report on Drug Use Among Adult and Juvenile Arrestees.* Washington, D.C.: U.S. Department of Justice.

U.S. Department of Justice. Drug Courts Program Office. 1997. *1997 Drug Court Survey Report: Executive Summary.* Washington, D.C.: American University.

U.S. General Accounting Office. 1991. *Drug Treatment: State Prisons Face Challenges in Providing Services.* Report to the Committee on Government Operations. U.S. House of Representatives. Washington, D.C.: U.S. Congress.

Unrau, Yvonne A. and Heather Coleman. 1997. "Qualitative Data Analysis." In Richard Grinnell Jr., ed., *Social Work Research and Evaluation,* 5th ed., 501–26. Itasca, Ill.: F. E. Peacock.

Vaillant, George E. 1995. *The Natural History of Alcoholism Revisited.* Cambridge, Mass.: Harvard University Press.

Van Ness, Daniel. 1986. *Crime and Its Victims: What We Can Do.* Downers Grove, Ill.: Intervarsity Press.

Velicer, Wayne F., James O. Prochaska, Joseph L. Fava, Greg J. Norman, and Colleen Redding. 1998. "Smoking Cessation and Stress Management: Applications of the Transtheoretical Model of Behavior Change." *Homeostasis* 38:216–33.

Vidmar, Neil. 2001. "Retribution and Revenge." In Joseph Sanders and Hamilton V. Lee, eds., *Handbook of Justice Research in Law,* 31–63. Dordrecht, Netherlands: Kluwer Academic.

Volberg, Rachel A. 1994. "The Prevalence and Demographics of Pathological Gamblers: Implications for Public Health." *American Journal of Public Health* 84(2): 237–41.

Warr, Mark. 1993. "Parents, Peers, and Delinquency." *Social Forces* 72:247–64.

Washton, Arnold M. 1989. *Cocaine Addiction: Treatment, Recovery, and Relapse Prevention.* New York: Harper and Row.

Weisburd, David, Elin Waring, and Ellen Chayet. 1995. "Specific Deterrence in a Sample of Offenders Convicted of White-Collar Crimes." *Criminology* 33:587–607.

Wells, Susan J. 1995. "Child Abuse and Neglect Overview." In Richard L. Edwards, ed., *Encyclopedia of Social Work,* 19th ed., 1:346–53. Washington, D.C.: National Association of Social Workers.

Wilson, James Q. 1983. *Thinking About Crime.* Rev. ed. New York: Basic Books.

Wilson, James Q. and Richard J. Herrnstein. 1985. *Crime and Human Nature.* New York: Simon and Schuster.

Wilson, James Q. and Joan Petersilia, eds. 1995. *Crime: Public Policies for Crime Control.* San Francisco: ICS Press.

Wolf, Rosalie S. 1995. "Abuse of the Elderly." In Richard J. Gelles, ed., *Families and Violence.* Minneapolis, Minn.: National Council on Family Relations.

Wolfgang, Marvin, Robert M. Figlio, and Thorsten Sellin. 1972. *Delinquency in a Birth Cohort.* Chicago: University of Chicago Press.

Yochelson, Samuel and Stanton E. Samenow. 1976. *The Criminal Personality.* Vols. 1 and 2. New York: Jason Aronson.